This book is the first in a major new series examining global economic institutions and contrasts regional economic integration in the Asia Pacific region and in Europe.

In the Asia Pacific region, regionalism is developing by means of 'open regionalism', constructed through the APEC (Asia Pacific Economic Cooperation) process. This is different from the regionalism which has developed in Europe, through the construction of a single European Market and Monetary Union within the European Union. In the light of this contrast, a number of important contemporary policy questions are considered by an international team of contributors. How should Europe and other parts of the world respond to the development of open regionalism in the Asia Pacific region? Can these regions develop a shared global agenda directed towards sustaining genuinely multilateral solutions to international trade policy problems over the coming years?

Peter Drysdale is one of Australia's foremost authorities on Australia's international trade and economic diplomacy. He is a professor in the Economics Division, Research School of Pacific and Asian Studies at the Australian National University (ANU) and Executive Director of the Australia–Japan Research Centre (AJRC). He is a member of the Order of Australia.

David Vines is the Director of the Global Economic Institutions (GEI) Research Programme of the ESRC. He is Fellow and Tutor in Economics at Balliol College Oxford, a Research Fellow of the Centre for Economic Policy Research in London and an Adjunct Professor of Economics at the Australian National University.

Europe, East Asia and APEC

A Shared Global Agenda

Global Economic Institutions

General Editor
David Vines
Balliol College, Oxford

The Global Economic Institutions Research Programme (GEI) is a series of sixteen linked research programmes funded by the Economic and Social Research Council of Great Britain. The programme focuses on how existing global economic institutions and regimes operate, how they might be improved and whether new institutions are needed. Its principal findings will be presented in a sequence of five volumes, to be published as the series **Global Economic Institutions**.

The topics covered by the five volumes will include the reform of global economic institutions, the International Monetary Fund, the World Bank, governance in the global economy, and Europe and Asia, and international economic development. Together the volumes will represent a major contribution to contemporary debates among economists, political scientists, politicians, business leaders and others with a shared interest in the growth and development of the global economy.

Europe, East Asia and APEC

A Shared Global Agenda?

edited by

Peter Drysdale

and

David Vines

CAMBRIDGE
UNIVERSITY PRESS

Published by the Press Syndicate of the University of Cambridge
The Pitt Building, Trumpington Street, Cambridge CB2 1RP, United Kingdom

Cambridge University Press
The Edinburgh Building, Cambridge CB2 2RU, United Kingdom
40 West 20th Street, New York, NY 10011–4211, USA
10 Stamford Road, Oakleigh, Melbourne 3166, Australia

First published 1998

Printed in the United Kingdom at the University Press, Cambridge

A catalogue record for this book is available from the British Library

Library of Congress cataloguing in publication data applied for

ISBN 0 521 63315 X   hardback

M.R.

Contents

Figures

Tables

Contributors

PETER DRYSDALE is a Professor in the Economics Division, Research School of Pacific and Asian Studies at the Australian National University (ANU) and Executive Director of the ANU's Australia–Japan Research Centre (AJRC). Professor Drysdale is one of Australia's foremost authorities on Australia's international trade and economic diplomacy. He has written extensively on Asia Pacific economic cooperation.

DAVID VINES is Fellow and Tutor in Economics at Balliol College, Oxford. He is also Adjunct Professor of Economics in the Research School of Pacific and Asian Studies at the ANU, a Research Fellow of the Centre for Economic Policy Research in London, and Director of the Research Programme on Global Economic Institutions of the Economic and Social Research Council. His research is on international economics, including regional integration in the Asia Pacific region, and European monetary union, and the future roles of the IMF, World Bank, and WTO.

KYM ANDERSON is Professor of Economics and Foundation Director of the Centre for International Economic Studies at the University of Adelaide, as well as Research Fellow of Europe's London-based Centre for Economic Policy Research (CEPR).

RON DUNCAN is Professor of Economics and Executive Director of the National Centre for Development Studies, Research School of Pacific and Asian Studies at the ANU.

ANDREW ELEK is Executive Director of Bellendena Partners, an economic consultancy specialising in international economic cooperation issues. He is also a Research Associate of the Economics Division of the Research School of Pacific and Asian Studies at the ANU and of the Department of Economics at the University of Tasmania.

CHRISTOPHER FINDLAY is an Associate Professor in the Department of Economics at the University of Adelaide and an Associate of the Australia–Japan Research Centre at the ANU. He is also co-Director of the Chinese Economy Research Centre, University of Adelaide.

JOSEPH FRANÇOIS is Professor of Economics and Chair of International Economic Development at Erasmus University, Rotterdam. He is also a senior fellow with CEPR in London, a fellow of the Tinbergen Institute in Rotterdam, and a senior economic consultant to the WTO.

ROSS GARNAUT is a Professor of Economics at the ANU's Research School of Pacific and Asian Studies.

BRETT HOUSE is a doctoral student in economics at University College, Oxford. He is also senior lecturer in economics at Keble College, Oxford.

TONY LAWSON has been a Visiting Fellow with the National Centre for Development Studies in the ANU's Research School of Pacific and Asian Studies since his retirement from the Australian Industries Commission in 1995.

PONCIANO INTAL, JR. is the President of the Philippine Institute for Development Studies (PIDS). Dr Intal is a member of the Program Committee of the Economy and Environment Program for Southeast Asia and of the Advisory Board of the Microeconomic Impact of Macroeconomic Adjustment Policies projects of the International Development Research Centre of Canada.

ROLF J. LANGHAMMER is Vice-President of the Kiel Institute of World Economics, and Head of the Research Department on Development Economics and Global Integration at the Kiel Institute of World Economics.

JUSTIN YIFU LIN is Professor and Founding Director of the China Center for Economic Research at Peking University, Professor at Hong Kong University of Science and Technology, and Adjunct Professor at the ANU.

WARWICK MCKIBBIN is Professor of International Economics and Head of the Department of Economics in the Research School of Pacific Studies at the ANU. He is also a non-resident Senior Fellow at the Brookings Institution in Washington DC and President of McKibbin Software Group Inc.

RICHARD POMFRET is a Professor of Economics at the University of Adelaide.

RICHARD PORTES is Director of the Centre for Economic Policy Research, which he founded in 1983, Professor of Economics at London Business School, and Directeur d'Etudes at the Ecole des Hautes Etudes en Sciences Sociales in Paris.

JIM ROLLO is Chief Economic Adviser at the Foreign and Commonwealth Office in London and External Professor of Economics at the University of Nottingham. He is a member of the steering committee of the Global Economic Institutions research initiative of the British Economic and Social Research Council.

HADI SOESASTRO is a Director at the Centre for Strategic and International Studies (CSIS) in Jakarta. He is the 1997 Okita Fellow at the Research School of Pacific and Asian Studies, ANU.

YONGZHENG YANG is a Senior Lecturer at the National Centre for Development Studies, ANU.

Preface

Over the past few decades, East Asia has grown more rapidly than any other part of the world economy. Its trade and industrial transformation has been built upon openness and integration into the world economy and a continual process of reform and liberalisation in a succession of East Asian economies. East Asian growth has been associated with transpacific economic integration and the emergence of the Asia Pacific economy as a new centre of international economic activity. This development has already had a profound impact on the world economy and it brings with it new interests and new responsibilities for East Asia and the Pacific in the management of the international economic system. The currency and financial problems of East Asian economies in 1997 served to underline their growing importance to the health of the international economic system.

The Asia Pacific Economic Cooperation (APEC) process has emerged since 1989 as the institutional process in which Asia Pacific reform and liberalisation is now being managed. It is driven by twin objectives: to secure an appropriate regional framework within which to manage integration between countries whose economies, societies and polities are diverse; and to secure a world order into which this regional integration process fits harmoniously.

The regionalism which is emerging as a result of this process is very different from regionalism in Europe and this difference is expressed by the description *open regionalism*. Such regionalism involves non-discrimination in trade. There is — and will be — no customs union such as Europe was built upon. There is no supra-national institutional authority for implementing the decisions of APEC leaders and their ministers. The goal of free trade and investment liberalisation by 2010 for advanced economies and by 2020 for developing economies is to be pursued by 'concerted unilateralism' — the actions of individual members of APEC encouraged by common commitment and peer pressure.

It may still surprise many European observers that the region in which this is happening, East Asia, is already a larger destination for European Union

(EU) exports than is North America. This is a new trans-regional structure for world trade, and so management of the world order requires new thinking about the direction of international economic policy and economic diplomacy.

The ASEM (Asia–Europe meeting) leadership dialogues thus began in Bangkok in 1996 with further, but related, objectives: to explore the extent to which Europe and East Asia share common objectives for the emerging world order, and also, for Europe, to explore whether the 'East Asian challenge' can be turned into an opportunity for European trade and investment.

There are many questions. How should Europe and other parts of the world respond to developments in the Asia Pacific region? Are there lessons here that might have application elsewhere — for example in Europe's approach to its periphery and to Russia? North America is a major player in APEC. Is there a tension between Western Pacific (East Asian and Australasian) commitment to open regionalism and the increasing tendency in the United States towards specific reciprocity in its trade policy dealings? Are the 'hubs and spokes' preferential trading arrangements between the European Union and its East European and Mediterranean partners, let alone countries in Latin America and Russia, sustainable? Will institutional rigidities and the economic and political costs of change frustrate the achievement of East Asia's economic ambitions, or of Europe's political and economic goals; or can these regions develop a shared global agenda? What is the relationship between ASEM and APEC? Can the APEC process and the fledgling ASEM dialogues play a role in developing and sustaining genuinely multilateral solutions to international policy problems over the coming years? In short, can they help to sustain and promote the World Trade Organization (WTO)?

These questions were all addressed in a series of meetings held in London, Brussels, Paris and Berlin in May 1996. Participants included economists and policy makers from throughout Europe, East Asia and Australia. The meetings themselves were the outcome of a long process of international collaboration during which the papers that now constitute this volume were commissioned. Initial planning took place at a workshop at the Australian National University (ANU) in Canberra in November 1995 and at a follow-up conference there in September 1996. Those first discussions set up collaboration between the Global Economic Institutions (GEI) Research Programme, the Australia–Japan Research Centre at the ANU and the CEPR (Centre for Economic Policy Research) in London; this was subsequently joined by ECARE (European Centre for Advanced Research in Economics) in Brussels, by CEPII (Centre d'Etudes Prospectives et Informations Internationales) in Paris, and by the Japanese–German Centre in Berlin. Financial support for the meetings was provided by the GEI Programme, the Australia–Japan Research Centre, the European Commission, the British

Foreign and Commonwealth Office, and the Australian Department of Foreign Affairs and Trade.

At the meetings, delegates presented radically divergent conceptions of what it means to be an economic region, discussed the risks and opportunities for trade liberalisation in their two parts of the world, and began to elaborate on a shared global agenda, which included an expression of resounding support for the WTO and the multilateral trading system.

The book which has emerged from these activities contains the papers presented at the meetings, revised in the light of the intense discussion.

Broadly, the conclusions of this book fit well with the call by the Vice President of the European Commission, Sir Leon Brittan, for a new round of global trade negotiations at the end of the millennium. They also echo the APEC call for global free trade by the year 2020 (something which was taken up by the previous British government's White Paper on International Competitiveness). They have been widely publicised in a report in the June 1996 newsletter of the GEI Research Programme. Already, they have fed informally into preparatory work for the second ASEM summit to be held in London in the spring of next year.

Our thanks to all those organisations and to a large number of individuals in bringing this work together in the volume that follows is manifold. Our colleagues, Richard Portes, André Sapir, Jean Pisani-Ferry, Jim Rollo and Wolfgang Brenn and their staff made possible the excellent discussions of these issues at the meetings held in Europe. The contribution of our colleagues from East Asia — Ponciano Intal, Takatoshi Ito, Justin Yifu Lin, Hadi Soesastro and Soogil Young — was critical to their success. We are especially grateful for the support of Andrew Elek and Brett House in launching and completing this work. Sir Leon Brittan and his Chef de Cabinet, Robert Madelin provided encouragement and support throughout the project. Our particular thanks go to Denise Ryan, Pamela Hewitt, Minni Reis and the staff of the Australia–Japan Research Centre for their patient labour in preparing this manuscript for publication. It has been an inspiration and an immense pleasure for us to be able to join in this truly global project.

Peter Drysdale and David Vines
Canberra and Oxford, December 1997

Part I

Context

1 Europe and East Asia: a shared global agenda?

PETER DRYSDALE, DAVID VINES AND BRETT HOUSE

The emergence of East Asia and the Asia Pacific economy, alongside the integration of Europe, have been among the most important developments in the world economy in the second half of the twentieth century. These developments have taken place in an increasingly integrated international economy with the institutional support of the General Agreement on Tariffs and Trade (GATT), now the World Trade Organization (WTO). They have also been associated with the growth of regionalism in international economic affairs, although the regionalism which is emerging in East Asia and the Pacific appears very different from the regionalism that earlier took root in Europe.

This volume sets out to explore how Europe and other parts of the world might respond to developments in the Asia Pacific economy and how, in particular, Europe might relate to East Asia and the process of Asia Pacific Economic Cooperation (APEC).

The essays collected here are the product of a European, East Asian, and Australasian collaborative research program that spanned the three continents. The objective here is to define the elements in a shared global agenda for Europe and East Asia. In this and the two following chapters — by Anderson and François, and Pomfret — we set the context, with a detailed examination of intra- and extra-regional trade and foreign investment flows in each region, as well as an analysis of the role of the European Union (EU) and East Asia in a tri-polar world in which the United States is the single most important national economy.

Regional origins and identities

Any discussion of trade relations between Europe and Asia, directed towards the issue of a shared global agenda, must begin with an understanding of the political and economic starting points of these two different regions of the world. We begin with some of the contrasts between the notion of open regionalism, which is developing within the APEC framework, and regionalism as it has emerged in Europe. The reasons for the differences between developments in Europe and Asia are explored in the context of existing international institutions and their relevance to the global policy agenda.

Regionalism in East Asia and the Asia Pacific

East Asia has been the most rapidly growing region in the world: it has had two decades of double-digit economic growth rates. Growth may drop sharply over the next few years in consequence of the currency and financial crises that originated in East Asia in 1997, but the medium- to long-term growth potential of developing East Asia remains strong. Growth has been based fundamentally on industrialisation for the *world* market: the proportion of trade which goes to and comes from trading partners outside the region is much higher than that for either Europe or North America. Most of the countries of East Asia are linked economically and politically with other nations rimming the Pacific. The APEC region is incredibly diverse, both culturally and geographically: it includes not only the ASEAN6 (Brunei, Indonesia, Malaysia, the Philippines, Singapore, and Thailand); Japan and Korea in Northeast Asia; China, Hong Kong and Taiwan; and Australasia; but also Canada, the United States, Mexico and Chile. Vietnam, Russia and Peru are also scheduled to join APEC over the next two years.

In this vast and diverse region, there is a regional project committed to the promotion of strength and peace for the Asia Pacific region as a whole. In the 1980s and the 1990s, the Asia Pacific became a region of strong states pursuing economic prosperity by means of market-friendly policies. The pursuit of economic prosperity is the means by which stability and peace are to be achieved, and this prosperity is to be realised through rapid economic growth. In turn, it is intended that economic growth will be promoted by means of sound macroeconomic policies, economic reform and trade liberalisation.

This volume focuses, more or less exclusively, upon trade policies and the chapters in it were written before the financial crises of the second half of 1997. Nevertheless, a word about the macroeconomic background to East Asia's trade relationships is necessary.

Macroeconomic policies, East Asian style, have essentially consisted of a high rate of national saving, a high investment rate and a competitive exchange rate. These form a coherent package which *supports* outward-oriented industrialisation. High savings support the investment that trade liberalisation and openness encourages. A high rate of savings also ensures that competitive exchange rates are not periodically jeopardised by periods of monetary restraint, high interest rates, and forces which encourage currency appreciation.[2] Until 1996, competitive exchange rates helped to underpin the profitability of investment for the world market and helped to preserve economic and political support for the policies of liberalisation.

In 1997, all this changed dramatically when a number of influences conspired to generate the East Asian financial crises. First, some analysts argue that the devaluation of the Chinese yuan in 1994 led to significant price under-cutting in many export markets. Second, and more importantly, the strength of the dollar against the yen and other major currencies led to a substantial nominal effective appreciation of currencies pegged to baskets with a high US dollar weighting. Third, domestic demand was allowed to rise too strongly in some Southeast Asian economies, driven by speculative capital in-flows, as well as unregulated and imprudent banking practices; this generated levels of inflation higher than international averages, which further appreciated real exchange rates. Finally, there was a slump in the world market for electronic products which sharply cut both the terms of trade and export sales of Thailand and other East Asian economies. As a result, export growth fell markedly.

This drop in export revenue fed anxiety about exchange rates which precipitated capital withdrawal and this change in sentiment fed upon itself, ultimately forcing retreat from pegged exchange rates to floating rates, accompanied by large depreciations. The necessary retreat from fixed exchange rates exposed a deeper problem in financial markets where large foreign borrowings were uncovered against the risk of devaluation.

The impressive Southeast Asian programs of macroeconomic reform, trade liberalisation and trade expansion in the 1980s and 1990s are challenged by the sharp adjustments and slower growth which will result from the financial crises of 1997. Protectionism is a common response for economies in times of slow growth. Significantly, this has not been the main initial response by ASEAN members, or in East Asia more generally, to the financial crisis. Early indications are that the APEC liberalisation agenda remains on track.[3] If protectionism is not the initial response, it is unlikely to be the response at any stage. The currency depreciations will again spur strong export expansion out of East Asia and, in combination with domestic expenditure restraint and lower investment levels, declines in the region's current account deficits. It appears at the time of writing that if the financial problems associated with debt overhang are decisively dealt with, then the macroeconomic conditions for the rapid expansion of exports which have characterised the East Asian growth experience may soon be re-established.[4] Indeed, it may not be long before the problems of a 'strong dollar' and 'strong euro' — the decline of the United States and European competitiveness relative to East Asia — are the issue, rather than those of a weak baht, ringgit, rupiah peso or won.

We now return to our main theme of trade liberalisation in East Asia. It has been pursued through a strategy of regional integration called 'open regionalism', an approach which has been officially promoted since 1989, when the APEC process was initiated at a meeting of foreign and trade Ministers in Canberra. Its intellectual origins stretch back much further, but the idea was entrenched through the Pacific Economic Cooperation Council (PECC) after 1980 (see Chapter 5). The meeting of APEC Heads of Government at Bogor, Indonesia, in November 1994 gave regional approval to a program of trade liberalisation which is designed to lead to free trade in the Asia Pacific region by the year 2010 for developed countries and 2020 for developing countries (see APEG 1994).

'Open regionalism' is a term whose very meaning is contentious.[5] In this introduction, we adopt a precise and specific use of this term which denotes 'concerted unilateral MFN (most favoured nation) liberalisation of trade' by a number of states (see Chapter 5; Drysdale and Garnaut 1994; Garnaut 1997a). Despite adopting this usage, we note ambiguities in meaning as we proceed.

'Open regionalism', in the sense of concerted unilateral MFN liberalisation, implies the creation of something very different from a preferential trading area like the customs union of the European Union, or the North American Free Trade Area (NAFTA). Such open regionalism is of particular interest because it is a new form of regionalism. The development of a kind of 'free trade club' along open regionalist lines will have significant implications, not only for the countries participating, but also for the global trading system. This approach has been adopted by the East Asian and Asia Pacific communities for a variety of reasons which are detailed below.

We explore the significance of each of the components of open regionalism: that it is carried out on an MFN basis, that it is concerted and that it is unilateral.

Liberalisation on an *MFN basis* means that increased access to domestic markets is afforded to all trading partners, regardless of their location or their individual trade policies. APEC's members are pursuing MFN-style liberalisation for three major reasons. First, MFN liberalisation does not cause trade diversion; after liberalisation, the member countries continue to trade both with the rest of the world and within the region on a level playing field. At least part of the impetus for the creation of APEC was a realisation in East Asia that it would be significantly hurt by trade diversion losses if it opted to develop a customs union. This is particularly true because, as already noted, a large proportion of East Asian trade occurs with countries outside the region (see Garnaut 1997a). Second, liberalisation of a preferential kind in the Asia Pacific region would put enormous pressure on the system of trade reform managed by the WTO. This is because Article XXIV of the WTO Charter allows the creation of preferential trading blocs only if they are all-or-nothing affairs. According to the Charter, participants must completely liberalise, across 'substantially all trade', according to an agreed timetable, and they must do this by negotiating a formal trading bloc, for which they obtain explicit sanction from the WTO.[6] Since it would be extremely difficult to agree on the terms of such a bloc in a region as diverse as the Asia Pacific, the most likely outcome would be a 'dirty bloc', in which there would be backsliding into partial preferential liberalisation, with a picking and choosing of the sectors to be liberalised, at different times, by different players, in bilateral deals. Such behaviour would fundamentally compromise the region's respect for WTO principles, which participants are determined to uphold. Third, because this liberalisation is not preferential, other countries which are not members of the formal process, are free to join implicitly in the process by liberalising in the same way. This is particularly important in a region where a succession of economies is committing to programs of internationally-oriented industrialisation, as well as the trade and economic reforms that success in this ambition requires. By contrast, if liberalisation were to be preferential, then membership of the trading bloc is an all-or-nothing affair. Could one imagine China or Russia as members of a formal bloc which includes the United States? Furthermore, a preferential bloc would be the subject of continuing accession pressure from countries outside the arrangement hoping to obtain access to the markets within it. This would exacerbate all of the difficulties described above (see Baldwin 1993).

Ruggiero (1996) notes that:

The choice between the alternatives is a critical one; they point to very different outcomes. In the...case [of preferential discriminatory arrangements], the point at which we would arrive in no more than 20 or 25 years would be a division of the trading world into two or three intercontinental preferential areas, each with its own rules and with free trade inside the area, but with external barriers still existing within the blocs. The [open regionalism] alternative, on the other hand, points towards the gradual convergence on the basis of shared rules and principles of all the major groups...[to an outcome in which] both regional and multilateral approaches will have contributed to full liberalisation in a free global market.

The proposed approach to trade liberalisation is *concerted* because participants do believe that collective action in trade liberalisation may assist in overcoming domestic obstacles to reform. Foreign liberalisation may support domestic policy reformers; in particular, more liberalisation may be chosen if it is known that other countries are liberalising simultaneously. With such 'concertedness' each national government knows that, as it opens its own markets, there will be increased market access available in partner countries. We are all familiar with such concertedness in conventional customs unions and free trade areas. In the creation of a conventional customs union, however, such concertedness must express itself as an all-or-nothing affair, for the reasons already explained. By contrast, trade liberalisation based on open regionalism is always intended to be MFN-consistent. Open regionalism allows participants to pick and choose the sectors to liberalise, and to do this at different times, in partnership with different players. Provided that all such actions really are carried out on an MFN basis, absolutely no pressure on WTO principles is implied by the gradual exploitation of this reciprocity. Of course, to the extent that sectoral progress focuses on those goods and services for which the origin and destination of trade is concentrated within the region, trade liberalisation will be concentrated in sectors of importance to players within the region and omit other areas of greater importance for those exporting into the region from beyond its boundaries. This is thus to concede that regionalism which is 'open' may nevertheless distort the liberalisation agenda towards those sectors of most importance to the liberalising region.

That the liberalisation should be *unilateral* means that it provides freedom of action for participants to proceed in their own way, at their own pace, without reference to formal international treaties. This may appear to reduce the pressure on policy makers to liberalise, but the reverse may be true since policy reform does not have to be held back by detailed multilateral negotiations. Under the APEC process, there is freedom for individual countries to liberalise ahead of international deadlines. Participants want this for three reasons. First, this form of liberalisation has been claimed to command greater political support in many East Asian countries than one which is driven by trade specialists negotiating international treaties. Second, it is favoured by East Asian participants on behavioural and cultural grounds. It has been described as the 'Asian Way of diffuse reciprocity through understandings rather than through formally binding treaties' (see Yamazawa 1992). For this reason the APEC process may be more grassroots-driven and responsive than are WTO rounds. Such global rounds can be thought — and are thought by some Asia Pacific players — to involve a loss of sovereignty. There may be a negative perception of the WTO in some East Asian countries because of a sense that it has placed an excessive emphasis on harmonisation. In contrast, the cooperative efforts associated with participation in a project of open regionalism can give East Asian countries the confidence to prepare for WTO negotiations, disciplines and bindings. Third, and perhaps most fundamentally, open regionalism allows participants a great deal of scope for domestic reform. This brings us back to one of the central questions in the political economy of trade reform. Trade liberalisation is not in the nature of a prisoner's dilemma, beneficial only if other parties undertake it. Unilateral trade liberalisation, when it is well managed macroeconomically, and with attention given to adjustment costs, is beneficial to the country undertaking it, irrespective of whether it is being undertaken elsewhere. It is thus vital that countries not enter into forms of international negotiation which induce participants to hold back on liberalisations which they would be independently willing to undertake, so as to use these as 'concessions' in treaty negotiations. Such negotiations could actually lead to pressures which maximise the 'cost' of reform, thereby reinforcing domestic protectionist pressures and slowing the process of liberalisation rather than accelerating it. Open regionalism passes this core test in a way that no other form of international regional trade association does. Because it does not require the negotiation of legally binding treaties, participants are free to pursue the twin-track strategy of international reciprocal negotiations about market opening on the one hand and unilateral internal domestic reform on the other.

Indeed, in a strategy of open regionalism, international concertedness and domestic unilateralism can complement each other. Because liberalisation is not tightly locked together with international negotiations, participants are free to pursue both strategies (international and domestic) hand-in-hand. Joining in the process of a regional liberalisation 'club' may be a means by which policy makers, who are in favour of free trade but subject to a protectionist polity, can actually gain access to a form of 'commitment mechanism' which enables them to counteract the influence of domestic protectionism. Thus, peer pressures actually are exerted within APEC to ensure countries keep liberalising domestically. Action Plans are publicly presented at heads of government summits for approval. This brings international pressure to bear on individual governments to produce Action Plans that are meaningful. The intense publicity which these plans are afforded then acts as a particular form of commitment mechanism: there is a lurking threat of shame awaiting any leader who would subsequently depart from announced plans. This may lead to more liberalisation than might otherwise be expected. The example of the radical Philippines liberalisation, announced in preparation for the Manila APEC Summit in November 1996, is a case in point: all tariffs are to be reduced to 5 per cent by 2004. Until very recently, such a prospect would have seemed highly unlikely. In Australia, where there has recently been protectionist back-sliding, the existence of the APEC commitments has meant that protectionist decisions have nevertheless left in place both the tariff cuts promised to APEC by Australia in the run-up to 2000, and the target of free trade in 2010.

APEC participants therefore claim that open regionalism creates the right structure for incremental, cumulative, self-sustaining liberalisation. Chapter 5 lays out a number of core principles which underpin this process, in particular comparability, continuous process, and flexibility.

Whether the APEC process really represents such a coherent and durable economic formation will, of course, become clearer over time. APEC style unilateralism may be simply the best system that can be achieved given the diversity of the APEC region. The crunch on hard trade issues, including agriculture, trade facilitation, and standard-setting is yet to come. Many of these issues will need to be negotiated in the WTO, and there APEC may play a valuable catalytic role.

The recent spate of currency turmoil and macroeconomic instability may yet threaten the virtuous circle of policy reform, peace and prosperity that open regionalism promises. But so far there is no sign of retreat on the core trade reform agenda. Instead, there has simply been a broadening of the agenda to encompass regional financial cooperation and financial market reform.

Regionalism in Europe

The contrast between the Asia Pacific region and Europe could not be stronger. The European Union is a much more inward-looking group of relatively homogeneous countries bound together by strong constitutional structures. This view is presented in Chapter 4 by Portes and Vines. The next few pages draw in detail on that chapter.

The Single European Market, and the European customs union within which it was established, should be understood as the core of the European project, and its rationale should be seen as political. Europe has lived through two horrific world wars this century; the overriding end of the architects of the European Common Market/European Community/European Union was to put an end forever to these bloody conflicts. For France, which has been invaded three times by Germany in a 70-year period, and for Germany, whose political process led to the grotesque aggression of the Second World War, these experiences produced a search for forms of integration which reassured the former and tied the hands of the latter. Thus, Monnet, Schumann and the other founders of modern Europe created the European Coal and Steel Community in the 1950s, whose explicit purpose was to internationalise — and so immobilise — the means of waging war. This project then progressed to the creation of a customs union, the common market, and alongside this a heavily protected agricultural sector; it has now moved further still.

Thus, the way in which the European region has attempted to craft peace and stability as foundations for prosperity could not be more different from the approach of the Asia Pacific region. East Asia has pursued peace through prosperity and prosperity through trade liberalisation between independent sovereign states. Europe has pursued peace and stability through a process of supra-national political integration. This means that trade liberalisation initiatives for Europe will inevitably have to be achieved through a process of supra-national negotiation and compromise, rather than being the outcome of the agendas and initiatives of individual states acting independently, as is the case in the Asia Pacific region.

From this realisation flows three key implications.

First, the supra-national institutions in Europe should be seen as an inevitable outgrowth of a natural evolutionary process in which the customs union led on to the structures of the Single European Market. By the early 1980s, unreformed domestic measures and regulations threatened to thwart the effects of the liberalisation of border barriers and this led to pressures for a more truly integrated market area. Thus was born the Single European Market. The creation of the Single European Market has led not only to the elimination of a large number of formal national trade barriers, the elimination of customs formalities at national borders, the replacement of these national trade controls by Community-level instruments and the passing of trade policy competence almost entirely to the European level (although not in services). It has also led to a Europe-wide process of harmonisation and standardisation: specifically, the construction of a Europe-wide apparatus of notification, mutual recognition directives, harmonisation and certification. The Single Market has also established freedom of trade in services as well as goods. Since such service provision is highly regulated throughout Europe, this has required the establishment of Europe-wide regulatory structures (in areas such as finance and transport services). In addition, the Single Market is in the process of removing internal barriers to public procurement, the completion of which requires regulatory discipline. There has been a Europe-wide competition policy since 1958, but in 1990 this policy was extended to cover mergers. Finally, the opening of the internal market in regulated industries (in particular, telecommunications and energy) is leading to the establishment of Europe-wide regulatory structures in these industries. The conclusion is that the creation of a genuine single market has required the establishment of supra-national structures both in standard-setting and regulation. These structures have been embedded in a supra-national system of law-making and the administration of justice. It can be argued that the creation of the Single European Market has led to a form of openness in Europe which is different from the MFN removal of external trade barriers characteristic of the open regionalism process. Mutual recognition has made European markets available to all producers, not just European companies. It has meant that foreign exporters into the Union, as well as foreign investors coming to produce in the Union, have only had to satisfy standards in one member country, rather than in all of them. Other aspects of the Single Market have benefited exporters to Europe and foreign investors in Europe in similar ways. Consequently, the European Union may be a great deal more 'open' than a casual assessment would suggest.

Second, the European Monetary Union (EMU) project has been an inevitable consequence of the Single European Market. The project had its origins in the following twin-forked logic. Capital market integration implies that quasi-fixed exchange rates are not sustainable. With the high degree of capital mobility now observed in the Single Market, European countries are incapable of maintaining a fixed relative exchange rate unless they entirely and permanently surrender their separate national monetary policies. Without this, fears of devaluation could be sufficient to provoke a depreciation which governments would otherwise have been able to avoid. That is, separate currencies might remain vulnerable to self-fulfilling speculative attack. This is a view which suggests that quasi-fixed exchange rate systems, such as the European Monetary System (EMS) of the late-1980s, are intrinsically vulnerable, and that upon their creation there is no way to stand still. With the advent of the EMS, Europe could only proceed forwards to EMU, or backwards to floating exchange rates again (see Portes 1993). Crucially, completion of the single market process has been viewed by many analysts as incompatible with any return to floating exchange rates. Notice that this is not just a story about the removal of modest transactions-cost triangles; it is an industrial economics story about market integration. Full integration requires the breaking down of market segmentation; the evidence suggests that the existence of different currencies is the most plausible explanation of why the Law-of-One-Price does not hold within Europe (see Goldberg and Knetter 1997). Notice, too, that if monetary union does lead to the further integration of the internal market in the way in which this argument would suggest, then this will, in effect, also make Europe more open: it will benefit both foreign exporters into the Union and foreign investors located within the European Union.

Third, and as a consequence, there has been no macroeconomic strategy in Europe of framing policies to support outward-oriented industrialisation in the manner of the Asia Pacific. Macroeconomic policies, European style, have boiled down to strategies for internal convergence with the objective of monetary union rather than the creation of an explicitly external orientation. One could argue, in keeping with the form suggested above, that after the formation of the EMU, the resultant integrated market will be one which foreign producers will find it easier to serve; hence the monetary union may lead indirectly towards increased openness in Europe. One could also argue that European fiscal consolidation, which monetary union will hopefully make possible, will pave the way for higher European savings rates and so make possible a more competitive European real exchange rate. This may facilitate an increasing orientation of European production toward the world market, thereby engendering greater enthusiasm for further liberalisation of Europe's external trade barriers. But, in contrast with countries in the Asia Pacific region, there has as yet been no organisation of macroeconomic strategy around this objective. And there are many risks in this approach, which are noted below.

Modelling the regional integration process and implications for trade policies

The third section of this book contains important and new evidence on trade liberalisation and regional integration. The ground-breaking modelling exercises in it were specially commissioned; they provide a fundamental re-examination of the EU and APEC approaches to trade liberalisation and the nature of their trade links with the rest of the world.

In Chapter 7 by Yang, Duncan and Lawson, the GTAP (Global Trade Analysis Project) CGE (Computable General Equilibrium) model is used to examine the implications of the two distinctive approaches to trade liberalisation which have already been discussed: the creation of preferential free trade areas (PTAs) and liberalisation through MFN policies. The former approach has been adopted in Europe while the latter is being pursued in the APEC region. In an interesting twist, Yang, Duncan and Lawson attempt to estimate the impact a switch of policies would have on EU, East Asian and global welfare. What would happen if the European Union adopted an MFN approach to trade policy, while the APEC economies began the creation of a preferential PTA?

In a world in which there is imperfect competition, whether due to market structure or simply, as in the GTAP model, because goods are imperfect substitutes, there is inevitably market power. In such a world, a country undertaking MFN liberalisation inevitably suffers a terms-of-trade loss. How big that terms-of-trade loss is (compared with the static efficiency gains of trade) determines, in a static neoclassical trade theory model like GTAP, whether unilateral MFN liberalisation is worthwhile. If more than one country adopts MFN free trade at the same time, then neither country will suffer a terms-of-trade loss on that part of their trade which is with each other, providing that their potential export structures, when trade is liberalised, differ sufficiently. If a large enough number of countries adopt MFN free trade at the same time (and their export structures are sufficiently different, which is likely the larger the group), then the terms-of-trade loss is necessarily small and countries will gain from MFN liberalisation.

In such a world, a country forming a PTA with one or more other countries inevitably achieves a terms-of-trade gain because, at the margin, it diverts demands away from foreign goods towards domestic ones. It also experiences static efficiency gains due to trade creation. But there are also static efficiency losses due to the trade diversion upon which so much emphasis was placed earlier. Whether the region gains from the formation of a customs union depends on whether the trade creation effects are large (which they will be if potential export structures are different) and whether trade diversion effects are small (which depends on a comparison of cost structures with those in the rest of the world). One would expect the terms-of-trade benefits to be small for very small regions and for regions which include most of the world and largest for regions occupying about half of the world; one would also anticipate that trade creation effects would grow, the larger the size of the PTA region; and that trade diversion effects would shrink, the larger the size of the region.

Yang, Duncan and Lawson show that in the GTAP model:

- the terms-of-trade losses from MFN liberalisation can be large and so even quite large numbers of countries conducting MFN liberalisation together can experience rather little gain, particularly if their export structures are somewhat similar;

- apart from particular identifiable effects, the trade diversion effects in these models are often rather small, so that PTAs are normally beneficial; and

- taking points (i) and (ii) together, the GTAP model suggests that a medium-to-large customs union can be more welfare-improving for participating countries than an area undergoing MFN liberalisation.

This set of results has policy implications which are discussed by Yang et al. in Chapter 7. In this kind of model, it appears that a customs union might be preferable to MFN liberalisation, for the above reasons.

For Europe the position is made much more complex by the issue of agriculture. If agriculture is excluded, a move towards a PTA in the form of a customs union with the Central and Eastern European countries (CEECs) leads to little change in welfare (since the CEECs are so small). If agriculture is excluded, however, overall MFN liberalisation leads to a very large welfare loss. This is a striking second-best result; the removal of protection in non-agricultural sectors, but not in agriculture, increases the relative protection of agriculture and leads to further encouragement of agricultural over-expansion.

If agriculture is included, however, everything changes radically. Agriculture is the area of most significant trade diversion in Europe. CEEC agriculture is low cost relative to that in the European Union but high cost relative to that in the rest of the world. Consequently, the inclusion of agriculture in an EU–CEEC customs union leads to massive trade diversion, so much so that overall there is hardly any resulting benefit from the very large changes in trade flows such a union would bring about. Additionally, whoever bears the subsidy costs of the increase in agricultural protection in the CEECs actually ends up worse off. By contrast, agriculture is also the area which would give Europe the greatest benefit from MFN liberalisation in the simulations. The extra efficiency gains from including agriculture far outweigh the terms-of-trade loss from its inclusion. Thus, for Europe, full MFN liberalisation is much better than a customs union with the CEECs when agriculture is included.

Having obtained results of this kind, how much weight should be placed on them? In their MFN versus PTA aspect, they appear to support the views of Bergsten (1997), a proponent of the PTA approach to liberalisation discussed later in this chapter, rather than the supporters of open regionalism. Yet there are three important reasons why one should not take results of this kind as evidence against the open regionalism project.

First, the GTAP model does not incorporate a mechanism whereby joining a club of open regionalists reduces domestic rent-seeking, of the sort identified by Krueger (1974) would suggest. Second, there is no modelling of the idea that trade liberalisation creates pressures for increased efficiency, both because it reduces monopoly power and also because greater competition increases the need to reduce costs. Third, it ignores the ideas, emphasised for example by Sachs and Warner (1995), that becoming more open to the world market actually leads to increases in investment and growth. All of these ideas give rise to important qualifications to modelling results such as these.

In another careful modelling exercise detailed in Chapter 8, McKibbin explores the third of these issues. He uses his Dynamic Intertemporal General Equilibrium model, the Asia Pacific G-Cubed (AP-GCubed) model, to provide empirical estimates of the long-run gains to trade liberalisation for a range of countries, primarily in the Asia Pacific region. Because this model is dynamic, intertemporal, and contains explicit treatment of foreign investment, the results which are obtained using it elaborate on those produced with the GTAP model which have just been described.

The investigations are carried out under a set of alternative assumptions about the group of countries undergoing unilateral liberalisation, liberalisation as part of the ASEAN regional grouping, liberalisation as part of the APEC regional grouping, or liberalisation as part of a multilateral trade reform process. It is found, in agreement with the results from the GTAP model discussed above, that gains emerge for any one country from other countries' liberalisation and that multilateral liberalisation leads to larger overall economic gains for each country.

It is also found, in opposition to the GTAP results discussed above, that even in the medium term, substantial gains are realised by a country if it liberalises on its own. These results turn very significantly on an important feature of the AP-GCubed model. It is assumed in the simulations that trade liberalisation involves reductions in tariffs on both imported consumption goods and imported capital goods. Reductions in the cost of the latter increase the rate of return on capital and encourage an output boom, which is part of the reason for the beneficial effects. The resulting boom, in the macro-economic policy regimes being considered, actually causes an appreciation of the real exchange rate and an improvement in the terms of trade in the short to medium term. This is the key reason why this model overturns the pessimistic conclusions about unilateral liberalisation obtained from the GTAP model.

Comparative analysis of the welfare effects of alternative strategies of trade liberalisation is clearly a fruitful area for further work. No attempt has yet been made in the AP-GCubed simulations to allow for the fact that in many of the economies under examination, capital goods have been exempt from tariffs. To add this detail might well make a difference to the simulations since the rate of return on capital might not then rise.

Furthermore, longer-term issues remain unresolved. In the long run, when capital is fully adjusted, it seems possible that the AP-GCubed results might look rather like those of the GTAP model. After all, investment simply magnifies the output-expanding effects of trade liberalisation which are picked up in the GTAP model, and this might be expected to exacerbate rather than improve the terms-of-trade loss on which the pessimistic GTAP results hinge.[7]

This review suggests that further important modelling work remains to be done in this area.

Linkages

Trade and investment flows between Europe and East Asia have been growing significantly over the last ten to 15 years in the absence of any formal inter-regional links. The economic centres of gravity in the world have also shifted considerably during this time. Europe continues to account for about one-third of world GDP and half of global international trade. East Asia, however, has nearly trebled its shares of both world GDP and trade, the former at the expense of North America and the latter at the expense of other developing and transition economies, as noted in Chapter 2 by Anderson and François.

Anderson and François also point out that East Asia now contributes more to global trade than the Americas. If one nets out the intra-bloc trade of industrial economies (intra-EU, intra-CEEC, intra-NAFTA and intra-CER

[Australia–New Zealand Closer Economic Relations]) from their trade and global trade figures, then East Asia's importance is even more obvious. From this perspective, East Asia's share of global extra-bloc trade exceeds the whole of Europe's. When the European Union is treated as a single trading entity, six of the top nine economies exporting to the European Union are East Asian, with their combined merchandise exports accounting for almost 30 per cent of the global total. Malaysia, Thailand and Indonesia are among the next eight.

With the relatively rapid growth of East Asia's trade, the importance for Western Europe and East Asia of their bilateral trade flows has been steadily converging. Between 1990 and 1995, the share of Western Europe's trade with Asia rose from 8.6 to 9.6 per cent, while the share of Asia's trade with Western Europe fell from 19.3 to 16.4 per cent.[8] These data imply bilateral export trade growth rates of about 12 per cent per annum from Western Europe to Asia (double Western Europe's total export growth rate) and 8 per cent per annum growth in the opposite direction over those five years (which was only two-thirds of Asia's overall trade growth rate). By 1995, about one-third of both regions' total extra-regional trade growth was with the other. In fact, over the past ten years, Europe's trade with East Asia has actually become larger than that with North America. Nonetheless, each region's share of the other's total trade is proportionately smaller than their respective shares of global trade. In fact, Anderson and François argue that Europe–Asia trade is only about two-fifths of what one might expect given the importance of each region in global goods trade and foreign direct investment (FDI).

This suggests that there is significant room for an improvement in trade relations between these two regions. The authors also use projections based on the GTAP model to examine the impact of several prospective developments on future trade outcomes: (i) the accession to the WTO of China and hence Taiwan; (ii) the extent to which the Uruguay Round commitments are implemented on time, particularly the Agreement on Textiles and Clothing; (iii) the extent to which the East Asian countries, and especially China, continue their rapid growth through export-oriented industrialisation; and (iv) the extent to which further MFN trade liberalisation in the Asia Pacific is achieved through the APEC process.

Anderson and François emphasise the small size of existing investment flows between Europe and Asia. There is a question about whether constraints on investment flows come from the supply or demand side. Some suggest that regulations on European pension funds hamper such investment flows, while others contend that the regulatory frameworks and underdeveloped fixed-income markets in Asia have been to blame. Hiemenz (1997) observes that 65–70 per cent of the Organisation for Economic Cooperation and Development (OECD) countries' GDP (gross domestic product) is derived from services, that expansion in European trade with Asia could be expected to come largely from service exports, that service exports require a foreign investment presence, and therefore that the development of satisfactory investment codes will be important for future progress on the trade front. Yet Hiemenz also warns that while many empirical exercises clearly show that FDI now has a hand in driving trade flows, it is still unclear what determines FDI by region. No robust theory or model of FDI exists, but further work in this area might allow us to derive more accurate conclusions about the potential for deeper investment and trade linkages between the European Union and APEC.

With this background in mind, the volume moves to the dissection of Europe–East Asian economic relations from the European perspective. Chapter 9 by Langhammer analyses Europe's recent economic performance in Asia and attempts to identify the driving forces behind Europe's increasingly keen interest in the region. The author identifies the major European actors involved in developing trade relationships with Asia, and presents some important stylised facts concerning the nature of Europe's trade and FDI flows with Asia. The chapter then goes on to outline the major characteristics of recent Brussels-led policy changes in external relations and their possible underlying economic motives. Finally, Langhammer analyses the extent to which East Asian fixed-income markets might provide an opportunity for European pension plans to engage in portfolio diversification, which could further enhance the emerging capital flows between Europe and East Asia.

Responsibilities and challenges for the Asia Pacific region

Preserving openness

A key question is how easy will it be for APEC to remain true to its goal of being an 'open club', especially as negotiations move to the difficult areas of standard-setting, trade facilitation and investment codes (see Chapter 5). This is because, even when a club is nominally open to new members, the very absence of these future members from the initial discussions negatively affects the likelihood of, and benefits from, future membership. Those institutions which do form, even loose groupings like APEC, will inevitably favour incumbent interests at the expense of those of future entrants. Chapter 6 by Intal and Findlay reviews these issues. A clear example of the problems involved is given by David and Steinmueller (1997), which contains a discussion of standard-setting in telecommunications. In telecoms, the 'old world', in which standards were set by international public-interest bodies like the

International Telegraphic Union, is gradually disappearing. In the 'new world', standards are increasingly set by private market players, often in consortia, in the pursuit of competitive advantage; there is often, then, a deliberate attempt to capture international public bodies and to use them to rubber stamp these private interest standards. This example suggests that APEC will need extreme vigilance to defend openness if it moves into areas such as standard-setting.

Drysdale, Elek and Soesastro (Chapter 5) highlight the fact that issues related to standard-setting, trade facilitation and investment codes will become more important as tariffs approach zero. It will be a challenge to see if open regionalism can be applied effectively to produce cooperation in these new areas where there are no significant multilateral disciplines against discrimination. Bindings may be necessary for further progress. The informal nature of APEC may be a problem in this regard. Such informality may be convenient for governments, but the uncertainty it engenders is bad for business. Yet, given the APEC countries' repeated commitment to WTO consistency, the loose APEC structure is also seen as a means of moving towards binding in the aforementioned areas. It should be noted, however, that the APEC approach does face competition from other international economic frameworks. For instance, the OECD is in the midst of forging a binding treaty on investment. As OECD members, Japan and South Korea must eventually accede to this treaty, and Singapore has also signalled its intention to sign it; this leaves little space for alternative APEC conventions on investment.

In a related vein, it is often the case that declining industrial sectors become the most protectionist and hence the greatest impediments to trade liberalisation. This suggests that pre-emptive binding on sectors that may face decline in the near future can be an effective way to lock in liberalising processes before such industries are able to warp national trade agendas. In APEC the public announcement of action plans serves to make them *de facto* binding agreements.

APEC and regional trade tensions

APEC has already become more than just a loose community of like-minded nations encouraging each other in a process of unilateral liberalisation. It has also become a structure, an umbrella, under which trade tensions within the East Asian region are managed.

Garnaut points out in Chapter 12 that APEC also has the potential to be similarly constructive in transpacific trade relations. The tendency of the

United States to conduct trade relations bilaterally and to seek bilateral reciprocity in its trade negotiations is well known. It is also understandable. For a hegemonic player — which the United States still is — there is a natural temptation to use muscle to force a market open (in the name of both self-interest and the general good). APEC has already been a forum in which tensions between the United States and Japan, resulting from such actions by the United States, can be multilateralised and calmed.

US involvement in APEC is one of the principal reasons for both Japanese and South Korean interest in the organisation. Yet Rollo observes in Chapter 11 that there US enthusiasm for the concept of open regionalism is seriously qualified by domestic calls for reciprocitarianism. If US interest is diverted elsewhere, into the creation of the FTAA (Free Trade Area of the Americas) initiative, for instance, can we be sure that Japan and South Korea will maintain their enthusiasm for the APEC process?

APEC can also play a constructive role in US–China relations. The 1996 APEC Summit in Manila provided a congenial setting for presidential talks to set US–China relations on a more productive course. APEC also established a role for itself in the management of transpacific tension by coupling its support for the liberalisation agenda in China with endorsement of China's entry into the WTO. In Chapter 10 of this volume, Lin analyses the case for China's entry, in relation to global political and economic concerns. China's accession to the WTO highlights the tensions and problems thrown up by its transition to a market economy. WTO membership will bring with it pitfalls and opportunities, both in China and abroad. Lin argues that the latter are the more prominent.

This leads to the interrelations between the three major world trade areas: Europe, Asia and the Americas. First, suppose that we think of the world as consisting wholly of these three regions, and that we think of their interrelationships visually as an inverted triangle.[9] Is APEC a 'pole' at the bottom angle of this inverted triangle, the place where the motor of East Asian liberalisation is located? Or is it an 'edge' along the right-hand side of this triangle, a structure for managing transpacific trade relations between the United States and East Asia? Second, if APEC is the edge on the right-hand side of this triangular world, then should we think of ASEM (Asia–Europe Meeting process) as the edge on the left-hand side (between Europe and East Asia)? But if APEC is not an edge but a pole, should ASEM somehow aspire to be 'not an edge'?

This is the subject of Rollo's examination of global trade liberalisation in Chapter 11. He considers a number of scenarios with an eye to their potential risks and opportunities and puts forward the view that multilateralism is the best way to resolve the inadequacies of US reciprocitarianism, EU inwardness and APEC open regionalist unilateralism. The role of the WTO remains pivotal, since free rider problems may abound in the process of multilateral liberalisation. This brings us to the last major challenge facing APEC.

Solving the free rider problem

The most significant test facing open regionalism concerns its implications for the rest of the world. Those who do not join an open region clearly gain from a reduction of tariffs by those who do, because liberalisation gives outsiders access to the markets of the liberalising group, but members of the group do not gain access to outsiders' markets. In the context of APEC, this has become known as the 'free rider' problem. It relates, concretely, to fears that truly open regionalism would offer Europe access to a liberalising East Asian market without any corresponding opening of markets being offered by Europe.

These fears have two related facets, one of which is economic and the other, political.

Economically, unilateral trade liberalisation may squander APEC's negotiating leverage with other countries and regions. Politically, it could doom the commitment to liberalisation in key APEC economies like the United States (Bergsten 1997: 12). In response to these fears, Bergsten suggests a modification of open regionalism which would have nearly all of the benign features described at the beginning of this chapter, but which, nevertheless, would not make members' liberalisation entirely MFN. They would afford this liberalisation only to those outsiders who offer similar liberalisation themselves. The requirement of reciprocal liberalisation has earned this approach the label of reciprocitarianism.

The proposal is structured as follows. Firstly, APEC should continue with its process of *concerted unilateral* liberalisation along the timetable agreed at Bogor in 1994 and reaffirmed at Seoul in 1995 (see APEG 1994; 1995). This would see APEC setting about unilateral tariff reductions of an MFN kind, with the objective of moving towards the ultimate objective of MFN free trade. However, APEC might collectively reserve the right not to make the last stage of the process multilateral *unless* the rest of the world joined it in a new WTO round of trade negotiations and so moved to global free trade. APEC could make clear that in the final stage of the trade liberalisation process it would move to a preferential free trade area rather than MFN free trade if outside countries failed to liberalise their trading regimes. The prospect that APEC would keep these external tariffs and would not remove them until the rest of the world joined with it would, it is argued, remove the incentive for outsiders to free ride in seeking access to the liberalising APEC market. The final choice of whether free trade or a free trade area is the endpoint of reform could be left until tariff reduction has reached its final stages. In the APEC process, this point is still a long way off, leaving much time for negotiation, and for 'constructive ambiguity' about the ultimate outcome.

Although perhaps initially persuasive, there are vital objections to such a proposal. First, it is entirely unfeasible in that there is no collective action mechanism by which this could be done within the loose APEC grouping. APEC is not founded on an international agreement, nor does it possess any supra-national authority which would allow it to take collective action of the kind presumed in Bergsten's calculations. Nor is there any prospect that this will change. APEC governments undertake actions on trade liberalisation or other matters individually (Drysdale 1997a: 15). Under Article XXIV of the WTO, as already noted above, such a policy would need to be set up as an actual formal bloc, with a formal membership and an agreed timetable, and this would need formal WTO approval. APEC has eschewed any moves in this direction. Second, even if the participating countries were to meet all of the requirements of Article XXIV, such an approach would add to the global proliferation of rules of origin, the 'spaghetti effect' of which Bhagwati (1996) has been so critical.

These objections appear to us to be decisive. Nevertheless, any analysis of APEC must address the issue of how the free rider problem can be dealt with, both at the level of perceptions and at the level of reality. We believe persuasion is preferable to threat as a negotiating approach, and that an alternative strategy is possible. This would bundle the final stage of APEC MFN liberalisation with a global round of MFN trade liberalisation. Such a round would make it possible to exert pressure on foreigners without the deep threat to the order of the global trading system implied by reciprocitarianism. Clearly, this strategy could have the effect of making the final stages of the APEC liberalisation process conditional on a successful global round of trade negotiations. But it will also be true that by then, just as members of APEC come to see the benefits of liberalisation, outsiders may also appreciate just how large these benefits can be. Progress along these lines could be achieved without threat to the integrity of the international trading system.

Drysdale, Elek and Soesastro (Chapter 5) propose that a positive response to APEC's lead on trade liberalisation, in which the European Union also commits itself to eliminating all border barriers to trade and investment by 2020, would set the stage for effective cooperation among both groups to achieve free and open trade and investment between them as well as within each region. If this were to occur, there would be no need for special arrangements between the European and Asia Pacific economies to liberalise border barriers. On a supporting note, Yang, Duncan and Lawson find that 'modelling demonstrates with robustness ...that there is a substantial free-riding problem with MFN liberalisation in both Europe and the APEC region'. If APEC and Europe react to this problem by reciprocating each other's MFN liberalisation, it will enhance the welfare improvements for both parties as well as for the rest of the world. It has been proposed that the WTO might be able to play a role in resolving the uncertainties hanging over unilateral liberalisation for both regions. Clearly, there seems to be good support for a multilateral approach to deepening EU–APEC trade relations. Fears of terms-of-trade losses and free-riding seem to be the key impediments to the multilateral agenda. Given the European Union's commitment to multilateral liberalisation through the WTO, this could be the venue through which new relationships can be forged with the APEC countries.

It is thus our view that the free rider issue can and should be dealt with in a way which continues to observe the MFN principle of liberalisation. To use a threat, even if only an implicit threat, that this principle might be abandoned involves paying too high a price for a leveraged negotiating position. APEC's commitment to open regionalism could play an important role in the run-up to the next round of WTO negotiations. As Garnaut asks in Chapter 12, 'What are the prospects for Asia to use the ASEM process as a forum to convince Europe to make a commitment to liberalisation?'

Responsibilities and challenges for Europe

Preserving openness

One unexpected challenge to Europe from the evolution of global trade relations concerns its ability to outgrow the customs union on which it was originally based. As the world moves towards globally free trade in goods and services at the beginning of the next century, and as the European customs union thereby withers away and the European Union loses one of its key competencies, will the European institutional structure be strong enough to transform itself? Or will statist protectionist pressures, familiar from the national level, ultimately prove to be an obstacle at the European level to Europe playing a constructive role in moving the world to really free trade?

Reforming relations with the European periphery

The APEC process makes possible a straightforward relationship between core countries and peripheral ones. Countries can pursue many of the policy initiatives and reap the same gains whether formally they are in or out of the club: open regionalism effectively excludes no-one, and it also encourages peripheral countries to liberalise unilaterally. In particular, the Asia Pacific structures, including APEC, are a framework in which a cumulative process of industrial relocation through foreign investment can take place: as development has occurred and real wages have risen in the most advanced centres, we have seen relocation from Japan and the original four newly industrialising economies or NIEs (Hong Kong, Korea, Singapore and Taiwan) first to Malaysia, Thailand, Indonesia, and parts of China, and later to the Chinese hinterland, to Vietnam, Pakistan and India. In an open regional system there is no institutional impediment to these ever-widening concentric circles of development.

In contrast with this, the European Union's relationship with its periphery appears fundamentally flawed. It will have been 15 years from 1989 to the time at which the first four of the ten CEECs are admitted to membership of the European Union. Meanwhile, these countries have been offered — and accepted — entirely unsatisfactory hub-and-spokes free trade arrangements with the European core. As Portes and Vines discuss in Chapter 4, these arrangements are not part of any coherent larger scheme and have the following four deep problems.

Zero-tariff status does not mean free access to EU markets. The European Union has a long history of imposing contingent protection such as anti-dumping and voluntary export restraints.

Second, rules of origin impede the use of inputs from third country low-cost suppliers (for example from the Asia Pacific region). Thus, quite independently of (declining) levels of tariff protection, they can block the effective integration of the CEECs into European and world markets. Since so much of world trade, especially exports from industrialising countries such as those in Eastern Europe, is globally vertically integrated and requires inputs from other countries, this may be a serious obstacle to developments in Eastern Europe.

Third, because the EU agreements are bilateral, they do not give producers in any one CEEC the right of access to the markets of other CEECs. Since EU firms, located in the hub of the agreements, have such access, this provides an incentive to service CEEC markets from within the European Union rather than from within any CEEC. These markets are not small and this trade structure could become a significant impediment to the development of indigenous industries in the CEECs.

Finally, agricultural trade is mostly excluded from the liberalisation. Yet agriculture is an obvious area of comparative advantage for the CEECs.

All of this places extreme difficulties in the way of CEEC producers developing the kind of vertically disaggregated production networks which have characterised the pattern of Asia Pacific integration and development. It is no surprise that, with some exceptions, inward investment and growth in these countries has been disappointingly slow.

These 'half-way problems' arise because the European Union's status as a customs union creates an impossible dilemma for the CEECs. Either they join the European Union, and get access to proper free trade with the European Union (even though the result will be trade diversion, and even though membership will require them to take a phenomenally large number of deep-integration steps extraordinarily rapidly, to adjust to the single market), or they choose MFN free trade with the global market and remain outside the European customs union, bedevilled by rules of origin and threats of contingent protection from their closest neighbours.

The worst of all outcomes is the current 'middle way': delayed membership and no MFN free trade. It results from foot-dragging by existing EU members. But this foot-dragging is not a chance outcome. In keeping with the discussion above, this is exactly the problem which APEC members would expect to bedevil the process of liberalisation, European style.

It is unclear how Russia fits into this scheme, given the politics and economics of its relations with Europe. Now that Russia will be admitted to membership of APEC, how will its economic relations with Europe, including the CEECs, evolve?

EU relations with North Africa have features which are perhaps worse still: no prospect of eventual membership of the European Union; trade diversion because these countries have lowered their very high tariff levels only towards the European Union; and quota ridden and contingent access to the European market, all of which encourage rent-seeking rather than expansion. This is not an institutional recipe for a constructive economic relationship between the European Union and North Africa. At least one hopeful sign has recently emerged from EU discussions. Recent decisions in Brussels suggest that Europe has shelved its ambition to create an ever-spreading range of such hub-and-spokes arrangements with other countries and regions such as Southern Africa and Mercosur.

Managing the risks of Economic and Monetary Union

The EMU project also presents large risks. This is because monetary union, begun to make possible the completion of the Single European Market, has become entangled in another issue — the need for fiscal consolidation in Europe. Throughout the 1980s and into the mid-1990s, deficits have averaged well above 4 per cent of GDP in the European Union. In the EU15, the ratio of government debt to GDP has risen from 40 per cent in 1979 to about

75 per cent in 1996. The EU15 budget deficit fell below 3 per cent of GDP only in 1989, a year of unsustainable growth. Given this history, countries in Europe are now simultaneously moving towards significant fiscal restraint. Such fiscal consolidation is certainly a necessary condition for the increased national savings necessary for any increase in European growth.

If the required large-scale fiscal restraint is not to cause unemployment, it must be accompanied by significant monetary loosening, but achieving such a policy mix remains problematic. The difficulty is that fiscal restraint needs to be decided at the level of the individual member nation whereas monetary loosening within EMU can only be achieved on a Europe-wide basis. Furthermore, there can only be monetary loosening if most countries do achieve the necessary restraint. Any individual country in Europe considering fiscal restraint has no guarantee that others will do the same, no guarantee that monetary policy will be loosened, and so no guarantee that unemployment will not emerge. Consequently, consolidation by an individual nation currently looks distinctly unattractive. Cooperation is required. The Maastricht fiscal convergence criteria, and the stability pact agreed in Dublin in December 1996, are best seen as devices to impose a 'cooperative' and coordinated fiscal consolidation on all members of the monetary union.

Success — in the sense of avoiding large unemployment adjustment costs and the threat these imply to the continuation of the consolidation process — requires a sustained, medium-term rise in private sector investment (or reduced private savings). The cut in interest rates required for this may need to be large and pre-emptive, and there may need to be a considerable fall in the value of the euro. The former would produce the fall in private sector savings and the rise in private sector investment that is required to avoid large-scale unemployment; the latter would augment this response by means of an increase in net exports. Success would be cumulative. The rise in net exports would promote further investment, further supply improvement, and could lead to a cumulative and sustained reduction in unemployment. This would involve the achievement, Europe-wide, of what has been achieved in Britain and the United States on the macroeconomic front in the last five years.

There is, however, a danger that European policy makers — and voters — might fail to understand the links in this chain of policy initiatives. In particular, there is no evidence that European Central Bankers understand the role which they need to play in this process. They appear to be preoccupied with the simple view that monetary tightness will be required to establish the anti-inflation credibility of the new European Central Bank. The risk therefore looms of a non-cooperative scenario, one in which the fiscal authorities do not cooperate with each other, and the Central Bank cooperates with no-one. There could be too little fiscal consolidation, with too little commitment, to persuade the European Central Bank to carry out the necessary monetary loosening. But there may be enough fiscal consolidation (albeit reluctant) to cause a fall in output. Under this scenario, investment falls rather than rises; the exchange rate does not depreciate, and net exports do not rise. Unemployment goes on rising, and investment will not recover. Tax revenues fall, and so the fiscal consolidation is under-done. In 1997 the French electorate roundly rejected austerity, and the Bundesbank publicly demanded macroeconomic rigour. The unsatisfactory scenario sketched above suddenly edged much closer to reality. The recent problems in East Asia and the large depreciation of East Asian currencies have tipped the balance in the same direction.

If EMU is underpinned by such flawed policies, it will be difficult for Europe to move towards increased openness in the manner discussed earlier in this chapter. Europe will find it hard to play a constructive role towards its periphery, in its relations with East Asia, and in a new WTO round; indeed in any shared global agenda at all. This is a recipe for a Europe which resists trade liberalisation.

Global issues: A shared commitment to multilateralism

The chapters in this book point toward a clear conclusion. EU inwardness, US reciprocitarianism, and APEC open-regionalism/unilateralism may all in themselves be dead ends.[11] The first approach could lead to a virtual colonisation of Eastern Europe and North Africa but no further, the second to a bilateral morass, and the third may run out of steam when countries must deal with increasingly difficult issues. The best way to resolve an impasse of this kind is multilateralism, especially when the enthusiasm for liberalisation has spread so far and so deep.

Two important steps forward seem possible, the first regional and the second global in scope. First, the countries on Europe's periphery might usefully adopt some of the methods of open regionalism. Clearly, such an approach would not be relevant to those for whom there is a prospect of accession to the European Union in the near future. For others, however, such as Bulgaria, Latvia, Lithuania or the Ukraine, or indeed Turkey and the North African states, the possibility exists for further integration into the global market through concerted but unilateral MFN tariff reductions to and below European levels, at the same time as any increased access to European markets is negotiated. They might then seek European assurances that this would not lead to the imposition of rules of origin or of contingent protectionism by the European Union. In seeking to do this, these countries might find natural allies in the East Asian countries, both as potential trading partners, and as mentors in the required process of institutional change. In fact, they might change the whole dynamic of intra-European trade relations. The prospective membership in APEC of Russia now suggests that these countries might even be able to use such an approach to propel the reform of trade relations with Russia high onto the international agenda.[12]

Second, there may be the potential for global alliances which could enable Europe, the United States and the other APEC participants to break out of the limitations of their respective approaches to trade liberalisation. It might be the case, for example, that the ASEM process could enable Europe and APEC's non-US members to find sectors in which there is shared interest in liberalisation, particularly as a means of defusing US fears about European free-riding. The recent agreement on information technology is a case in point; there may be other areas of environmental or medical technology, for instance, which could yield similar success. More speculatively, Europe and APEC could consider the adoption of a strategy to promote a whole new round of global trade negotiations. If Europe and APEC were to do this, it might completely change the manner in which trade negotiations are conducted well into the next century.

Notes

1 The authors are grateful to Jim Rollo and Ross Garnaut for very helpful comments on a draft of this introduction.
2 These issues are discussed in a paper by Peter Drysdale (1997).
3 APEC, Ninth Ministerial Meeting Joint Statement, Vancouver, 21–22 November 1997.
4 These points are elaborated in Ross Garnaut, 'ASEAN and the regionalisation and globalisation of world trade', mimeo, Australia National University, November 1997.
5 Bergsten (1997) reviews the ambiguities associated with this term.
6 The reasons for this are entirely understandable. Formal constraints on bilateral liberalisation are essential if the MFN principle which underpins the WTO rules for a liberal world trading system is to be protected. The particular set of rules embodied in Article XXIV states that non-MFN liberalism is allowed if and only if it seeks to create a fully integrated market such as exists within a single country.
7 McKibbin also provides some valuable results concerning short-run dynamics. In the short run, unilateral liberalisation (admittedly undertaken with a non-accommodating monetary exchange rate policy) can cause a Keynesian-type slump because the reduction of demand for import-competing goods is not outweighed by the effects of increased investment, whereas it does not cause a slump if other countries expand their demand for exports at the same time as the country switches its demand towards imports. Thus, even if unilateral liberalisation does increase

output and welfare in the long run, liberalisation by other countries may help to reduce short-run adjustment costs.

8 Ulrich Hiemenz noted that the data on which these figures are based include statistics on both manufacturing and agricultural sectors. He argued that the apparent decline in importance of Western Europe for East Asia may be due to price effects obscured by this aggregation.

9 This is Simon Broadbent's contribution, made initially at the London conference in May 1997.

10 What follows in this and the next section draws on Chapter 4 by Portes and Vines.

11 A point we owe to a contribution from Hugh Patrick at the London conference.

12 A point suggested by Ponciano Intal.

References

Asia–Pacific Economics Group (APEG) (1994) *Asia Pacific Profiles*, Canberra.

—— (1995) *Asia Pacific Profiles*, Canberra.

Baldwin, R. (1993) 'A domino theory of regionalism', Discussion Paper No. 857, CEPR, London.

Bergsten, C.F. (1997) 'Open regionalism', mimeo, Institute of International Economics, Washington DC.

Bhagwati, Jagdish (1996) 'Preferential trade agreements: the wrong road', *Law and Policy and International Relations* 27(4).

David, P.A. and W. Edward Steinmueller (1997) 'Standards, trade and competition in the emerging global infrastructure environment', *Telecommunications Policy 20(10), December.* Also published in P. David and T. Shaiman, 'Standards setting and the global information infrastructure', Newsletter, Global Economic Research Programme No 4, CEPR, London, pp. 2–7.

Drysdale, P. (1988) *International Economic Pluralism: Economic Policy in East Asia and the Pacific*, Columbia University Press & Allen and Unwin.

—— (1997a) 'APEC and the WTO: complementary or competing?', paper presented to the Institute of Southeast Asian Studies APEC Roundtable, Singapore.

—— (1997b) 'Tigers won't be tamed', *Compass*, National Australia Bank, November, pp. 20–23.

—— and R. Garnaut (1994) *Asia Pacific Regionalism: Readings in International Economic Relations*, HarperEducational in association with Australia–Japan Research Centre, Canberra.

Garnaut, R. (1996a) *Open Regionalism and Trade Liberalisation*, Sydney: Allen and Unwin.

—— (1997a) 'Open Regionalism: An Asia Pacific contribution to the world trading system?', mimeo, Institute of Southeast Asian Studies, Singapore.

—— (1997b) 'ASEAN and the regionalisation and globalisation of world trade', mimeo, Australian National University, Canberra.

Goldberg, P.K. and M.M. Knetter (1997) 'Goods prices and exchange rates: what we have learned', *Journal of Economic Literature* 35(3), pp. 1243–72.

Hiemenz, Ulrich (1997) Comment on 'Europe and East Asia in an Integrating World Economy: Retrospect and Prospect' by Kym Anderson and Joseph F. François, mimeo.

Krueger, Anne O. (1974) 'The political economy of the rent-seeking society", *American Economic Review* 64(3) pp. 291–303.

Lee Jong-Wha (1993) 'International trade distortions and long-run economic growth', *International Monetary Fund Staff Papers* 40(2) pp. 299–328.

Portes, R. (1993) 'EMS and EMU after the fall', *The World Economy* 16(1), pp. 1–16.

Ruggiero, R. (1996) 'Implications for trade in a borderless world', speech of the Director-General of the WTO to the World Trade Congress, Singapore, April.

Sachs, Jeffrey D. and Andrew Warner (1995) 'Economic reform and the process of global integration', in William Brainard and George Perry, eds, *Brookings Papers on Economic Activity*, No. 1, August, Washington, The Brookings Institution, Washington, DC, pp. 108–18.

Yamazawa, Ippei (1992) 'On Pacific economic integration', *Economic Journal* 102(415), November, pp. 1519–29.

2 Commercial links between Western Europe and East Asia: retrospect and prospects

KYM ANDERSON AND JOSEPH FRANÇOIS

Introduction

Over the past 15 years, regional and global economic integration both took important forward steps. During the period 1985–94, the ratio of world trade to gross domestic product (GDP) rose three times faster than in the preceding ten years and nearly twice as fast as in the 1960s. Since 1985, the flow of foreign direct investment (FDI) as a share of global GDP has doubled (World Bank 1996). This internationalisation is due to a considerable extent to unilateral trade and macroeconomic reforms and associated falls in international transport and communications costs. But those reforms themselves were stimulated by and contributed to regional integration initiatives in Europe, North America and smaller regions. Moreover, the most comprehensive of multilateral initiatives, the Uruguay Round, also promises to contribute to globalisation during its implementation over the next few years. All these developments have made and will continue to make the national economies of the world more interdependent, although the nature and extent of the contributions to integration vary considerably across regions.

In an important survey paper, Winters (1996) makes clear that, despite a massive research effort, neither theoretical models nor empirical studies are yet able to answer unequivocally Bhagwati's memorable question as to whether regional integration agreements (RIAs) are stepping stones or stumbling blocks to global economic integration and welfare improvement, such are the complexities of the economics and political economy involved. Even if attention is focused on just one RIA, such as the European Union (EU) and its effects on outsiders, analysts are unable to agree on whether the rest of the world is better or worse off with than without the European Union — not least because we are unsure of the counterfactual.

Bearing this in mind, the present paper has two modest aims. The first is simply to examine the history of regional and global economic integration of

Europe, East Asia and elsewhere, as reflected in actual intra and extra-regional trade and investment data, and to see what this historical pattern has meant for bilateral trade and investment flows between Western Europe and East Asia. With that as background, the second aim of the paper is to analyse empirically the total and bilateral trade growth prospects of East Asia and Western Europe over the next dozen years. The analysis is conducted in the context of regional and global economic growth, Uruguay Round implementation, and possible additional APEC (Asia Pacific Economic Cooperation) and other trade liberalisations. We work with a forward-looking numerical model (a global Computable General Equilibrium or CGE model) to provide those projections of the world.

Several potential developments will influence these prospective trade and FDI outcomes and their effects on economic welfare. One of the more important is the accession to the World Trade Organization (WTO) of China (and hence Taiwan) and its impact on China's economic growth. A second is the extent to which the Uruguay Round commitments are implemented on time, particularly with respect to the Agreement on Textiles and Clothing. A third is the challenge of delivering further most favoured nation (MFN) trade liberalisation in the Asia Pacific through the APEC process. The fourth is a possible new WTO round of multilateral trade negotiations. Section 2 of this paper is devoted to exploring the historical record. We then turn, in sections 3 and 4 of the paper, to an examination of prospects under various scenarios. The final section of the paper is devoted to drawing out policy implications from this empirical exercise.

International economic integration in Europe and Asia: some facts[1]

During the past three decades, the economic centres of gravity in the world have shifted considerably. While Europe continues to contribute about one-third of world GDP and half of global international trade, East Asia has nearly trebled its shares of both GDP and trade. Its GDP share has grown at the expense of North America and its trade share at the expense of other developing and transition economies (Table 2.1). East Asia's share of world trade now exceeds North America's. If one nets out the intra-bloc trade of the industrial economies from theirs and global trade, then East Asia's share of global extra-bloc trade now exceeds the whole of Europe's. When the European Union is treated as a single trading entity (as it often now is by compilers of world trade statistics), it turns out that six of the top nine exporting economies are now East Asian, their combined merchandise exports

Table 2.1   *Relative importance of Europe, North America and East Asia in global GDP and trade, 1963 and 1996, per cent*

	GDP		Trade[a]	
	1963	1995	1963	1996
Europe	34	35	50	48
NAFTA	45	28	18	18
East Asia	9	24	9	24
Rest of world	12	13	23	10
Total	100	100	100	100

Note: a Total of merchandise exports plus imports.
Source: Updated from Norheim, Finger and Anderson (1993) using World Bank (1997) and WTO (1997).

accounting for almost 30 per cent of the global total, and Malaysia, Thailand and Indonesia are among the next eight (WTO 1997).

What about the regionalisation of international trade and investment flows? For Europe (East and West combined), the intra-regional trade share has been remarkably stable for the 160 years for which data are readily available. The share was two-thirds throughout the nineteenth century, it dropped to two-fifths in the middle half of this century, and has since crept up to around three-quarters. But for most of that long period the ratio of Europe's trade to GDP has been increasing — so much so that the share of Europe's GDP that is traded with the rest of the world quadrupled during the 100 years to 1930, and it has remained at around one-eighth of GDP since then (Anderson and Norheim 1993).

Nonetheless, compared with other regions, both Eastern and Western European trades have been much more concentrated in their own regions. Western Europe's intra-regional share of total trade has risen steadily from 50 to 70 per cent since the 1950s, and Eastern Europe's jumped from less than 20 to more than 60 per cent with the formation of the CMEA (Council for Mutual Economic Assistance) before crashing back to below 20 per cent following the CMEA's demise in the 1990s. By contrast, the intra-regional trade shares have been fairly steady at around a much lower one-third for North America, no more than one-fifth for the rest of the Americas, and until recently around two-fifths (now one-half) for Asia (Table 2.2).

Table 2.2   *Share of intra-regional trade in each region's total trade,[a]*
1928 to 1995, per cent

	1928	1958	1968	1979	1990	1995
Western Europe	51	53	63	66	72	69
Eastern Europe & FSU	19	61	64	54	36	19
North America	25	32	37	30	32	36
Latin America	11	17	19	20	15	21
Asia[b]	46	41	37	41	45	51
Africa	10	8	9	6	6	10
Middle East	5	12	8	6	8	8

Notes: a Total of merchandise exports plus imports.
       b Asia includes Australia and New Zealand plus the Southwest Pacific
       islands.
Source: Revised and updated from Norheim, Finger and Anderson (1993) using
       WTO (1996).

One would expect Asia's intra-regional trade share to have grown simply because East Asia's share of global trade has grown so dramatically. The impact of the latter can be netted out by calculating the index of intensity of intra-regional trade. That index is defined approximately as the share of intra-regional trade in a region's total trade as a ratio of the region's share of global trade.[2] Between 1958 and 1990 that index increased by 15 per cent for both Western Europe and North America and rose by more than 40 per cent for Eastern Europe/former Soviet Union (FSU), but it *fell* by 27 per cent for Asia (Anderson and Norheim 1993). That might suggest the intensity of Europe's trade with itself is being reinforced by its regional integration agreements, whereas the absence of substantial inward-looking agreements in East Asia is having the opposite effect on Asia's trade pattern.

But what about the share of GDP that is traded extra-regionally? For Western Europe, North America and Asia, those shares are currently remarkably similar at around 15 per cent. North America's share doubled over the past two decades because of the rise in its overall trade-to-GDP ratio but the others have changed little. For the world as a whole the extra-regional trade share of GDP has increased since the 1960s from one-eighth to one-sixth (Table 2.3). But notice that within Asia, the developing countries have raised substantially their share of GDP traded extra-regionally, from one-fifth to one-third over that period. What has been happening to bilateral trade flows

Table 2.3   *Shares of regional GDP traded extra-regionally,[a] 1928 to
1995, per cent*

	1928	1958	1968	1979	1995
Western Europe	17	16	13	16	15
North America (incl. Mexico)	8	6	6	13	15
Asia[b] of which:	17	16	14	16	14[c]
Developing Asia	22	19	20	28	34[c]
World	15	13	12	19	16[c]

Notes: a Total of merchandise exports plus imports.
          b Asia includes Australia and New Zealand plus the South-west Pacific
          islands.
          c 1993.
Source: Updated from Norheim, Finger and Anderson (1993).

between Europe and Asia? With the relatively rapid growth of Asia's trade,
the importance of each to the other has been converging steadily. For
example, between 1990 and 1995 the share of Western Europe's trade with
Asia rose from 8.6 to 9.6 per cent while the share of Asia's trade with Western
Europe fell from 19.3 to 16.4 per cent. Those data imply bilateral export
trade growth rates over those five years of about 12 per cent per annum from
Western Europe to Asia (double its total export growth rate) and 8 per cent
annual growth in the opposite direction (two-thirds of Asia's overall trade
growth rate). By 1995 each region was trading with the other just on one-
third of its total extra-regional trade. However, the share of each in the other's
total trade is only about two-fifths as large as the other's share of global
trade, suggesting much room yet for improving trade relations between the
two regions (Table 2.4).

Much the same is true of trade between Asia and Central and Eastern
Europe plus the FSU. That trade has grown much slower than each of those
region's total trade. Indeed, there has been virtually no growth in exports
from Asia to those economies in transition over the five years to 1995. The
former Comecon economies still trade very intensively among themselves
(albeit less than in 1990) and with Western Europe (which, in the data in
Table 2.4, includes eastern Germany). The share of their exports to Asia is
less than half Asia's share of world trade, and the share of Asia's exports to
them is only one-third the latter's share of world trade.

Table 2.4   *Regional shares in and growth of Europe's and Asia's trade,[a] 1990 to 1995, per cent*

Distribution of region's exports	Western Europe	C. and E. Europe & FSU	North America	Asia[b]	World
Western Europe					
1990	70.2	3.7	8.0	8.6	100.0
1995	68.9	4.4	7.4	9.6	100.0
C. & E. Europe & FSU					
1990	42.5	38.7	2.1	7.5	100.0
1995	57.3	18.9	4.8	12.8	100.0
Asia[b]					
1990	19.3	1.7	24.4	45.1	100.0
1995	16.4	1.0	23.8	50.9	100.0
Regional shares of world trade (X + M)					
1990	48.6	3.2	16.9	21.1	100.0
1995	44.2	3.0	17.3	25.8	100.0
Growth in trade value (per cent p.a., 1990–95)					
Western Europe					
Exports	5	9	5	12	6
Imports	5	10	5	8	5
C. & E. Europe & FSU					
Exports	10	-8	25	6	8
Imports	9	-8	3	-1	5
Asia[b]					
Exports	8	-1	8	16	12
Imports	12	6	10	16	12

Notes: a Total of merchandise exports plus imports.
   b Asia includes Australia and New Zealand plus the Southwest Pacific islands.
Source: Compiled from WTO (1996) data.

FDI flows have grown much faster than trade flows during the past decade or so, but the growth has not been uniform across regions. Outward FDI has grown relatively slowly from the ageing economies of Western Europe and Japan during the 1990s, especially compared with North America, Australasia and Asia's newly industrialising economies whose inward FDI also has grown rapidly (Table 2.5). During the present decade China has been more than four times as important as a host to FDI than all of Central and Eastern Europe plus the FSU. In 1995 it accounted for one-eighth of global FDI inflows,

Table 2.5   *Annual volume of inward and outward foreign direct*
investment, various regions, 1984 to 1995, current US$ billions

	1984–89		1990–94		1995	
	Inward	Outward	Inward	Outward	Inward	Outward
EU15	37.7	62.6	78.7	108.2	111.9	132.3
Other Western Europe	2.1	5.3	3.7	8.8	3.7	9.6
C. & E. Europe & FSU	0.0	0.0	3.8	0.2	12.4	0.3
Japan	0.0	20.8	1.6	29.3	0.0	21.3
Hong Kong	1.4	1.8	1.6	10.5	2.1	25.0
China	2.3	0.6	16.1	2.4	37.5	3.5
Other East Asia	6.0	2.7	15.9	7.2	22.7	13.0
North America	48.6	21.5	40.9	47.8	71.4	100.3
Australia & New Zealand	4.5	3.6	6.7	3.7	15.6	6.7
Rest of world	12.8	2.7	23.7	3.8	37.6	5.8
World	115.4	121.6	192.7	221.9	314.9	317.8

Source: Compiled from United Nations (1996, Annex Tables 1 and 2).

equal in value to more than one-quarter of all of Western Europe's or one-
third of North America's FDI outflows. Historically, Hong Kong has been a
major supplier of investment funds for China.

In the decade to 1995 the importance of FDI in gross fixed capital formation rose by more than a third globally but little of that change is evident in
OECD (Organisation for Economic Cooperation and Development)
countries. By contrast, that indicator for developing Asia rose from 2.6 to 8.2
per cent for inward FDI and from 1.4 to 5.0 per cent for outward FDI, taking
it from well below the global average of 3.2 per cent in 1984–89 to well
above the global average of 4.0 per cent in 1995 (United Nations 1996,
Annex Table 2.5).

The regional distribution of FDI stock data in 1992 and their growth since
1980 are reported in Table 2.6. The European Union has invested only a
small proportion of its funds in East Asia, and of the FDI funds invested in
the European Union, only a small proportion came from East Asia. In each
case the shares by 1992 amounted to only 4 per cent of the EU total, or
around 8 per cent if intra-EU FDI is not counted. The numbers in parentheses
in Table 2.6 suggest these shares changed little between 1980 and 1992,
although they may have increased in the 1990s (OECD 1996; European Commission and UNCTAD 1996; UNCTAD 1996). Those 4 per cent shares are
much smaller than East Asia's shares of global FDI stocks, both outward and

Table 2.6   *Regional shares (and their growth since 1980) in stocks of outward and inward foreign direct investment, EU12, East Asia and North America, 1992,[a] per cent*

	EU12	East Asia	North America	Rest of world	Total
Outward FDI from:					
EU12	48	4	28	18	100
	(14)	(-2)	(-5)	(-6)	
East Asia	16	24	40	15	100
	(7)	(-11)	(14)	(-9)	
North America	38	11	23	24	100
	(4)	(5)	(4)	(-4)	
[Share of world FDI					
inward stock]	*40*	*10*	*28*	*22*	*100]*
Inward FDI into:					
EU12	49	4	25	20	100
	(12)	(2)	(-15)	(-1)	
East Asia	14	48	19	17	100
	(-5)	(6)	(-4)	(12)	
North America	44	19	23	12	100
	(5)	(15)	(-18)	(-3)	
[Share of world FDI					
outward stock]	*45*	*16*	*30*	*9*	*100]*

Note: a Numbers in curved parentheses are the percentage changes in the shares of FDI from 1980 to 1992.
Source: Compiled from Bora (1996) and UNCTAD (1996, Annex Tables 3 and 4).

inward (16 and 10 per cent, respectively). The story is similar from the viewpoint of other regions: East Asia had by 1992 around 16 per cent of its outward FDI invested in EU12, and almost the same share (14 per cent) of its inward FDI had come from the European Union — but at a time when the European Union accounted for 45 and 40 per cent of global outflows and inflows of FDI, respectively. So while it is true that the European Union has been much more important to East Asia than vice versa in terms of the volume of FDI, that is what is to be expected given the European Union's greater importance in global FDI stocks. Again, as with goods trade, these relative shares suggest that the European Union is less than two-fifths as important to East Asia's FDI as the European Union is to the rest of the world, and likewise for the importance of East Asia to the European Union. It needs to be kept in mind, however, that small changes in these shares mask huge growth in levels of foreign direct investment. Between 1981–83 and 1991–93, the ratio of FDI to GDP grew for OECD countries from 0.9 to 1.6 per cent and for East Asia's developing countries from 0.7 to 1.1 per cent (World Bank 1996, Figure 2).

In short, these merchandise trade and investment data make clear that the world is becoming more integrated, not only within regions but also between the major regions, despite the fact that there has been an unprecedented proliferation of regional integration agreements this decade, especially in Europe. This conclusion probably would not change greatly if it had been possible to include services trade data. That does not mean those agreements are necessarily a good thing for the world economy, however, because even more inter-regional integration and economic growth may have occurred without them. Certainly the data in Tables 2.4 and 2.6 suggest there is still considerable scope for expanding European–Asian trade and investment, given the importance of each region in global trade and FDI. That raises the question to be addressed in the next section: to what extent will economic growth and the trade liberalisations in prospect for the next decade raise bilateral flows and shares and improve economic welfare in the two regions?

Numerical projections to 2010

We now turn from historical fact to numerical conjecture. To this end, we work with a global CGE model that employs the GTAP (Global Trade Analysis Project) data set (see below) and IMF (International Monetary Fund) and World Bank projections for GDP in 2010 (see Anderson et al. 1997a, b and IMF 1997).

The interaction of open economies is complex, involving both trade flows and investment flows. It is even more complex if we consider intertemporal interactions, as they spill over to accumulation mechanisms, affecting the stock of capital and hence the evolution of the structure of production. Given enough data, one could construct and estimate an econometric model of the world economy that allowed formal estimation of all of these effects. However, the current state of data and theory precludes such an approach. While econometrically based linked macro models are the accepted compromise for macroeconomic trends, this precludes analysis of general equilibrium effects across industries. As our interest is in multi-sector interactions, we follow the recent literature (Anderson et al. 1997a, b) and employ a calibrated six-sector, 14-region multi-region general equilibrium model of the world economy. The present application differs in two important ways from the recent projections literature: the model involves endogenous capital accumulation, and it also includes stylised representations of scale economies and imperfect competition. We provide only a brief description of the model here, referring the interested reader to detailed technical references.[3]

The central feature of CGE models is the input–output structure, which explicitly links industries in a value-added chain from primary goods, over continuously higher stages of intermediate processing, to the assembling of goods and services for final consumption by households and governments. The link between sectors may be direct, like the input of steel into the production of cars, or indirect, via intermediate use in other sectors. Sectors are also linked through competition for scarce resources (primary factors of production such as land, labour and capital). Our model, which is a projections version of the same general equilibrium model employed by the WTO secretariat for assessment of the Uruguay Round, is no exception. At the firm level, production involves primary factors adding value to intermediate inputs. Formally, production in the model involves a nested production function, consisting of CES (constant elasticity of substitution) value added and Leontief intermediate demand. Heavy/intermediate industrial sectors are modelled as imperfectly competitive and subject to large-group monopolistic competition (that is constant mark-ups and free entry). We also model the service and extraction sectors as being subject to modest scale economies, modelled through declining average costs and average cost pricing.

Demand for firm-differentiated products at the intermediate and final product level is based on a CES aggregation function, along the lines of Ethier (1982) and Krugman (1980). For competitive sectors, import demand is modelled with a (non-nested) Armington-type CES aggregator. Both the firm-level differentiation and the Armington differentiation imply two-way trade in products differentiated either at the firm or regional level. Final demand, at the upper tier, is defined over regional households, and is modelled as Cobb-Douglas. Trade also involves trading costs (a mix of trade and transport services), which are modelled explicitly.

We assume that savings rates are fixed, so that changes in the pool of regional savings (due to income changes) result in changes in investment spending. Changes in regional investment levels in turn lead to changes in steady-state capital stocks. Capital markets are modelled as regional markets, to match the stylised facts about long-run capital accumulation patterns. In the model, changes in incomes therefore feed through to endogenous changes in the capital stock and thereby in the structure of production.

Social accounting data are taken from the final revision (August 1996) of the GTAP version 3 data set. That GTAP data set includes information on national and regional input–output data, bilateral trade flows, final demand patterns, and government intervention, and is benchmarked to 1992. Its protection estimates are based on detailed World Bank and WTO data on pre- and post-Uruguay Round protection levels (McDougall 1997). Our regional aggregations, spanning all sectors of all economies of the world, are shown in Table 2.7, along with the pre- and post-Uruguay Round protection rates.

In projecting a baseline data set for 2010, the world economy as described above for 1992 is re-calibrated to the 2010 baseline GDP levels, using the rates of growth shown in Table 2.7, assuming no changes to existing trade and other policies. In doing so, the effective labour supply is adjusted to reflect both expected labour supply growth (based on World Bank projections) and labour productivity gains, while physical capital stock projections are based on the long-run accumulation closure and the stock of land is held constant.[4] The implications of these projections for the geographic distribution of GDP are illustrated in Figure 2.1. From the figure it can be seen that East Asia is expected to continue to increase substantially its share of global GDP during the next decade or so, while Europe's is expected to fall somewhat.

The baseline scenario for 2010 is then altered to reflect implementation of the Uruguay Round (as detailed in the various papers in Martin and Winters 1996). That requires specifying the associated commitments including cuts

Figure 2.1   *Regional shares of global GDP, 1992 and 2010*

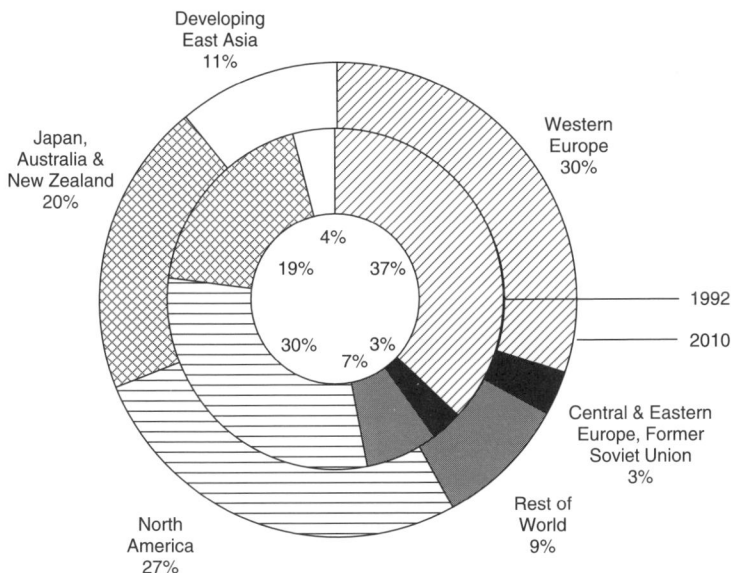

Table 2.7   *Rates of protection and GDP growth assumed for 1992–2010*

	Average pre-Uruguay Round tariff (%)	Average post-Uruguay Round tariff (%)	Annual GDP growth rate (%)
Indonesia	15.8	14.5	6.6
Malaysia	17.2	10.2	9.0
Philippines	31.0	23.4	5.1
Thailand	40.3	29.6	8.0
China, mainland	35.0	35.0	7.8
Hong Kong & Singapore	1.3	0.7	6.1
Taiwan	14.6	14.6	6.1
Korea, Rep.	24.3	12.7	6.7
Japan	21.3	14.3	2.8
Australia & New Zealand	12.7	8.9	3.4
North America (incl. Mexico)	5.3	4.1	2.6
Western Europe	6.5	5.3	2.5
C. & E. Europe & FSU	9.9	8.5	3.5
Rest of world	24.4	22.8	3.5

Sources: GTAP database (McDougall 1997) and World Bank projections (see Anderson et al. 1997b).

in tariffs, tariff equivalents of non-tariff import restrictions, and export subsidies agreed to under the Round. Reform of the system of MFA (Multi-fibre Arrangement) textile and apparel quotas is an especially important part of the Uruguay Round reforms for East Asia. In the present application, MFA restrictions are represented as export tax equivalents.[5] The non-agricultural information is obtained largely from the WTO's Integrated Database (Reincke 1997), while the expected agricultural protection cuts are based on extensive research conducted at the World Bank (Hathaway and Ingco 1996). These modelled reforms explicitly exclude protection cuts in China and Taiwan initially (since they are not yet WTO members). In addition, we do not assume that MFA quota elimination will automatically be extended to China. Instead, we consider these separately when we examine the implications of China and Taiwan both joining the WTO.

Figures 2.2 and 2.3 illustrate Western Europe's and developing East Asia's total and bilateral trade patterns as they were in 1992 and as projected for 2010 after the implementation of the Uruguay Round. The most striking change is the increased importance of East Asia's developing economies for West European exports. Our projections suggest that by 2010 the region will over-take North America as the most important regional destination for Western Europe's extra-regional trade, its share rising from 13 to 22 per cent. Not surprisingly, developing East Asia is also the most rapidly growing destination of exports from individual economies of East Asia. Hence, while the relative importance of East Asia for Western Europe grows dramatically, the relative importance of Europe for East Asia grows very little. This state-ment masks important growth in the absolute level of trade between develop-ing East Asia and Western Europe: as illustrated in Figure 2.4, we project a dramatic expansion in the volume of trade in this relationship as a result of the combined impact of economic growth in Asia and the implementation of the Uruguay Round agreements.

Figure 2.2   *Regional shares of Western European extra-regional exports, 1992 and 2010*

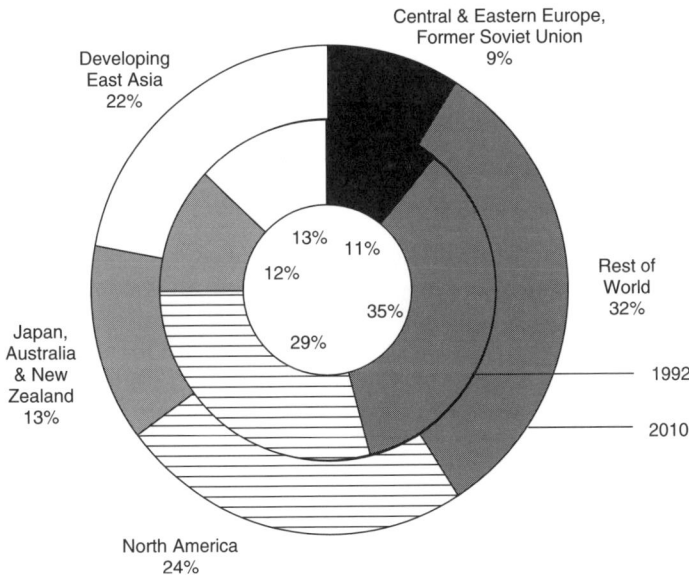

Figure 2.3   *Growth in Western European–developing East Asian trade, 1992 to 2010*

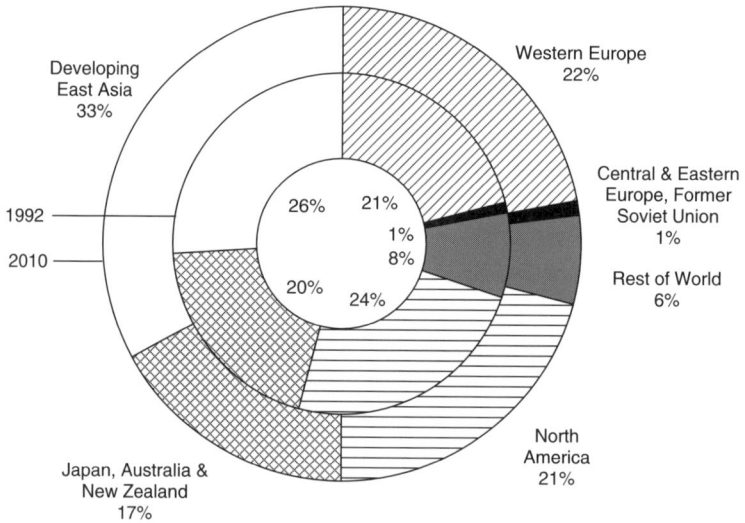

Post-Uruguay Round policy reforms

We next turn to examine a number of post-Uruguay Round scenarios. Tables 2.8 and 2.9 present a comparison of the Uruguay Round implementation (due to take place through to 2005), with additional possible post-Round liberalisations. These include:

• accession of China and Taiwan to the WTO;

• a transatlantic initiative aimed at closer economic integration of Western Europe and North America (modelled as a preferential trade agreement);

• open regionalism in the APEC region (involving a reduction in trading costs as well as elimination of tariffs); and

• another WTO round, involving a 50 per cent reduction in tariffs as well as a reduction in trading costs valued at 2 per cent of trade.

Table 2.8   *Real income effects of trade liberalisation in 2010, based on projected GDP and measured in 1992 US$ billions*

	Uruguay Round	China/ Taiwan in WTO	TAFTA	APEC	New WTO Round
Indonesia	3.6	0.9	-1.1	1.3	23.0
Malaysia	86.2	1.8	-5.8	133.7	171.3
Philippines	8.7	0.1	-0.3	21.1	19.3
Thailand	40.5	3.0	-3.5	196.9	184.4
China, mainland	4.1	7.8	-1.8	93.5	116.7
Hong Kong & Singapore	11.1	9.8	-1.0	79.1	64.8
Taiwan	9.6	11.3	-1.3	58.0	55.4
Korea, Rep.	28.1	2.9	-1.4	57.2	64.8
Sub-total, developing East Asia	**191.9**	**53.8**	**-16.2**	**640.8**	**699.7**
Japan	58.5	9.6	-3.5	155.6	140.3
Australia & New Zealand	-0.2	0.5	-0.4	4.9	8.7
North America (incl. Mexico)	28.0	8.6	22.4	105.3	130.3
Western Europe	32.7	9.7	55.5	32.5	182.7
C. & E. Europe & FSU	0.4	0.1	-0.6	0.2	16.7
Rest of world	17.1	-0.2	-5.4	18.9	179.0
Total, world	**328.4**	**66.0**	**51.7**	**958.2**	**1,357.5**

Note: TAFTA is Transatlantic Free Trade Area.

Source: Authors' model results.

Table 2.9 shows that implementation of the Uruguay Round would add nearly 1 per cent to global GDP by 2010, or US$328 billion per annum in 1992 dollars. This is bigger than the estimates produced by other studies using the GTAP model (for example Anderson et al. 1997a, b), mainly because the version of GTAP used in the present study includes the realities of imperfect competition and increasing returns to scale (but also because the present study is looking at 2010 rather than 2005, when the world economy would be smaller). WTO accession for China and Taiwan would add considerably to that gain, however. In our accession scenario, we assume a 50 per cent reduction in tariffs by China and Taiwan on an MFN basis, as well as the removal of non-tariff restrictions on China's exports of textiles and clothing. That degree of liberalisation would add a further US$66 billion per year or one-fifth more to the global economic welfare gains from the Uruguay Round. Even neighbouring economies in East Asia are projected to gain, despite

Table 2.9   *Real income effects of trade liberalisation in 2010, per cent of projected GDP*

	Uruguay Round	China/ Taiwan in WTO	TAFTA	APEC	New WTO Round
Indonesia	0.8	0.2	-0.3	0.3	5.1
Malaysia	35.2	0.5	-1.7	39.1	50.1
Philippines	7.3	0.1	-0.3	16.1	14.8
Thailand	10.4	0.7	-0.8	45.1	42.2
China, mainland	0.3	0.5	-0.1	6.4	8.0
Hong Kong & Singapore	3.2	2.6	-0.3	20.9	17.1
Taiwan	1.6	1.8	-0.2	9.2	8.8
Korea, Rep.	2.9	0.3	-0.1	5.7	6.5
Japan	1.0	0.2	-0.1	2.7	2.4
Australia & New Zealand	0.0	0.1	-0.1	0.8	1.5
North America (incl. Mexico)	0.3	0.1	0.2	1.0	1.3
Western Europe	0.3	0.1	0.5	0.3	1.6
C. & E. Europe & FSU	0.1	0.0	-0.1	0.0	1.8
Rest of world	0.4	0.0	-0.1	0.4	4.1
Total, world	0.9	0.2	0.1	2.5	3.5

Source: Authors' model results.

being competitors with China and Taiwan in many markets. This contrasts with results in, for example, Anderson et al. (1997b), where assumptions of constant returns to scale and perfect competition ensure there is less scope for at least ASEAN (Association of Southeast Asian Nations) economies to gain from China/Taiwan expansion through intra-industry specialisation; indeed some were projected to lose slightly. The only projected loss from Chinese accession in the present study is a very slight one for other developing countries, which face stronger competition in apparel markets from China. Western Europe is a major winner from Chinese WTO accession (adding almost one-third to its GDP gain from the Uruguay Round), as are the United States and Japan.

The 'TAFTA scenario' (Transatlantic Free Trade Area) assumes a preferential transatlantic free trade agreement is implemented, as well as preferential trade facilitation measures yielding a reduction in trading costs equalling

2 per cent of the value of trade.[6] Such an agreement yields classic trade diversion effects, with European and North American gains generally accruing at the expense of the rest of the world, including East Asia. (It also yields investment diversion effects — see Baldwin and François 1997 for further discussion.) The trade facilitation assumed is enough to ensure that the world as a whole is expected to gain, but the projected loss to the excluded economies is greater than the gain to North America.

In contrast, the 'APEC scenario', which involves open regionalism (and hence MFN-based tariff reductions), yields unambiguous gains to all regions. In this scenario we assume the developed economies of the APEC region honour their commitment to remove all trade barriers by 2010. The developing economies have until 2020 to meet their commitment to free trade, but for simplicity we assume they also reach that target by 2010. Should that eventuate, the gains to the global economy are huge, at US$958 billion per year. This dwarfs the global gains from a TAFTA; and North America is nearly five times better off in this case. Even Western Europe gains sizeably from APEC, at US$33 billion as compared with US$55 billion per annum from a TAFTA. In addition, the rest of the world also gains from APEC, whereas all excluded regions would lose from a TAFTA. The two scenarios thus present contrasting implications of preferential regional integration and open regional integration. They also indicate that there will be large barriers to trade still remaining in the APEC region even after the Uruguay Round is fully implemented.

Finally, we present in the last column of Tables 2.8 and 2.9 the benefits of a hypothetical new WTO round of multilateral trade reductions which is assumed to be implemented by 2010. (Negotiations for some areas, such as agriculture, services and TRIPs [trade-related intellectual property], are required under the Uruguay Round agreements to begin by 2000.) This new round is assumed to involve a 50 per cent reduction in all post-Uruguay Round tariffs, and (as in the two previous regional reform scenarios) a reduction in trading costs equal to 2 per cent of the value of trade. For East Asia (and North America), this yields benefits comparable to those from APEC. That is, completely free MFN trade within the Asia Pacific would benefit those APEC economies by about as much as a 50 per cent MFN trade reform globally. For Western Europe, however, a new WTO round yields much greater gains than either a TAFTA or the APEC initiative: US$183 billion compared with US$55 billion and US$33 billion per annum in 2010. This is because Western Europe benefits more from its own tariff reductions in the new WTO round scenario than in the TAFTA scenario. It also benefits more from tariff reductions by non-Asian trading partners in the new WTO round.

Conclusions

The historical evolution of bilateral trade and investment flows between Western Europe and East Asia seems likely to continue, according to the above numerical projections analysis conducted in the context of regional and global economic growth and Uruguay Round implementation. The results demonstrate, though, that several strategic issues will influence the prospective trade outcomes and their effects on economic welfare. One is the accession to the WTO of China and hence Taiwan. Another is the (now seemingly unlikely) prospect of a transatlantic free trade agreement. A third is the extent to which the APEC economies can deliver on their promise to free their trade on an MFN basis of the next decade or so. A final challenge is delivering further MFN trade liberalisation through a new WTO-sponsored multilateral round.

Several conclusions are worth highlighting from the projection exercises. First, both the Uruguay Round and the continuing rapid growth of East Asia's developing economies ensure that those economies will continue to increase their shares of Western Europe's trade. East Asia, by contrast, will not see a comparable rise in the share of its trade involving Western Europe. As East Asia's importance in world trade keeps rising, its intra-regional trade will also continue to rise in importance. Given the current low degree of European–East Asian integration, as reflected in Tables 2.4 and 2.6, this suggests there will remain ample room over the next decade for the ASEM process (Asia–Europe Meeting) to contribute to trade and FDI growth between the two regions.

Second, while Western Europe is projected to benefit from the regional APEC liberalisation initiative, European interests are much better served by drawing East Asia into another global WTO round than by waiting for improved market access from an MFN-based initiative in the APEC region. Europe's economic interests are also tied to fast-tracking the WTO applications for the former centrally planned economies, and especially China.

The estimates presented above are conservative in several respects: they do not include any liberalisation of services trade and investment; nor do they include the key dynamic effects of reform elucidated in the new endogenous growth theory; and effects of numerous other dimensions of the Uruguay Round such as the TRIPs agreement also are ignored.

Finally, one other likely development that has not been mentioned above but will influence European–East Asian trade and investment flows is eastern enlargement of the European Union. Inviting the ten Central and East European former communist countries into the European Union, while almost certainly a good thing for both east and west (see Baldwin, François and Portes 1997), would cause some EU trade and investment diversion away from East Asia, particularly in labour-intensive manufactures. The negative effect on real incomes in East Asia is estimated in one recent study to amount to less than 0.2 per cent of the region's GDP, however, depending on the extent to which sensitive products fr om Eastern Europe (food, textiles, clothing, steel) are allowed free access to EU markets (Baldwin and François 1996).

Notes

*   An earlier draft of this paper was presented at a conference on 'Europe, East Asia, APEC, and the ASEM Process', London, 20–21 May 1997. Thanks are due to Ulrich Hiemenz for helpful comments and to the Centre for Economic Policy Research, the Australia–Japan Research Centre and the Australian Research Council for financial assistance.

1   This section draws on Anderson (1997).

2   See Anderson and Norheim (1993) for the precise definition and detailed calculations of the intra-regional trade intensity index.

3   Versions of this model have been implemented in both GAMS/MPSGE and GEMPACK. Model codes for both are available at the following website: http://www.intereconomics.com/handbook. In terms of model structure and implementation, the critical difference is that François et al. (1996) work with the GAMS/MPSGE version of the model, while for this application we work with GEMPACK. The theory remains the same.

4   The calibration of projection models is more art than science. In the present application, we are working with external (IMF/World Bank) estimates of overall GDP growth. Combined with the underlying structure of the model, we estimate a mixture of capital accumulation and labour productivity gains consistent with these projections. Of course, capital stocks may also adjust because of foreign investment flows, and GDP projections may or may not be exactly consistent with underlying capital stock trends as implied by historical data. In the end, the slack is made up for by our appeal to factor productivity growth. Ideally, a fully specified intertemporal model with sufficient sectoral data on historical physical and human capital stocks and the like would be used. However, like the fully specified multi-sector econometric model we alluded to earlier, this ideal is unachievable given the current state of data and theory. All we can do is reassure the reader that the projections presented here are relatively robust, qualitatively, with respect to alternative calibrations.

5   See François, McDonald and Nordstrom (1996; 1997) for applications involving explicit modelling of agricultural and MFA textile quotas as quantitative restraints.

6   See Baldwin and François (1997). These trading costs estimates are based on recent assessments of the European Single Market Program and APEC initiatives.

References

Anderson, K. (1997) 'Prospects for closer economic relations between Europe and East Asia', CIES Policy Discussion Paper 96/10, University of Adelaide, revised July.

——, B. Dimaranan, T. Hertel and W. Martin (1997a) 'Asia–Pacific food markets and trade in 2005: a global, economy-wide perspective', *Australian Journal of Agricultural and Resource Economics* 41(1), pp. 19–44, March, Discussion Paper No. 1474, CEPR, London, September.

——, B. Dimaranan, T. Hertel and W. Martin (1997b) 'Economic growth and policy reforms in the APEC region: trade and welfare implications by 2005', *Asia–Pacific Economic Review* 3(1), April, Discussion Paper No. 1605, CEPR, London, March.

—— and H. Norheim (1993) 'Is world trade becoming more regionalized?', *Review of International Economics* 1(2), pp. 91–109, June.

Baldwin, R.E. and J.F. François (1996) 'Scale economies, imperfect competition, and the eastern expansion of the EU', paper presented at the conference on Modelling New Challenges for Agriculture and Agribusiness in Europe, Giessen, 15–17 October.

—— and J.F. François (1997) 'Preferential trade liberalization in the North Atlantic', Discussion Paper No. 1611, CEPR, London, March.

——, J.F. François and R. Portes (1997) 'The costs and benefits of eastern enlargement', *Economic Policy* 24, April.

Bora, B. (1996) 'Foreign direct investment', in B. Bora and C. Findlay, eds, *Regional Integration and the Asia–Pacific*, London: Oxford University Press, Chapter 6.

Ethier, W. (1982) 'National and international returns to scale in the modern theory of international trade', *American Economic Review* 72(3), pp. 389–405, June.

European Commission and UNCTAD (1996) *Investing in Asia's Dynamism: European Union Direct Investment in Asia*, Brussels: European Commission.

François, J.F. (1994) 'Global production and trade: factor migration and commercial policy with international scale economies', *International Economic Review* 35(3), pp. 565–81, August.

——, B. McDonald and H. Nordstrom (1996) 'A user's guide to the Uruguay Round assessments', Discussion Paper No. 1410, CEPR, London, June.

——, B. McDonald and H. Nordstrom (1997) 'Trade policy and the capital stock in a multilateral framework', in R.E. Baldwin and J.F. François, eds, *Dynamic Issues in Applied Commercial Policy Analysis*, Cambridge and New York: Cambridge University Press, forthcoming.

—— and D.R. Roland-Holst (1997) 'Scale economies and imperfect competition', in J.F. François and K.A. Reinert, eds, *Applied Methods for Trade Policy Analysis: A Handbook*, Cambridge and New York: Cambridge University Press, forthcoming.

Hathaway, D. and M. Ingco (1996) 'Agricultural liberalization and the Uruguay Round', in W. Martin and L.A. Winters, eds, *The Uruguay Round and the Developing*

Economies, Cambridge and New York: Cambridge University Press, Chapter 2.

Hertel, T.W. ed. (1996) *Global Trade Analysis: Modeling and Applications*, Cambridge and New York: Cambridge University Press.

IMF (1997) *Global Economic Outlook*, Washington DC: International Monetary Fund.

Krugman, P. (1980) 'Scale economies, product differentiation, and the pattern of trade', *American Economic Review* 70(5).

Martin, W. and L.A. Winters eds (1996) *The Uruguay Round and the Developing Economies*, Cambridge and New York: Cambridge University Press.

McDougall, R.A. ed. (1997) *Global Trade, Assistance, and Protection: The GTAP 3 Data Base*, West Lafayette: Center for Global Trade Analysis, Purdue University, January.

Norheim, H., J.M. Finger and K. Anderson (1993) 'Trends in the regionalization of world trade, 1928 to 1990', in K. Anderson and R. Blackhurst, eds, *Statistical Appendix in Regional Integration and the Global Trading System*, Ann Arbor: University of Michigan Press and London: Harvester Wheatsheaf.

OECD (1996) *International Direct Investment Statistics, 1983–95*, Paris: OECD.

Reincke, U. (1997) 'Import tariffs on merchandise trade', in R.A. McDougall, ed., *Global Trade, Assistance and Protection: The GTAP 3 Data Base*, West Lafayette: Center for Global Trade Analysis, Purdue University, January, Chapter 13.

UNCTAD (1996) *Sharing Asia's Dynamism: Asian Direct Investment in the European Union*, Geneva and New York: United Nations.

United Nations (1996) *World Investment Report* 1996, Geneva and New York: United Nations.

Winters, L.A. ed. (1995) *Foundations of an Open Economy: Trade Laws and Institutions for Eastern Europe*, London: CEPR.

Winters, L.A. (1996) 'Regionalism versus multilateralism', paper prepared for a CEPR conference on Regional Integration, La Coruna, Spain, 26–27 April.

World Bank (1996) *Global Economic Prospects and the Developing Countries*, Washington DC: The World Bank.

—— (1997) *World Development Indicators* 1997, Washington, DC: World Bank.

WTO (1995) *Regionalism and the World Trading System*, Geneva: World Trade Organization.

—— (1996) *International Trade Statistics*, Geneva: World Trade Organization.

—— (1997) *International Trade Statistics*, Geneva: World Trade Organization, forthcoming.

3   Regionalism in Europe and the Asia Pacific economy

RICHARD POMFRET

International trade diplomacy since the 1940s has shifted from US leadership to US–EU hegemony in the 1970s and 1980s to a pluricentric system in the 1990s, with East Asian countries playing an increasingly active role as their share of world trade mounts. This chapter analyses the potential role of the European Union (EU) and of East Asian countries in a world where the United States is the sole superpower and has the most important national economy, but where progress in establishing acceptable world trade regimes will involve policy makers from all three regions.

The first section analyses Asian reactions to the trade policy dilemma which emerged in the late 1980s as a choice between regionalism and multilateralism. The catalysts were fears of a Fortress Europe emerging from the European Union's 1992 program (EC92) and of the spread of the Canada–US Free Trade Agreement (CUSTA) to cover most of the Western Hemisphere. Asian reactions consisted of moves to strengthen existing regional trading arrangements, the creation of new regional organisations, and a renewed commitment to multilateralism. The third was the most important, but the emergence of Asia Pacific Economic Cooperation (APEC) as a new institutional element is also relevant to discussion of East Asia's trade policy options.

Section 2 focuses on the dynamics of inter-regional negotiations. The last General Agreement on Tariffs and Trade (GATT) rounds were largely concluded through US–EU agreements which were accepted by other countries. Such a situation is becoming less acceptable to these other countries, which are now major trading nations. Proposals for a Transatlantic Free Trade Area (TAFTA) likewise arouse concern in excluded countries. A neglected aspect of APEC is that its summits are the first major international meetings from which European countries have been excluded. The First Asia–Europe Summit (ASEM) in March 1996 was a belated attempt to establish a Europe–Asia link. APEC, TAFTA and ASEM are all unsatisfactory as institutions for addressing global trade issues because each excludes important trading nations.

At the same time as the regionalism–multilateralism debate and the emergence of regional umbrella organisations, trade talks have been extended to include new areas. The Uruguay Round, for example, dealt with trade in services, intellectual property rights and trade-related investment measures. The metamorphosis of GATT into the World Trade Organization (WTO) is one reaction to the perceived need for greater institutional capacity to deal with the new areas. The inclusion of regulatory issues and competition policy in regional arrangements such as the Closer Economic Relations agreement (CER) between Australia and New Zealand and, especially, in the EC92 program has highlighted the question of whether the new areas can best be tackled initially at a regional level, and perhaps subsequently be globalised.

The fourth section argues that despite the current publicity given to new areas, there is important unfinished business with respect to the old areas of trade taxes and quantitative restrictions on trade. These transparent trade barriers were the central concern of GATT and they have been substantially liberalised, but they have not been eliminated. APEC is uniquely well placed to lead the world to global free trade by outlawing trade barriers in the old areas.

The final section draws some conclusions about the policy options and roles open to the European Union and East Asia in future world trade diplomacy.

East Asian reactions to EC92

For East Asian policy makers the key issue in international commercial diplomacy during the late 1980s and early 1990s was how to react to the spectre of regional trading blocs in Europe and in the Americas. Regionalism had not been a major feature of Asian economic relations during the second half of the twentieth century; even the more formalised regional trading arrangements such as the Association of Southeast Asian Nations (ASEAN) or those between Australia and New Zealand had little impact on trade flows. The EC92 program, the Canada–US Free Trade Agreement and the initiation of negotiations to expand the latter to include Mexico stimulated a re-evaluation of this situation. Asian reactions to this challenge were threefold: the strengthening of regional trading arrangements, the creation of umbrella regional organisations, and renewed commitment to multilateralism.

ASEAN is the most prominent regional trading arrangement in Asia. Since the early 1980s, some of the ASEAN members (Singapore, Malaysia, Thailand and Indonesia) have been among the fastest growing economies in the world. This rapid growth has been based on outwardly-oriented development strategies, but the trade policies have been essentially non-discriminatory. Attempts to promote intra-ASEAN trade during the late 1970s and early 1980s through preferential tariffs and joint industrial policies had little impact, and the trade expansion during the 1980s was mainly with partners outside Southeast Asia.[1] Apart from the arrangements between Australia and New Zealand, which were strengthened by the 1983 Closer Economic Relations agreement, other regional trading arrangements in Asia existed on paper but had minimal or zero economic impact before the 1990s. Although the Economic Cooperation Organisation (ECO) had been revived in 1985 and the South Asian Association for Regional Cooperation (SAARC) was launched in 1985, neither had adopted any practical measures, while the South Pacific Forum and the Gulf Cooperation Council (GCC) had some economic impact but involve small populations (Pomfret forthcoming).

ASEAN, ECO and SAARC all renewed their efforts towards regional integration in the early 1990s. In January 1992 the ASEAN members signed accords aimed at establishing by 2008 an ASEAN Free Trade Area (AFTA) with intra-ASEAN tariffs on manufactures reduced to 0–5 per cent and elimination of non-tariff barriers. AFTA was given greater credibility than the earlier preferential trading arrangement, but still required a relaunch in October 1993 and a new deadline (2000) was set at the 1995 ASEAN summit. Despite high-level commitment, uncertainty remains about whether trade barriers on sensitive items will in fact be reduced when the deadline approaches. Besides the attempted strengthening of ASEAN trade links, the association has also expanded to include Vietnam in 1995 and Laos and Myanmar (Burma) in 1997. Cambodia's accession, also scheduled for July 1997, was put on hold by ASEAN after the Hun Sen coup, but ASEAN's expansion to ten members is expected in the near future.

The three original ECO members (Iran, Pakistan and Turkey) signed a Protocol on Preferential Tariffs in 1991. They agreed to offer one another a 10 per cent preferential tariff reduction on selected commodities, but the offer lists were extremely limited. ECO was revitalised by the collapse of the Soviet Union, after which the six Islamic former Soviet republics and Afghanistan joined ECO in 1992. The new members were invited to participate in the preferential trading arrangements, but they did not respond.[2] SAARC announced a similar preferential tariff reduction program in 1995, but implementation has been even more limited than in ECO. Thus, despite much talk and initiating action, preferential trading arrangements in Asia remain limited.

It is possible to construct a scenario of Asian trade in the early twenty-first century conducted by seven large blocs: the ASEAN10, SAARC, ECO, the

Russian Federation, greater China (including Hong Kong, Macau and Taiwan), a reunified Korea, and Japan — only Mongolia, Armenia and Georgia are outside these blocs and they could conceivably be pressured into preferential arrangements with Russia. In practice, this is an extremely implausible scenario.[3] Many of the forces working against regional cooperation in Asia in the past still remain. Even on a more narrowly economic evaluation, the trade diversion costs of preferential trading arrangements which undermined earlier ASEAN schemes are preventing even mild discrimination within ASEAN and ECO today.[4]

The most immediate Asian reaction to the perceived threat of large trading blocs in Europe and the Americas was the formation of the APEC forum and the East Asian Economic Caucus (EAEC) in 1989. Initially, both were essentially defensive reactions and lacked a positive agenda, but their conceptions differed on membership and content. The Malaysian-sponsored EAEC defined East Asia to include the ASEAN members, China, Japan, and the northeast Asian newly industrialising economies (NIEs), while APEC took a wider geographical view to include Australasia and countries of the eastern Pacific. The EAEC became identified with a more discriminatory outlook favouring intra-Asian trade as a counterpart to the European Union or the proposed Free Trade Area of the Americas (FTAA), while APEC was promoted as a non-discriminatory association and considerable effort went into defining the concept of 'open regionalism'.[5] In practice, the EAEC made no progress due to Japanese coolness towards any arrangement that might discriminate against the United States. Consequently Japan embraced APEC, and the United States also responded positively to APEC and hosted the first APEC summit in late 1993.

APEC is not a regional trading arrangement. Some commentators dismiss it as a mere talking shop, although talking shops have their value (as ASEAN, for example, has demonstrated in its ability to defuse tension in a previously unstable part of Asia). APEC has tried in its initial summits to make progress in two areas; as a workshop for devising rules for deep integration (for example an investment code) and as a forum for promoting trade liberalisation in the region on a multilateral basis. These initiatives will be analysed further in section 3.

Despite the publicity given to regional trading arrangements and to the regional umbrella organisations, the most substantial Asian response to the perceived threat of regionalism in world trade was increased commitment to the multilateral trading system. In the Uruguay Round, for the first time, Asian countries played an active role in multilateral trade negotiations, either individually or together with other nations with similar interests (for example as members of the Cairns Group of agricultural exporters). This coincided with a period of unilateral trade liberalisation in many Asian economies.

Unilateral tariff elimination has a strong basis in economic theory, but the main impetus in practice has been the demonstration effect of the association between openness and rapid economic development in the high-performing Asian economies. The relationship between trade liberalisation and rapid growth in the original NIEs was opaque, because trade policies ranged from almost free trade in Hong Kong to interventionist policies in South Korea; advocates of free trade and advocates of interventionist trade policies could both find support for their theories from the NIEs. In the second-generation NIEs of Southeast Asia the relationship between trade policy liberalisation and accelerated growth is more clear cut, and the rapid growth in Thailand, Malaysia and Indonesia since the mid-1980s has proved to be a powerful demonstration of the benefits of unilateralism (Pomfret 1995).[6]

The benefits of an open trade regime have become increasingly accepted in Asia, especially following the success of the second-generation NIEs since the early 1980s. After being for the most part free riders in GATT, Asian countries participated more actively in the Uruguay Round and show an increasing commitment to the rights and obligations of GATT/WTO membership. For the poorer Asian GATT signatories, this involved reappraising views of GATT as an instrument of rich-country imperialism. Several of them did, however, begin to seek redress against US or EU measures through GATT. Japan was slower to follow this route, but began to do so after 1995, claiming that WTO dispute settlement procedures were a big improvement over their predecessors.

Most of the larger Asian trading nations are already WTO members, and most of the non-members have applied for membership. Working parties to consider accession have been established for China (1987), Nepal (1989), Taiwan (1992), Russia (1993), Cambodia (1994), Vietnam (1995), the Kyrgyz Republic and Kazakstan (1997), and other Central Asian countries have applications pending. If all of these applications were successful, then the common acceptance of WTO rules would provide a mutually beneficial basis for intra-Asian trade. The completion of Mongolia's accession arrangements in 1996, five years after establishment of the working party in 1991, suggests that the problems of WTO negotiations with economies in transition from central planning are not intractable.

Across-the-board trade liberalisation is often easier to implement in practice than preferential tariff reductions such as those involved in the ASEAN, ECO and SAARC preferential trading schemes; the selectivity of the latter leads to negotiations becoming mired in bilateral bargaining where vested interests can manoeuvre to ensure exemption of their products. The process of non-discriminatory trade liberalisation can, however, be enhanced if there is an appearance of reciprocity to rally exporters and other vested interests in support of trade liberalisation, which will be inevitably opposed by people involved in import-competing activities. Thus, APEC might play a positive role in promoting trade liberalisation on a non-discriminatory basis, by measures such as the simultaneous announcement of liberalisation 'offers' at the 1995 Osaka summit.[7]

APEC, ASEM, TAFTA and the WTO

GATT was a US-led institution. The original negotiations were between the United States and the United Kingdom with some Canadian participation, but the institutional form was determined by the failure of the US Congress to ratify the Havana Charter for the International Trade Organisation. The first GATT rounds were essentially vehicles to reduce US tariffs from their high post-1930 levels. With the ending of most quantitative restrictions and the establishment of current account convertibility in Western Europe, tariff cuts by the Europeans appeared on the agenda by the late 1950s, and in the 1964–67 Kennedy Round, the European Community (EC) gave a strong signal of its willingness to join the United States in leading trade liberalisation. Other GATT members were on the sidelines; whether they cut their own tariffs or not was left open, with many developing countries and Australia choosing to free ride on the European and North American tariff cuts without reciprocating. Trade disputes between the United States and the European Community were settled bilaterally, while trade disputes involving one of the major players and third countries were often settled by grey measures such as voluntary export restraint (VER) agreements.[8]

The GATT era saw tremendous trade liberalisation which was universally beneficial. Even the targets of the grey measures, notably Japan and the newly industrialising economies of East Asia, clearly benefited from the GATT system. The real losers were countries which chose to limit their participation in the global economy. Thus, the US–EC hegemony was tacitly accepted.[9]

The United States and the European Community also dominated the other major economic institutions. The heads of the World Bank and the International Monetary Fund are respectively US and European, and their offices are in Washington DC. The Organisation for European Economic Cooperation was converted into the OECD (Organisation for Economic Cooperation and Development) in 1960 by the addition of the United States and Canada, and its headquarters are in Paris. The annual G7 summits bring together the US President and four EU leaders, with the Japanese and Canadian leaders often in the background. The OECD has expanded to include Japan, Australia, New Zealand, Mexico, South Korea and Central European countries, but Asia remains under-represented given the economic importance of China, the NIEs and ASEAN. In the United Nations (UN), power is more diffused (although the United States, France and the United Kingdom hold three of the five permanent Security Council seats, with accompanying veto power), but the UN economic bodies are less influential than other international economic institutions.

The symbolic importance of APEC was that it broke this mould. The point was underlined in 1993, the 'Year of APEC' for the United States. Asia had not figured prominently in the priorities of recent US Presidents or Secretaries of State.[10] In stark contrast, at the December 1993 Blake Island APEC Summit, President Clinton welcomed all of the East Asian leaders, apart from the recalcitrant Dr Mahathir, to a get-together in plaid shirts and spectacular scenery.[11] For the first time since the creation of a world economy, the Europeans were left out of a major economic summit.

The European reaction was to build its own links with Asia, culminating in the March 1996 Asia–Europe Summit meeting in Bangkok, and to revive the Atlantic connection. ASEM created an institutional link, but little else. It fuelled discontent among excluded countries, notably Australia and New Zealand, and the South Asian countries, which had also been excluded from APEC. In fact, the Asian contingent at ASEM corresponded to the EAEC, so that the ASEM process may have contributed some legitimacy to this grouping. This may, however, be a temporary phenomenon, as the participants at the second ASEM Summit are widened to include at least the Australasian countries and India.

The lack of achievements by ASEM reflects more fundamental disagreements about what should be on the global agenda. Both the European Union and the United States emphasised new areas of trade liberalisation when they launched the Uruguay Round, but APEC has become associated with the old area of tariff elimination. The Bogor Declaration had an echo at the Summit of the Americas in December 1994, but the European Union refuses to make a parallel commitment to tariff elimination by 2010. The European Union points to a similar target date in its Euro–Med initiative, but that is only for eliminating tariffs on trade in Western Europe and the Mediterranean Basin. The European Union remains wedded to preferential tariffs and zero MFN (most favoured nation) tariffs preclude that option.

The EU Commissioner welcomed a 1995 proposal by Canadian Prime Minister Jean Chrétien to link NAFTA (North American Free Trade Area) and the European Union in a Transatlantic Free Trade Area.[12] The United States, however, was cool to the idea, which became diluted to talking about an Atlantic Market Place. This may be a harbinger of a US return to multilateralism and commitment to MFN treatment after its affair with bilateralism since the early 1980s.[13] The United States may also be more aware than the Europeans appear to be of the negative reaction in Asia which

TAFTA would certainly generate. A further example of the European Union's continued attachment to preferential tariffs and its blindness to their negative reception by third countries is the discussion of extending the European Union's network of preferential trade agreements with Eastern European countries to include Ukraine and Russia; the latter would be a red rag to the United States and to others.

The US–EU hegemony is eroding and institutional arrangements will have to evolve to reflect this. APEC is a symptom of this reality, but it is important to recognise the danger of exclusion. The European Union will react to being left out of a more influential APEC, just as Asian countries resent their under-representation or lack of influence in existing international economic institutions and would be aghast if TAFTA were implemented.

Old areas, new areas, and appropriate fora

From 1947 to 1994 multilateral trade negotiations, dispute settlement and other international aspects of trade liberalisation were achieved by a small GATT secretariat.[14] Success with minimal institutional support was possible because the issues were relatively straightforward as long as the focus was on simple transparent trade barriers such as tariffs (which had to be non-discriminatory and no higher than their bound level) and quantitative restrictions (which were generally illegal). GATT signatories recognised the benefits of free access to other countries' markets and could be induced to overcome domestic resistance to reducing their own tariffs if simultaneous tariff cuts could be negotiated with important trading partners.

As tariffs dropped, other trade impediments assumed greater importance. The Tokyo Round addressed contingent protection such as anti-dumping and countervailing duties and new areas such as public procurement. The guide-lines and codes which emerged from the Tokyo Round were less satisfactory than the clear-cut rules which applied to tariffs and quantitative restrictions. In the Uruguay Round the United States and the European Union pushed for the inclusion of more new areas such as services, trade-related investment measures and intellectual property rights. In the 1990s environmental, labour and other regulatory issues have moved on to the trade policy agenda. The new areas typically involve more complex issues, and one argument behind the establishment of the World Trade Organization (WTO) in 1995 was the need to build up a secretariat which could provide support in analysing new issues and in monitoring compliance with codes in these areas.

An argument in favour of regional agreements concerns the advantages of dealing with new areas on a regional basis. A subset of geographically close or culturally similar countries may be more likely than a global organisation to reach agreement on common regulations. The European Union has clearly progressed furthest towards deep integration via a mixture of harmonisation and mutual recognition of rules and standards, but as the Union becomes closer there is a question of whether this should be considered a regional agreement or the creation of a federal organisation. If several regional groups reach distinct solutions to regulatory and other trade-related issues, the potential problem is of incompatible standards at the global level.

A related argument in favour of progressing on a regional rather than a global basis is the opportunity to test alternative approaches to regulatory reform. Regulatory competition could help to identify the benefits and costs of alternative approaches. The best approach could eventually become the global standard and be supervised by the WTO.[15]

The WTO is better suited to coming in at a later stage because its secretariat has a limited capacity to analyse feasible alternatives. The European Union, with its large central bureaucracy and links to national administrations, is well placed to undertake serious preparatory studies. Other bodies could play this preparatory role, as the OECD has done with its codes on capital movements[16] or as UNCTAD (UN Conference on Trade and Development) is trying to do with respect to foreign investment.[17] APEC, too, has taken steps to define an investment code. The problem with this approach to international regulatory reform is that the drafters of the code are unlikely to be neutral so that their composition will influence the content of the code in ways which are likely to be unacceptable to other groups of countries.

Devising an appropriate institutional framework for dealing with new trade issues in the coming decades must begin from the existing situation. The luxury of devising a blueprint from scratch as the Anglo-American policy makers did in 1942–47 is not available. The WTO will expand its activities beyond those of GATT and in some areas (for example monitoring actual trade policies and providing a more effective dispute resolution procedure), this should be beneficial. At the same time, however, it is important to remember that one reason why GATT worked well was its narrowly defined scope, which helped it to avoid becoming embroiled in unsolvable matters where failure to find a solution would have undermined its legitimacy. It is also important to recognise that not all areas affecting international trade flows are appropriate matters for international regulation. Trade exists because of differences between national economies; differences in climate or soils do not constitute unfair trade, and it is far from obvious that different regulatory environments require harmonisation (Bhagwati and Hudec 1996). This is not a case for ignoring all the new areas which have emerged in recent trade policy debates, but it is an argument for caution in setting up a panoply of international arrangements which may only provide the seeds for conflict.

Moreover, for some of the new areas, appropriate international fora with global membership (or global access to membership) already exist, for example the International Labour Organisation (ILO) to address labour issues, World Intellectual Property Organisation (WIPO) on intellectual property rights, the International Organisation for Standardisation (ISO) on standards or the United Nations Environment Programme (UNEP) on the environment. This may still leave some institutional gaps, which could be filled by organisations such as APEC or ASEM or an Atlantic Market Place, but a universal forum is likely to be preferable to a regional forum in order to avoid the drawbacks of excluding participants from the drafting room. Here the European Union may have one advantage; it is the only regional organisation positively working to weld national economies into some form of federal state with internal supra-national institutions. In this setting, experiments in creating, say, a supra-national competition policy may have useful lessons for the global debate.

Unfinished business

APEC's philosophy gained a label, 'open regionalism', long before it was defined. The main thing agreed upon is that open regionalism should be non-discriminatory; APEC will not be a free trade area or customs union, and is therefore not regionalism in the sense used in this chapter. The positive content of open regionalism has been the commitment made at the 1994 Bogor summit to eliminate tariffs by 2010 in the more developed APEC members and by 2020 in the less-developed APEC members. This was followed up at the 1995 Osaka summit by APEC members' presenting their lists of concrete steps towards the Bogor target.

The significance of the Bogor declaration is easy to question. The fundamental issue of whether tariffs will be reduced on an unconditional MFN basis or whether they will be reduced conditionally on imports from countries making equivalent tariff cuts may be resurrected if important APEC members appear to be dragging their feet on unilateral trade liberalisation. The demand for reciprocity appears to be strongest in the United States, although revival of conditional MFN treatment would be a step backwards after having been abandoned by the United States in 1919 due to the trouble-making potential of conditionality. Conditional MFN treatment is contentious in part because (short of complete free trade) it is difficult to agree as to whether reductions are equivalent. It is also incompatible with commitments to third countries based on unconditional MFN treatment. In practice, insisting upon conditionality is tantamount to running a discriminatory trade policy.

Even aside from the reciprocity issue, there is widespread scepticism about whether APEC members will deliver on zero tariffs when it comes to the crunch. Protectionist pressures are still strong, but there are countervailing forces. The commitment to liberal trade policies has strengthened rapidly since the mid-1980s across Asia (see section 1 above), and within the policy-making establishment there is a greater commitment to trade liberalisation as something which is in their own country's best interests (rather than a necessary concession to secure access to other countries' markets).[18] The second positive sign is that the Bogor declaration was made at the highest level by the presidents and prime ministers of APEC members.

If the Bogor line is followed, then the significance of APEC could be as the standard bearer of multilateralism in finishing the business of eliminating trade taxes. Tariffs are low in most countries but peaks remain and they are not irrelevant. A further multilateral round may be a poor way to remove remaining tariffs and a straightforward target of zero tariffs may be the best way forward. APEC is a particularly appropriate forum for publicising such a target because it contains most of the world's major trading nations. The main exception, the European Union, is wedded to internal and external tariff preferences, which are incompatible with zero MFN tariffs.[19] The leader of trade liberalisation within GATT, the United States, is shackled in moving to zero tariffs by the authority of Congress, which is particularly susceptible to pressure from sectional interests. Other APEC members are better suited to implementing tariff elimination given the temporary absolutism of governments in Westminster democracies or more permanent absolutism of other governments in the region. Moreover, APEC governments rely to only a small extent on trade taxes for their revenue, so that tariff elimination will not have the negative fiscal and macroeconomic consequences which have accompanied, or hindered, trade liberalisation in South Asia and in Africa.

The scenario envisages continuing implementation of measures consistent with the Bogor targets by a critical mass of APEC members, so that the laggards are drawn along. Some smaller members have close to zero tariffs already (Hong Kong, Brunei, Singapore). New Zealand and, to a lesser extent, Australia have shown how quickly tariffs can be cut in a Westminster system by a determined government. Canada could do the same, and tariffs make little sense when so large a proportion of Canadian trade is already conducted duty free under NAFTA. Other Asian countries still have high bound tariffs, but applied tariffs are much lower; even in China with its high published tariff rates, pervasive exemptions lead to a low ratio of tariff revenue to imports.[20]

The potential demonstration effect has already been illustrated by the adoption of Bogor-like targets by American leaders at the December 1994 Summit of the Americas. European leaders, on the other hand, although willing to announce similar targets on a preferential basis (as in the Euro–Med target of free trade in the Mediterranean region by 2010), have been unwilling to announce targets for eliminating all tariffs.

The plausibility of this scenario will be tested soon in Southeast Asia, where economic change is rapid and a potential confrontation is looming over automobile trade. Malaysia's Proton has enjoyed special access to other ASEAN markets under various schemes. The proposed Indonesian national car is unlikely to be internationally competitive. Meanwhile, Honda is basing assembly of its Asia car in Thailand and Ford and General Motors have announced huge investment projects in Thailand, joining all the other major car producers. Although Thailand is the third largest market for new cars (after the United States and Japan), the huge capacity being built up in the country is clearly premised on large-scale exports. Thailand will not need preferential treatment to be competitive, but will Indonesia and Malaysia invoke special clauses to keep cars out of AFTA or will they consent to opening of their car markets?

Conclusions

The Uruguay Round coincided with several other major developments in the evolution of the international trading system. The EC92 program and CUSTA/NAFTA created concerns about the break-up of the world trading system into regional blocs. This episode was potentially dangerous, but by the mid-1990s it seemed to have had a happy ending. The EC92 program did not create a Fortress Europe, the United States did not retreat into Western Hemisphere isolationism, and neither EC92 nor NAFTA prevented the successful conclusion of the Uruguay Round. In Asia, too, the outcome was positive, with no significant regional trading arrangements and with the dominant umbrella organisation (APEC) committed to supporting unconditional MFN treatment. Behind the big stories, however, is a subtext of dynamic Euro–Asian interaction. The United States remains the single most important actor in international diplomacy, and to some extent Euro–Asian interaction is over creating an agenda which the United States will accept; can the European Union and Asia find common ground or are they offering competing visions on directions for the world trading system after the Uruguay Round?

Europe and East Asia are less crucial to one another than the United States is to each of them. On the other hand, both the Europeans and the Asians are too important to the world economy to be left out of negotiations. EC92 and NAFTA created fears of a world divided into three large blocs — fears which were quashed by the successful conclusion of the Uruguay Round. APEC, TAFTA and, to some extent, the OECD create concerns that future pre-negotiations in new areas of trade negotiations will take place within a cabal of eminent countries. That is a dangerous model because the prime lesson from discriminatory trading arrangements is that those feeling most affected are from the excluded countries. Even if it is efficient for the OECD or APEC to devise an investment code which could then be globalised, such a procedure will be perceived as unfair by those countries which are omitted.

The European Union and APEC could still play important leadership roles in pushing a positive global trade agenda. The European Union provides a natural experiment in developing regimes for many of the new areas which entered global trade policy debates during the Uruguay Round. Creation of a single European market involves regulatory harmonisation, a common competition policy and many other changes which go beyond what is desirable at the global level, but the European experience will provide evidence on the pitfalls and benefits of taking (at least) one path to the eventual destination. APEC, by contrast, can play a leadership role in ensuring that old areas of trade policy do not slip off the agenda before the business is finished. In particular, APEC is uniquely well placed to sponsor an effort to outlaw trade taxes and other transparent measures which discriminate between domestic and foreign goods and services.

Notes

* Earlier versions of this chapter were presented to a preparatory conference held at the Australian National University in Canberra on 28–29 August 1996 and at the CEPR/ESRC/GEI onference on 'Europe, East Asia, APEC and the Asia–Europe Meeting' Process held in London on 20–21 May 1997. I am grateful to partici pants in the lively discussion at both conferences and especially to Christopher Findlay and to David Vines for recording the comments at the London confer ence, which I could not attend. The chapter draws on my forthcoming book, *The Economics of Regional Trading Arrangements* (Clarendon Press, Oxford), and from a larger research project on regional trading arrangements in the Asia Pacific region, undertaken with financial support from the Australian Research Council.
1 Intra-ASEAN trade was lower in 1989 than it had been in 1970 (Ariff and Tan 1992: 254). Pomfret (1996) provides a fuller assessment of ASEAN's history.
2 Pomfret (1997) discusses ECO's prospects.
3 Pomfret (forthcoming) analyses in greater depth the various scenarios for regional trading blocs in Asia.

4 Some observers (for example Tang 1995: 198) paint a picture of growing region alism in Asia by also including the emergence of sub-regional zones and the for mation of APEC in their calculations, but this does not compare like with like. Sub-regional zones (such as that involving Singapore, Johor and Riau) are not the result of discriminatory policies and APEC is explicitly non-discriminatory. The important distinction, emphasised by Lorenz (1991), is between regionalism and regionalisation.

5 Garnaut and Drysdale (1994) and Bora and Findlay (1996) bring together articles on regional initiatives in the Asia Pacific region. In APEC's evolution there has been a tension between proponents of 'open regionalism' as a discriminatory pro cess and the non-discriminatory view which came to prevail in the mid-1990s. In the first three sections of this chapter I treat open regionalism as being non-dis criminatory, but the 'unfinished business' section raises the question of whether the tension between competing interpretations is indeed resolved.

6 Unilateral liberalisation in New Zealand and Australia was even more pronounced, but the growth consequences were less dramatic and thus the episodes had less international impact.

7 China used the 1995 APEC Summit in Osaka to announce a package of tariff cuts which went some way to removing obstacles to China's WTO accession; the occasion allowed China to display constructive participation in trade liberalisation in the Pacific region, without appearing to bow to foreign pressure over the WTO negotiations. There has also been a 'shaming effect'; when countries took their first offers to APEC preparatory meetings and found them overshadowed by other countries' offers, they revised their offers — this is especially potent when the host nation is involved (illustrated by the Philippines in 1996).

8 Sectors which the majors wished to exclude from trade liberalisation, notably agriculture and textiles and clothing, were taken outside the GATT system. VERs were not so pleasant even for the importer in the long run, as they tended to prolif erate (notably in textiles and clothing, but also in steel and in autos), leading to trade diversion and ever-increasing resource misallocation. By the 1980s, anti-dumping duties were the preferred safeguard measures, and in the Uruguay Round the United States and European Union conspired to keep anti-dumping reform off the agenda.

9 Winham (1986: 371) describes the Tokyo Round negotiating as a process whereby 'issues would first be negotiated bilaterally between the larger powers (US and EC) and then later multilateralised as the negotiations went on'. Other countries did play a more active role in the Uruguay Round than in previous rounds, but the key to successful conclusion of the Uruguay Round was a US–EU bilateral deal in 1993, after which everything else fell into place.

10 James Baker was hardly in Asia apart from his Mongolian hunting trips, and George Bush's most famous Asian photo-op was when he choked on his dinner at a banquet in Japan.

11 The choice of a Pacific island in Washington state emphasised the Pacific face of the United States. Canada followed the US example by selecting British Columbian sites for the 1997 APEC summit and its preparatory meetings; despite

its name, BC is by far the most Asian-oriented Canadian province and its largest city revels in the epithet Hongkouver, by which it is sometimes known in the more Europhile Toronto or Montréal.

12 The TAFTA proposal may well have failed to attract EU support (the French leadership was notably unenthusiastic about such a link), but my point is that although the European Union was willing to consider the proposal, by 1996 such a discriminatory arrangement was a non-starter in the United States.

13 Bergsten (1996) argues that this was already true in 1993, when US support for APEC gave a signal that the United States was not committed to dividing the world into regional trading blocs, as some people were interpreting the NAFTA and FTAA proposals.

14 Enforcement was based on the threat of approved retaliation. Despite the adverse publicity given to GATT's failure to settle disputes, this mechanism was suffi cient to avoid major trade wars, in part because blatant contraventions of GATT trade law were fairly transparent as long as the focus was on tariffs and quotas.

15 Some observers, particularly those with a penchant for intervention, worry that regulatory competition will result in a race to the bottom with minimal regula tions dominating. The contributors to Bhagwati and Hudec (1996) demonstrate that this outcome is not inevitable, although they also argue that regulatory harmonisation is generally undesirable because differences in regulations reflect differing national preferences and trade are an appropriate response to such diver sity.

16 The OECD codes on Capital Movements and on Current Invisible Operations have the force of treaty obligations for OECD members. Through the OECD Dec laration on International Investment and Multinational Enterprises, OECD mem bers make a non-binding commitment to grant each other national treatment. Acceptance of all Codes and Declarations is a condition for OECD membership (as was made clear during the Czech accession negotiations in 1995), so a menu approach to adherence (as is permissible with GATT/WTO codes) is not possible.

17 The dangers of establishing binding rules in an area where views can change is illustrated by the long-standing effort to establish under United Nations' auspices a Code of Conduct for Transnational Corporations (TNCs). The proposal, initi ated by developing countries in an era of suspicion of TNCs, was overtaken by events as countries vied to attract rather than regulate TNCs and the exercise was abandoned in 1992 (Low and Subramanian 1995: 421).

18 Unfortunately this statement seems shakiest with respect to two of the largest APEC countries, the United States and China, which both formulate trade poli cies in ways which emphasise national autonomy and which can be sensitive to protectionist pressures.

19 The European Union is also hampered by a decision-making structure based on compromises among national governments, which makes 'zero' a difficult target to agree upon. Several European commentators at the London conference argued that the European Union is not very discriminatory given its low average tariff and has played a positive role in recent multilateral trade liberalisation negotia tions. These positions confuse the benefits of trade liberalisation with those from

non-discrimination (which may or may not be complementary, as customs union theory demonstrates), and ignore the huge philosophical difference between some and no discrimination. The argument that the European Union is finally drawing a line on discriminatory trade policies is inconsistent with the tangle of arrange ments with would-be members and neighbours, which are unlikely to disappear soon; indeed, the dynamics of queue-jumping and negotiation of quasi-contrac tual arrangements on sensitive products tend to make discriminatory elements more rather than less complex.

20 The World Bank (1996: 7) estimates that '[O]only 15 percent of total imports are subject to tariff and non-tariff barriers, including import rights, licensing and quantitative restrictions'. In 1994, on merchandise imports valued at US$95.3 billion, the customs tax collected amounted to ¥27.3 billion (<US$3.2b), that is an average tariff rate of 3.2 per cent.

References

Ariff, Mohamed and Gerald Tan (1992) 'ASEAN–Pacific trade relations', *ASEAN Economic Bulletin* 8, pp. 258–83.

Bergsten, C. Fred (1996) 'Globalizing free trade', *Foreign Affairs* 75, May–June, pp. 105–20.

Bhagwati, Jagdish and Robert Hudec eds (1996) *Fair Trade and Harmonisation*, 2 vols, Cambridge MASS: MIT Press.

Bora, Bijit and Christopher Findlay eds (1996) *Regional Integration and the Asia Pacific*, Melbourne: Oxford University Press.

Garnaut, Ross and Peter Drysdale eds (1994) *Asia Pacific Regionalism: Readings in International Economic Relations*, Pymble NSW: HarperCollins.

Lorenz, Detlef (1991) 'Regionalization versus regionalism — problems of change in the world economy', *Intereconomics*, January, pp. 3–10.

Low, Patrick and Arvind Subramanian (1995) 'TRIMs in the Uruguay Round: an unfinished business?', in W. Martin and L.A. Winters, eds, *The Uruguay Round and the Developing Economies*, Discussion Paper No. 307, Washington DC: World Bank.

Pomfret, Richard (1995) 'Strategic trade and industrial policy as an approach to locational competitiveness: What lessons from Asia?', in Horst Siebert, ed., *Locational Competition in the World Economy*, Tübingen: J.C.B. Mohr: Paul Siebeck, pp. 205–26.

—— (1996) 'ASEAN always at the crossroads?', *Journal of the Asia Pacific Economy* 1, pp. 365–90.

—— (1997) 'The Economic Cooperation Organisation: current status and future prospects', *Europe Asia Studies* (formerly *Soviet Studies*) 49(4), June.

—— (forthcoming) 'US–EU regionalism from the Asian perspective', in Jens van Scherpenberg and Elke Thiele, eds, *Towards Rival Regionalism? US and EU Regional Economic Integration Policies and the Risk of a Transatlantic Regulatory Rift*, Baden Baden: NOMOS Verlag.

Tang Min (1995) 'Asian economic co-operation: opportunities and challenges', in Kiichiro Fukasaku, ed., *Regional Co-operation and Integration in Asia*, Paris: OECD, pp. 195–221.

Winham, Gilbert (1986) *International Trade and the Tokyo Round Negotiation*, Princeton NJ: Princeton University Press.

World Bank (1996) *The Chinese Economy: Fighting Inflation, Deepening Reforms*, Washington DC: The World Bank.

Part II

Regional identities

4   European integration: retrospect and prospect

RICHARD PORTES AND DAVID VINES

Introduction

Vantage point

There have been many studies on the past and future of European integration. Why write another?

This chapter was written in the context of the conference on Europe, East Asia and the Asia–Europe (ASEM) process. At this conference, economists and policy makers from Europe and from the Asia Pacific (and particularly from East Asia) met to discuss with each other areas of mutual interest. The early stages of such a dialogue must inevitably involve the participants on each side explaining to the other side the nature of their project. Thus the aim of this chapter is to explain the European project to an Asian Pacific audience, and more generally to a foreign audience. It contains a mixture of history, analysis, defensive argument, and criticism, and, most particularly, participant-observation anthropology. We want to say 'This is what the European integration seems to us to be', and 'here is how, and here is the extent to which, the project seems to us to make sense'.

Writing a chapter of this kind has had a personal motivation. One of us (Vines) regularly travels between Europe and Australia (and particularly between Oxford and the Australian National University [ANU]). This sometimes feels like travelling between two planets: there is the European (and in particular the British) view of the world in which 'EMU: to be or not to be' seems to be the Big Issue. But get off the plane in Jakarta or Sydney and 'APEC — the Next Steps' is where the issues seem to be. Of course everyone is interested in his or her own concerns. But why, say friends in that region, are these projects so different? Why has the European common market evolved into the Single European Market? Why now *monetary* integration? The other one of us (Portes) regularly travels between London, the Continent and the east coast of the United States. Friends in America are also surprised and ask similar questions.

To describe the European project to our colleagues in the Asia Pacific and in the United States is the aim of this chapter.

The global context and European issues

We would argue that the three most significant things to have happened in the world economy in the past ten years are:

- the rise of the Asian newly industrialising economies (NIEs) and of emerging-market economies elsewhere, the opening up and reintegration of much of the third world into the growth of world trade following the debt crisis of the 1980s and, more broadly, the progressive globalisation of the world economy;

- the success of the United States, at least against some criteria, in industrially restructuring in the face of this challenge, and in pursuing a macroeconomic policy which has facilitated this; and

- the collapse of the former Soviet Union and of communism in its East European satellites, meaning that the form of US reconstruction is into a multi-polar rather than into a Western Economy, of which it is the acknowledged hegemonic leader.

Against this background, we identify the following five key features of the European economy and European economic policy:

- From the mid-1980s, major European efforts have been directed towards developing the European 'customs union project' begun with the Treaty of Rome in 1958, and even before that, with the European Coal and Steel Community, into the Single European Market. This has involved trade liberalisation on a massive scale within a very large market, which was initially highly fragmented. This has been done in tandem with a global trade policy in which Europe has played a major constructive part in the negotiation of the Uruguay Round of global trade negotiations but has continued to resist the liberalisation of agricultural trade and to maintain some aspects of industrial protectionism.

- By the late 1980s, the European Monetary System was deemed to be a success, and European Monetary Union (EMU — also known as Economic and Monetary Union) was adopted as the vehicle for the next stage of European integration. The Maastricht treaty of 1991 laid out the framework of this process, and EMU is due to commence on 1 January 1999.

• Since 1989, Europe has set about constructing a new relationship with the nations to its east, and particularly with the ten 'Associated Countries' of Central and Eastern Europe.

• Europe's macroeconomic performance has been unsatisfactory recently. The share of investment in GDP (gross domestic product) is low, at least compared with some parts of the world, growth rates are low, and unemployment is high. Fiscal deficits are endemic, and the ratio of government debt to GDP has been on a rising trend which major policy efforts have only begun to reverse.

The challenge to Europe from its friends abroad

The puzzlement with which our foreign friends greet the European strategy can be summarised in the following five sets of questions. We will attempt to give an answer to these questions in the sections which follow.

First, is not European agricultural policy simply indefensible?

Second, why pursue a form of regional trade integration — a customs union and now a single market — when it is so widely known that this leads to trade diversion? This project was begun before Meade and Viner were understood. Is it not time to have, at least as an objective, the abolition of border barriers to trade?[1]

Third, is Europe actually constructing a good and durable relationship with the East? Or is it instead one of hub-and-spokes integration, leading to trade diversion amongst the spokes?

Fourth, can EMU be a sensible policy when Europe is clearly not an 'optimal currency area'? How can this policy be appropriate when Europe appears to have neither the wage flexibility, nor the labour mobility, nor the capacity for fiscal redistribution which are necessary to buffer asymmetric shocks? Does Europe have the degree of political integration necessary to discipline the budgetary process in its member states? Is there not a significant risk that EMU will become both generally inflationary (because of insufficient overall general discipline) and unduly deflationary in its effects on particular countries and regions which suffer from idiosyncratic or asymmetric shocks?

Finally, can current policies begin to address Europe's macroeconomic malaise?

Key points

The structure of our argument is as follows.

The Single European Market, and the European customs union within which it is established, should be understood as the core part of the European project. There is no orderly way from where we are now to a Europe of a kind in which 'open regionalism' in the Asia Pacific sense is possible. The only way in which this is currently imaginable is if the European project were to break down. From this point flow our other two main conclusions.

First, the EMU project is an inevitable consequence of the Single European Market: capital market integration implies that quasi-fixed exchange rates are not feasible, and full integration requires breaking down market segmentation, and this is not possible with floating exchange rates. But the EMU project contains very significant risks. Managing these risks will require very great skill in the conduct of European fiscal *and* monetary policies.

Second, it is inevitable that many nations of Eastern Europe will be part of this core European project. A way must be found to reconcile the following conflicting demands: the desires of many of these countries to join; the fears within the existing European Union that the European project will be swamped by too many such new members; and the need of these East European nations, whether inside or outside the European Union, for rapid moves towards very much freer trade, not only with the rest of Europe, but also with the rest of the world.

Agriculture

The agricultural protectionism embodied in the Treaty of Rome (1958) was essentially an income distribution policy. In the postwar period, European countries were in the process of industrialising (first for the domestic market and then for export), a process which naturally led to real incomes in industry rising faster than those in agriculture, a consequence which was reinforced by specialisation in international trade. Agricultural protectionism was deliberately designed to stand in the way of this 'natural' process of changing income distribution. The income distribution arguments for protectionism were bolstered by arguments following Keynes and Rosenstein-Rodan, which asserted that because the Common Agricultural Policy (CAP) would lead to an increase in agricultural incomes, it would thereby provide a market for the increasing industrial output.

External observers (including many inside Europe) now regard the latter kind of Keynesian reasoning as passé[2] and see the negative effects of the income distribution policy on efficiency as especially damaging.

Such observers, including especially the Cairns group, have endlessly reiterated the costs to Europe itself of the CAP: it has caused the over-expansion of the relatively inefficient European agricultural sector; it has consequently diverted resources from sectors in which Europe has a comparative advantage, thereby increasing industry's costs; and it has therefore reduced the level of savings available for investment and growth. Such external observers also point to the welfare costs of the CAP for the rest of the world because it leads to trade suppression and trade diversion, both of which lower world prices and impose welfare costs on food exporters.

These observers are also bitter that the CAP seems so impenetrable to efforts towards reform. After endless setbacks, hopes were eventually high towards the end of the Uruguay Round: the MacSharry reforms of 1992 began to push reform in the direction of income support and away from price support. Ultimately, however, these negotiations did not produce the anticipated reform of the CAP.[3] The levels from which reductions in support were to be achieved turned out to be abnormally high, because the years chosen for reference (1986–88) were years of abnormally low agricultural prices in which intervention payments, income support levels, and export subsidies were high. Some regard this outcome as a consequence of technical negotiating mistakes on the part of non-European parties; others believe that only with such a fudge could the Round have been concluded.

It is hard to see any way in which European agricultural policy can be defended. It is of course possible to point to historical and contemporary parallels.[4] But these do not provide a defence, and we do not offer one. We merely note that Commissioner Fischler would clearly like to go further in the direction of income support,[5] which is much to be encouraged, and observe that reform of the CAP forms part of the new British government's objectives.

The customs union and the Single European Market

The challenge

External critics, particularly from Asia Pacific region, have come to regard the kind of customs union embodied in the Treaty of Rome as an old-fashioned form of liberalisation. Trade theory, so they argue, teaches that unilateral most favoured nation (MFN) liberalisation is in a country's interests. Certainly a customs union leads to trade creation. However, so the argument goes, it also leads to trade diversion. This has real resource costs, both for the countries within the region and for those excluded. By contrast, these critics argue, unilateral liberalisation does not lead to trade diversion, because exporters in the rest of the world and importers within the region are on a 'level playing field' in supplying imports to the liberalised markets.

Much has been written about trade creation and trade diversion in Europe. Winters (1996) surveys this evidence. The central thrust of this literature has been to argue that, apart from agriculture, trade creation has dominated trade diversion. The European Commission has recently undertaken an economic evaluation of the Single Market program. There were forty background studies for this report, including one by Alasdair Smith on trade creation and trade diversion and two other studies by British economists on external access to the European market. All of these studies concluded that there had been little diversion. However, some evidence for diversion may be found in Bayoumi and Eichengreen (1995)[6] and Sapir (1997),[7] but the evidence may not be as clear cut as it seems. (See Chapter 13 in this volume by Garnaut.)

Opponents of customs union formation go further. They point out that because a customs union violates the MFN principle which is at the core of the General Agreement on Tariffs and Trade/World Trade Organization (GATT/WTO) system, WTO surveillance contains an 'all-or-nothing' requirement for such a union: participants must *completely* liberalise, across 'substantially *all* trade', according to an *agreed timetable*, and must do this by negotiating a *formal bloc* which is presented to the WTO. As a consequence, these critics argue, there are incentives for members to hold back 'concessions' as coin in negotiations on trade liberalisation, and it is argued that this can actually reinforce domestic protectionist pressures and slow down the process of liberalisation. By contrast, moves in individual countries towards unilateral liberalisation (without negotiation of a liberalisation schedule amongst all countries, covering substantially all trade, ratification by national processes and presentation to the WTO) enable some countries to start before others, and enable progress to be made in some sectors before others. A customs union, it is argued, is the wrong structure to achieve incremental, cumulative, self-sustaining liberalisation (see Garnaut 1997).

An explanation

The original European customs union was much more than a vehicle for the realisation of gains through trade by means of inter-Europe trade creation.

Europe has lived through two world wars this century, the horrific magnitude of which is almost impossible to imagine. The overriding end of the architects of the European Common Market/European Community/European Union has been to put an end forever to these bloody conflicts. For France, which had been invaded three times by Germany in a 70 year period, and for Germany, whose political process produced the grotesque aggression of the Second World War, the lesson was to search for forms of integration which reassured the former and tied the hands of the latter. Thus for Monnet, Schumann and the other founding fathers of modern Europe created the European Coal and Steel Community in the 1950s, whose explicit purpose was to internationalise — and so immobilise — the means of waging war. This lesson was connected with a reading of European history which claims that the existence of the nation state is a major explanation of Europe's wars, and a deeply held view that moves to enmesh the nation state in wider structures would erect bulwarks against future conflict.

A revealing contemporary restatement of the German version of this view was given by Karl Lamers (1996), foreign affairs spokesman for the Christian Democrats in the Bundestag, in an interview in the *Times* during a visit to Britain in 1996:

Germans…say that there has long been a supranational reality created by our European civilisation. Common problems spawn common interests: our vital interests are identical…Germans are convinced of the need to make Europe strong and effective in all major policy areas: effectiveness can only be achieved through majority decision making…Borders and geography will steadily lose significance.

If such moves are not forthcoming, Lamers argues:

politics will cease to be effective. A community only makes sense if it can begin to solve its existential problems. If the nation state can no longer do that by itself, its failure undermines its political legitimacy. To secure its legitimacy it has to go a step higher than the nation state…Looked at this way, the question is whether the British, the Germans and other Europeans are ready to submit themselves to a common institution that operates above the level of the nation state. When it came to the single market we were all ready to take that step. At the intergovernmental conference we must consider whether we can accept Community procedures on other common issues.

Garton Ash (1993) has documented how recent German foreign policy has been underpinned by such arguments. Modern Germany, so these arguments run, because it is democratic and peaceful, no longer has interests which are different from those of the European countries which surround it, and because of this similarity of interests, political integration is desirable in order to solve common problems.[8] Statements by Chancellor Kohl over the course of the past year, in the run-up to the 1996–97 inter-governmental conference on European political developments, also argue such supra-national political integration is necessary in order to tie the hands of German and other nationalisms which might otherwise undermine democracy and peace.

Jacques Chirac movingly launched his campaign for the May 1997 French elections with a speech illustrating French resonances with such themes. 'This is an election about Europe', he said. For 50 years we have lived in a peaceful Europe, and this is so because of the integration which we have achieved.

British views of the lessons to be learned from the twentieth century have always differed, and British visions for the future of Europe tend to differ correspondingly. Twice, salvation was obtained with help from transatlantic friends and from Empire. As a result, British conceptions of security tend to involve the coupling of the pursuit of prosperity with the NATO (North Atlantic Treaty Organisation) guarantee of a North American defence umbrella. The pursuit of prosperity tends to be viewed as separable from the pursuit of peace. In this, as in other ways, the British tend to find the view in continental Europe difficult to understand and tend to be in a minority.

If we accept the majority view[9] of the European Union's deep inner purpose — which we can call its political purpose for want of a better term — then the supra-national institutions of the Single European Market, and the European customs union within which it is established, should be understood as the core part of the European project. Thus, the only conceivable way in which we could go from where we are now to an 'open regionalism' would be if the European project were to break down. There is the possibility of this happening in the next decade, given the risks of the EMU project: these are discussed in the final section of the chapter.

It is necessary, therefore, to recognise the European project clearly for what it is not.[10] This is not to say that this project is straightforward. The supra-national structure being created in Europe is on the one hand more enmeshing than a mere set of intergovernmental treaties, but on the other hand it is less enmeshing than a full-blown federation. To this end, this structure has been called — not entirely enlighteningly — a confederation.

Deepening and the logic of the European Single Market

Over the 30 years following the Treaty of Rome, the commitment to the creation of a real customs union led increasingly to pressures to establish a more truly integrated market area, so that domestic measures and regulations could not thwart the effects on liberalisation of the reduction of border barriers.

Thus was born the Single European Market of 1992, the initiative for which came in the early 1980s, and the requirements for which were set out in the Single European Act, agreed at an Intergovernmental Conference in 1986. The creation of this single European market has led to the elimination of a large number of formal national trade barriers, the elimination of customs formalities at national borders and the replacement of these national trade controls by Community-level instruments. It has led to a form of Europe-wide competition policy and the passing of trade policy competence almost entirely to the European level (although not in services).

Before the internal market program, the European market was characterised by a proliferation of standards and technical regulations that had the effect of segmenting the market. This was a barrier to access into national markets both of products from outside the European Union and from other member states. This has given way to a Europe-wide process of harmonisation and standardisation. That has required the construction of a Europe-wide apparatus of notification, mutual recognition directives, harmonisation and certification. The Single Market has also established freedom of trade in services as well as goods. Since such service provision is highly regulated, this has required the establishment of Europe-wide regulatory structures. Examples are finance and transport services. The Single Market is also in the process of removing internal barriers to public procurement, the enforcement of which requires regulatory discipline.

There has been a Europe-wide competition policy since 1958, but in 1990 this was extended to merger policy. In addition, the opening of the internal market in regulated industries (in particular, telecommunications and energy) is in the process of leading to the establishment of Europe-wide regulatory structures in these industries. The conclusion is that the creation of a genuine single market has required the establishment of supra-national structures: both standard-setting and regulatory apparatus. This has been embedded in a supra-national system of law making and the administration of justice.

The Single Market and qualified majority voting

The transnational governance of the European Single Market is complex, since Single Market legislation covers the wide range of issues mentioned above. For our story, two features are important. First, in the light of its existing institutional history, it was natural that the European Community took the view that this transnational governance should be conducted under the existing European political framework.[11] Second, the European Community took the view in the negotiation of the Single Market that this governance could not be carried out by means of the hitherto adopted form of inter-governmental cooperation, in which each member state retained a veto. Here was the origin within Europe of qualified majority voting.

Intrinsic difficulties: the domino effect

The most important difficulty associated with customs union integration is the instability of the 'domino effect' which it induces, and its particularly awkward consequences.

The instability issue is as follows. A developing customs union is attractive for others around its borders to join, in order to gain access to the market within the union. Baldwin (1993) has called this a domino effect, and argues that it is driven by 'jealousy'. 'In business, what matters is relative competitiveness. A firm's profits and sales are lowered by anything that lowers its rival's costs.' This is his explanation for the pressures that have manifested themselves in Europe, for those around the edges of the European Union to become a part of the customs union, a process which has seen membership grow from 6 to 9 to 12 to 15 members.

Thus, in the early 1960s, as barriers within the European Community (EC) customs union began to fall, political economy pressures grew from producers outside the union for access to it, particularly within the European Free Trade Association (EFTA: Denmark, Finland, Ireland, Iceland, Norway, and the United Kingdom).[12] This pressure resulted in defection from the EFTA to the European Community by the United Kingdom, Denmark and Ireland in the early 1970s. Then, in the 1980s, three new southern members were added (Greece, Portugal and Spain), all of whom saw integration within the European Community as a route to prosperity and growth as they emerged from periods of authoritarian government. More recently, three northern Europeans (Austria, Finland and Sweden) have joined, again for generically similar reasons. Those remaining in EFTA after the earlier defections decided that they must react,[13] and they sought and obtained the European Economic Area (EEA) which was negotiated in the late 1980s. The purpose of that arrangement was essentially to give those in EFTA access to the market of the European Community. What emerged, however, was an extraordinary and unstable arrangement.[14] In fact, virtually none of the EFTAns was prepared to live with the EEA as it was negotiated. Even before the negotiations were completed, Austria, Finland, Norway, Sweden and Switzerland had applied for membership of the European Union itself.

The awkward consequences which flow from this domino process are as follows.

First, the newly joining members essentially have to adapt themselves to the incentives and cost structures of the EU core (since at each stage they are relatively small and so their joining has relatively little effect on this overall cost structure). This structure may not be an appropriate one for the joining country's best integration into the world economy and may give rise to particularly strong incentives for trade diversion.[15] This issue is described by Pomfret in Chapter 3.

The negotiations to bring in the newcomers can give rise to extensive side-payments. Adding three new southern members in the 1980s (Greece, Spain and Portugal) meant the construction of a new grouping, the 'poor four' (Ireland, Greece, Portugal and Spain). All these countries had large agricultural sectors whose output was competitive with that of the existing beneficiaries of the CAP. To limit opposition from incumbent farmers, and also from workers in sensitive areas, the European Community insisted on long transition periods. For example, quotas on Iberian iron and steel were in place for seven years, and Spanish fruits, vegetables and vegetable fats obtained free access to the EU market only in 1996. Migration rights were restricted for five years. 'The increased structural spending served an important… purpose. While the Iberians received second-class treatment in terms of market access and the labour market, they were offered better than first class treatment on the Structural Funds. This balanced the impression that Spain and Portugal were joining as second class members' (Baldwin 1994: 201). As a result, in 1992, nearly a third of the EU budget (31.6 per cent) was devoted to structural funds, in addition to the 53.7 per cent devoted to the CAP (Baldwin 1994: 162).[16] This spending is set to increase again. In particular, a special cohesion fund was agreed by heads of state at the Maastricht meeting at which the Treaty on European Union was agreed. This has a budget rising to 2.5 billion ECU (European currency unit) by 1997. It was established to fund projects exclusively in the four poorest EU states.[17] This agreement again seems to have been unrelated to generally perceived need, but to a requirement to get agreement on the European agenda as part of the Maastricht process. These developments have turned the European system into one with not just three but four legs: not just agricultural support, a customs union, and a single market, but also redistributive spending.

Furthermore, the increasingly wide membership of the customs union (which, for reasons touched on above, is an all-or-nothing membership) puts at risk the negotiation of further liberalisation by the core members of the union. This is a kind of median-voter-theorem problem. Adding more members at the edge of the union involves bringing in members whose concerns regarding liberalisation are different from those in the core, possibly making it harder for liberalisation decisions to be reached. Deadlock can then result because of the inability within the all-or-nothing framework to do liberalisation at variable speeds. This problem could limit the European Union's capacity to play a leading or even constructive role in the process of global trade liberalisation.

Finally, negotiations to bring in the newcomers may give rise to difficulties for incumbent members, especially now that there is qualified majority voting. The prospect of the dilution of the ability to form blocking coalitions on one or a few key issues can then induce incumbent members to block the membership of, and thus the prospects for trade liberalisation in, peripheral countries. This takes us on to our next concern.

Integration with the east

The collapse of the former Soviet bloc has brought a demand for EU membership by members of that bloc. This has happened for historical and geopolitical reasons.[18] It has also happened for domino reasons similar to those discussed above, namely to give the Central and Eastern European countries (CEECs) access to the internal market to assist in their economic transformation.

Progress has been exceptionally slow. To go from the revolutions of 1989 to the prospect of enlargement to include a small group of front runners in around 2004 — a 15-year period — seems unacceptable, and has been unacceptable for quite some while. How did Europe get to this point?

After an initial delay into the early 1990s, 'Association Agreements' were negotiated with a few of the countries of Central Europe. These have been extended to a total now of ten countries, and those ten are now on the list for eventual membership. The Copenhagen European Council of summer 1993 laid out certain criteria for entry — the Copenhagen Criteria — which involved (i) having political democracy, (ii) having a functioning market economy and (iii) being able to assume the obligations of EU membership. Little was done then until the European Council meeting in Essen (December 1994), which set out a 'pre-accession strategy', including the financial assistance program (Phare), a 'structured dialogue' between the European Union and the candidates, and a White Paper on the Single Market. This was a useful compendium of the European legislation of various kinds in the Single European Market area, but it gave no clear sense of priorities for implementation, nor did it indicate for these accession negotiations to come what issues were negotiable.

Nevertheless, there is a commitment to add the following ten CEECs to the European Union: the Visegrad four (the Czech Republic, Hungary, Slovakia, Poland), Slovenia, the three Baltics (Estonia, Latvia, Lithuania), and Bulgaria and Romania, along with Cyprus and Malta (if it wishes). And there is already the realistic prospect that five or more of these may be brought into the accession negotiations which are to begin in early 1998.

The EU–CEEC Association Agreements, negotiated in the early 1990s, are bilateral agreements with the economic objective of establishing bilateral free trade between the European Union and the CEECs. In these the European Union has removed tariffs and quantitative restrictions on most industrial products, and the CEECs have engaged in phased liberalisation which is almost complete. Nevertheless, these association agreements have three major faults (see Baldwin 1994). They institutionalised delay, they left out agriculture, and they left great scope for contingent protection, which has acted as a deterrent on investment in these emerging economies (see Messerlin 1996 for further discussion).

Consider first the conditions of access for industry.

The bilateral hub-and-spoke arrangements with the European core are not part of a coherent larger scheme. This creates two kinds of problem for the participating CEECs. First, because the agreements are bilateral, they do not give producers in any one CEEC the right of access to the markets of other CEECs. Since EU firms located in the hub of the agreements have such access, this provides an incentive to service CEEC markets from within the European Union rather than from within any CEEC country. Second, and perhaps more important, rules of origin may mean that a product assembled in two or more of the CEEC countries may not count as originating in any of them. Such rules may make it difficult to source inputs from third-country low-cost suppliers (for example from the Asia Pacific region), or from each other, meaning that producers in any particular CEEC may need to source inputs from higher-cost producers in the European Union. This places difficulties in the way of CEEC producers' developing the kind of vertically disaggregated production networks which have characterised the Asia Pacific region.[19]

Zero-tariff status does not mean free access. The European Union has a long history of imposing contingent protection such as anti-dumping and voluntary export restraints, and this has been applied to the CEECs under the association agreements, for example in steel.

One consequence of these two features, in our view, has been the disappointingly low levels of foreign direct investment (FDI) in the CEECs since 1989. Moreover, Baldwin (1994: 135) has argued convincingly that these first two kinds of problem may generate permanent 'hysteresis effects': problems in the early stages of liberalisation making difficulties for the subsequent emergence of industries and industrial concentrations which would have appeared without these initial disabilities. Too little attention has been devoted to trying to get a good equilibrium for these countries: faster progress towards accession, without this contingent protection, would have fed upon itself and would have locked in more tightly a process of more rapid institutional reform. This would, in turn, have given the kind of environment and security necessary for more rapid growth of direct investment.

Turning to agriculture, we encounter the third difficulty. Agricultural trade is mostly excluded from the liberalisation. Provisions in the agreements explicitly state that they 'shall not restrict in any way' the agricultural policies of the CEECs or the European Union. Since agriculture is an obvious area of comparative advantage for the CEECs, such a position is not sustainable in the longer term.

These 'half-way problems' arise because of the European Union's status as a customs union, which it is understandable that the CEECs wish to join for both political reasons and domino-economic reasons. But membership of the European Union for these countries does not look like an easy solution and there is likely to be further delay. On the one hand, it will lead to difficulties for existing EU members: the changed character of the European Union may well lead to pressures to slow down the achievement of further integration, not least because of the budgetary costs involved.[20] On the other hand, full membership of the European Union by these countries will require them to take a large number of major steps extraordinarily rapidly, steps of institutional adaptation which the core EU members took gradually over a period of 35 years; this too may lead to delay. Still, membership is necessary — in the absence of any other trade liberalisation strategy — to ensure the 'good equilibrium' of higher FDI, institutional reforms, faster growth of output and real wages, and incentives to accumulate domestic human and physical capital.

Economic and Monetary Union

The sceptical challenge

Outsiders register continued surprise that Europe could come to see monetary union as the appropriate vehicle for the next stage of European integration. They argue[21] that Europe is not appropriate for a common currency (it has neither the wage flexibility, nor the labour mobility, nor the capacity for the fiscal redistribution which is necessary to buffer asymmetric shocks) and also that Europe is unlikely to have sufficient political integration for the necessary budgetary discipline to be exercised over its member states. In these circumstances, the risk is that EMU might become overly rigid and deflationary, as attempts are made to enforce discipline, both by means of the 'stability pact' on European fiscal policy and through the European Central Bank (ECB).

How could this have happened, these outsiders ask?

False explanations

There appear to us to be two wrong or incomplete answers to this question. The first false trail is history. The distrust of floating exchange rates has a long intellectual history: British readers know Keynes (1971) and Nurkse (1945) on this subject, but there is a long French tradition of scepticism about floating exchange rates. The attempt to do something practical about the problems of floating exchange rates within Europe also has a long history: the Werner plan of 1970 for monetary union, the introduction of the 'snake' in the early 1970s (which soon failed, so that the 1970s was a decade of currency turbulence), and the launch of the European monetary system in 1979. By 1988 this had succeeded in making Europe a zone of exchange rate stability. In its early years, frequent and sometimes large realignments were required to hold the system together, but by the late 1980s the system appeared to have evolved from an original soft form into a hard zone in which currencies did not change. By this stage economic justifications of the European Monetary System (EMS) abounded, in terms of: (i) reduced transactions costs from exchange rate stability, (ii) the institutionalisation of macroeconomic policy cooperation which an integrated monetary system would bring, and (iii) the benefits to inflation-prone countries of hitching their monetary policy making to that of Germany. Indeed, by 1989, many were prepared to agree with Jacques Delors that the EMS was such a historical success that it could be used as the vehicle for the next stage of integration.

The second false trail is the view that the monetary union project was not born from a coherent strategy for Europe, but arose merely from a tactical deal involving the national interests of the two key European players. Along these lines, it could be argued that Delors's move was a 'French' one, in that a move towards European monetary union would enable French policy makers both to regain some control over French interest rates and to regain global monetary influence (Mélitz 1994), and that it also revealed a 'preoccupation with German economic might…a desire of the French to clutch to the Germans and to influence them' (All Souls College 1997: 1). It may also be argued that this move connected well with German fears of 'bad Germans' —

that monetary union would be a part of the wider structures which, by anchoring Germany in the way previously discussed, might address these fears.[22]

One market, one money

The strongest argument as to why support was forthcoming to transform the EMS into the EMU is as follows. The argument has two parts.

First, integration implies (especially in the absence of capital controls) that fixed exchange rates are just not feasible. The reasoning is partly familiar from Mundell-Fleming: with a high degree of capital mobility, a country is incapable of maintaining a fixed exchange rate unless it entirely surrenders control over its monetary policy. In addition, the work of Obstfeld (1986; 1991; 1994; 1996) and others has shown that this may not be enough. It may also need to be believed that a country has entirely surrendered the *possibility* of running an independent monetary policy. Otherwise, fears that it might devalue could be sufficient to provoke a depreciation which, without such fears, the government might have been able to avoid.[23] This is a view of the EMS in the late 1980s, the 'hard' EMS, which suggested that fixed exchange rate systems are intrinsically vulnerable (including to self-fulfilling attacks) and so there was 'no way to stand still, only forwards to EMU, or backwards to floating again' (Portes 1993).

Second, the completion of the Single Market process was seen as incompatible with the maintenance of any move back to floating exchange rates. This is not just a story about the removal of modest transactions cost triangles, it is rather an industrial economics story about market integration. Full integration requires the breaking down of market segmentation. The evidence suggests that the existence of different currencies is the most plausible explanation of why the Law-of-One-Price does not hold within Europe.

With the middle ground of quasi-fixed exchange rates ruled out and the move backward to floating also ruled out, only the move forward to EMU remained open.

Notice that this is not a story about optimal currency area theory. One can agree with the claim that Europe is not an optimal currency area (in the normal sense of that literature discussed above) but nevertheless still be in favour of the EMU project (see Wyplosz 1997).[24]

Are we to argue to our Asia Pacific friends that when you get this far you, too, will be thinking about monetary integration?

Requirements for a successful EMU project

There are, however, a number of problems which must be overcome if a monetary union project of this kind is to be successful. We identify four of these. The first two we discuss in detail, and the last two we only touch on briefly.

Fiscal consolidation, the Maastricht criteria, and the importance of monetary policy

The first problem is the medium-term problem of deficits and debt in Europe mentioned in the introduction. Right through the 1980s and 1990s, budget deficits have averaged well above 4 per cent of GDP. In the EU15 the ratio of government debt to GDP has risen from 40 per cent in 1979 to about 75 per cent in 1996. Only in one year, the year of unsustainable growth in 1979, did the EU15 budget deficit fall below 3 per cent of GDP. As a result, all countries in Europe have recently moved towards fiscal restraint. But there is a danger that governments underestimate the difficulties of fiscal consolidation in an area as large as Europe and underestimate the complexities of doing this at the same time as forming a monetary union. Success would require a sustained, medium-term rise in private sector investment (or reduced private savings). This is unlikely to happen automatically.

The Maastricht criteria for entry to EMU, which have enforced this consolidation, are usually seen as an imperfect response to the need to guard against a financial crisis within EMU resulting from 'excess deficits' in one country. The limits on deficits recently imposed in the 'stability pact' (strictly the 'Stability and Growth Pact')[25] have been given similar justification. This usual rationale results from the idea that such a crisis would impose externalities on other countries which would be especially large within a monetary union. The argument rests, in turn, on the view that a no-bail-out rule for the central bank could not remain credible in such circumstances: inevitably, so the argument goes, all European countries might be drawn into the solution of such a crisis, so firm rules are needed to guard against it. However, these ideas do not take seriously enough the fact that the risk of actual sovereign insolvency in European countries is very small. If that is so, then arguments for the Maastricht conditions and a 'stability pact' must be found elsewhere.

It is our view that there are strong rationales for such rules, because the generally shared objective of fiscal restraint and consolidation in Europe may need to be brought about by coordinated means within EMU. The problem with carrying out fiscal consolidation within a monetary union is that membership of the union makes consolidation a prisoner's dilemma, which is not the case with floating exchange rates. This is because, even if each country desires fiscal consolidation, a single country acting on its own within a monetary union cannot accompany its own fiscal consolidation with its own tailor-made 'matching' monetary expansion. If the consolidation is Europe-wide, the costs can be avoided. Thus, each country might well prefer 'tight' fiscal policy only if others pursue tight fiscal policy. Consolidation — according to this argument — becomes something which has to be coordinated.

Empirical simulations in Allsopp et al. (1997), using McKibbin's MSG2 model, show this prisoner's dilemma problem to be important empirically for EMU. The short-term unemployment costs (over two or three years) of a fiscal consolidation by a single country such as France within EMU can be *four times* as large as those which would occur if the consolidation were undertaken under floating exchange rates. Furthermore, additional simulations show that were there to be a cooperative consolidation of the same size by all EMU players, then short-term unemployment costs could be reduced to the same size as those ruling in a single country consolidating on its own under floating exchange rates.

A necessary part of such a benign coordinated outcome is a cut in interest rates and a fall in the value of the euro. The former would produce the fall in private sector savings and the rise in private sector investment that is required; the latter would augment this response by means of an increase in net exports. If there were such an outcome, then all could participate in a situation of lower interest rates, increasing investment and output, and rising tax revenues — a process in which the consolidation becomes self-reinforcing. Indeed, the outcome could tip Europe on to a path of higher investment, higher growth, and steadily falling unemployment, so helping to solve the macroeconomic problem identified at the beginning of the chapter. This is a benign scenario in which monetary union, embarked on essentially for reasons to do with completing the Single European Market, could help to solve the European macroeconomic malaise.

Notice that concerted fiscal restraint alone is not enough; it must be accompanied by sufficient monetary relaxation. In its absence, consolidation might become damaging and the rules of the stability pact might be quite unsuitable — one country's fiscal consolidation causing another country's output and tax revenue to fall — threatening higher unemployment and maybe even lower investment (so exacerbating the longer-term problem of macroeconomic malaise which the stability pact was designed to help solve). To avoid such problems, a pre-emptive cut in interest rates might be necessary, as might be a deliberate policy of engineering a sufficient fall in the euro.[26]

There are three related risks. First, it is hard to see how a good outcome can be achieved if the ECB sticks to a narrow view of its remit. An ECB committed only to building credibility for an 'inflation first' strategy is unlikely to manage this task in a satisfactory way.

Second, even a more 'flexible' ECB might be unwilling to risk the required monetary loosening if it doubts the credibility of the commitment by European fiscal authorities to consolidation. And, in turn, the fiscal authorities might doubt whether the ECB will allow the required monetary loosening. A non-cooperative game of 'chicken' might then emerge between the fiscal authorities and the ECB (see Artis 1997), whose outcome was not enough consolidation, and yet still not enough monetary loosening to prevent that consolidation from causing unemployment. There are grounds for fearing such an outcome: attempts by the French government to renegotiate the stability pact earlier in this year, coupled with doubts expressed by many commentators about whether the constraints of the stability pact are in fact as tight as had been intended, could indeed give the ECB grounds for opposing the necessary monetary relaxation.

Third, the ECB's task may be even more difficult if a growing international status for the euro leads to portfolio shifts that favour euro appreciation (see Alogoskoufis and Portes 1997; Alogoskoufis, Portes and Rey 1997); we discuss this below in the section on accommodating the euro as an international currency.

Leaving room for fiscal stabilisation

The second issue arises because fiscal policy will actually need to be more actively used for short-term stabilisation in a future EMU common currency area. This is necessary since individual countries will no longer have the freedom to lower interest rates or to devalue in order to counteract recession.

Contrary to 'fiscal federalist' fears, such stabilisation should not involve centralisation, but can be carried out at the national level. Normally in a recession the 'automatic stabilisers' allow tax revenues to fall, supporting income and counteracting the downturn. Furthermore, normally individual countries partly offset shocks by the flexible use of budgetary policy. Simply allowing the operation of the stabilisers, and perhaps some limited budgetary flexibility, would do much to stabilise the economies of the countries in EMU.

Of course, the proper role for fiscal policy will need to be carefully defined. Such fiscal policy is only an appropriate response to shocks in domestic demand, and must not be used to prop up uncompetitive economies. Fear and mistrust that it will be used for such illegitimate purposes lie behind Germany's attempt to drive a hard bargain on the stability pact.

Nevertheless, there are serious difficulties. Without care, stabilisation of shocks will be prevented by the stability pact, which provides that countries can expect significant penalties if they run a deficit larger than 3 per cent of GDP. There is only a narrow range of 'exceptional and temporary circumstances' under which countries can escape these penalties. (There will be automatic exemption if the country has experienced a fall in GDP of more than 2 per cent in the previous year – which would be exceptional – and the possibility of exemption if output has fallen over the previous year by between 0.75 per cent and 2 per cent, but no exemption otherwise.)

These figures can be put in context by again noting that, for the EU15 as a whole, the public sector deficit has been less than 3 per cent of GDP in only one year since 1979 (which was the boom year of 1989 when tax revenues were unsustainably high) and has averaged over 4 per cent. What has been agreed constitutes a serious straitjacket. To leave sufficient margin for deficits to rise in a recession, so that there is room for stabilisation over the cycle, will require yet further consolidation, perhaps to the point where the norm for the deficit is perhaps 1 per cent or even lower. This will require that European fiscal and monetary authorities manage yet a further large round of fiscal consolidation.

Accommodating to the euro as an international currency

It is possible that soon after its establishment, the euro will become a significant international currency. Indeed, providing the first two macroeconomic risks which we have discussed above are met, this seems likely. Alogoskoufis, Portes and Rey (1997) discuss some of the issues involved. One of the interesting questions that arises is as follows.

There may initially be a shortage of euro assets, and a strong portfolio demand for them. This could have the benign effect of bidding up euro asset prices, effectively lowering market yields and interest rates. But it could also have the effect of appreciating the exchange rate, which could partly undo increases in profitability and competitiveness. Which of these effects dominates will be important. The first outcome will assist with the process of macroeconomic consolidation discussed above, helping to get the share of investment and the European growth rate up, in harmony with budget tightening. But the second outcome will work in the opposite direction. Which possibility emerges will partly depend on the conduct of European monetary policy by the ECB: these considerations will make the task of that body even more demanding than has been suggested above.

EMU, the outs, and the new EU members

Finally, EMU will have an effect on the widening process discussed above. If EMU is not well handled and is deflationary, then this effect will be damaging to the countries around the EU core. It would also be likely to affect negatively negotiations on further liberalisation of trade between these countries and the European Union, and to upset and complicate the timetable for the widening of the European Union.

If EMU is well handled, however, there remain technical issues. At present there are plans to require that countries in the 'queue' to join EMU should join a new Exchange Rate Mechanism (ERM II). In our view, it would be preferable if such a requirement were not imposed, but instead fitness were judged according to whether a mix of fiscal and monetary policy had satisfactorily controlled deficits and inflation. Nevertheless, this requirement may prove possible to manage without the kind of speculative crisis which shook ERM I in 1992. First, the bands will be wide (plus or minus 15 per cent). Second, it is less likely that these countries will be burdened with overvalued exchange rates in the way which caused the problem in 1992. We are mainly talking about countries in which labour costs are low and industrialisation relatively rapid. As Portes (1997) discusses, such countries are likely to experience rising (not falling) real exchange rates, a phenomenon which can be met either with nominal appreciation or with somewhat more rapid inflation.

Conclusions

In this chapter we have reviewed the European project for an external, non-European audience, in particular for an Asian Pacific one. We have attempted to explain the political imperatives which have driven Europe in a direction which has taken it from customs union to single market to monetary union. We have also highlighted two crucial requirements for this project to continue to succeed.

First, Europe must find policies that improve the outlook for growth and thus for investment, leading to greater labour absorption and a solution to the European unemployment problem. At the macroeconomic level, this will require continued pressure for even higher national savings, and perhaps even lower budget deficits than those envisaged in the Maastricht criteria and the Growth and Stability Pact. It will require that the ECB allow lower European interest rates and a more competitive European exchange rate. At the microeconomic level it will require continued commitment by Europe to the process of global trade liberalisation, a commitment, however important, that will be difficult to sustain because of the complex balance of interests within the ever-growing European customs union.

Second, Europe must find a way in which its periphery in Eastern Europe and North Africa can radically cut tariffs and other trade barriers and so embrace freer trade, not just within the European market but also with the rest of the world. The Asia Pacific lesson is that it is in the interests of these peripheral countries to move as far and as fast as possible, collectively, towards free trade. Squaring this interest with their current remorseless moves towards inclusion within the European Union will not be easy. It may well require quite radical moves towards *globally* freer trade.

Notes

* This chapter was written for a AJRC/CEPR/GEI conference on 'Europe, East Asia, APEC and the ASEM (Asia–Europe meeting) Process' on 20–21 May 1997. We are grateful to Chris Allsopp, George Alogoskoufis, Heinz Arndt, David Currie, Ross Garnaut, Helène Rey, David Robertson and André Sapir for discussions on these matters.

1 As proposed, for example, in the recent British White Paper on international trade.

2 The Rosenstein-Rodan big-push story has been revived by Krugman and by Vishny, Shleifer and Murphy as a theory of development. But although it might have important things to say about how to get development going, it cannot be used to support or justify continued agricultural protectionism.

3 For a useful account, see Croome (1995).

4 Such an intervention has been historically common at the stage of industrialisation which continental Europe had reached; as for example in Britain before 1832, and in Japan and Korea in the recent past. It is the obverse of the protection of manufacturing in newly developing peripheral countries such as the US northeast in the nineteenth century, and Latin America, Australasia and South Africa in the twentieth century.

5 This is the form of support which prevailed in the United Kingdom prior to entry into the European Community.

6 'EFTA was heavily trade creating, but the EEC [European Economic Community] promoted intra bloc trade through a combination of trade creation and trade diversion. This conclusion is reinforced by our results for the first two enlarge-

ments of the Community, for which we also find both trade creation and trade diversion effects (the accession of Portugal and Spain, by contrast led to little if any trade diversion).'

7 Sapir charts how exports of the EFTA countries to the European Union fare 'less well' (than would have been expected from a double-log gravity model) in the period 1960–72; the effect being relatively small for Nordic countries which traded mostly within EFTA, and relatively large for Alpine members and the United Kingdom, which shipped more than 50 per cent of their Western European exports to the European Union. The result, argues Sapir, was the set of applications for membership of the European Union (see below).

8 His study contends that Germany's own interests in foreign policy have been pursued 'in Europe's name' (the title of his book) by means of precisely this kind of argument.

9 So far we have ascribed the view that Europe has a supra-economic purpose only to France and Germany. Many in Italy, Spain, Greece, Portugal subscribe to a vision of Europe which transcends economic reasoning. The last three countries were emerging from periods of authoritarian government at the time that they joined the (then) European Community, and they looked to their inclusion in the European market as a guarantee for their fledgling democracies. For Italy, there has always been a strong strand of thought which has seen membership of the European Community and the European Union as a device to discipline economic policy.

10 It is worth noticing the contrast here between the way in which economic and security issues are intertwined in Europe and the way in which they appear to be intertwined in the Asia Pacific region. In the latter region, security issues have long been a major concern. Twenty-five years ago they focused around the issue of communist insurgency, and more recently they have focused around the two Chinas problem (and the two Koreas problem). The Association of Southeast Asian Nations (ASEAN) was founded as an institution with the former security issue uppermost in mind. But subsequent economic cooperation structures have been viewed as policies for security only indirectly, through their effects on prosperity and thereby on stability, rather than as directly providing means to the institutionalisation of political cooperation. This seems inevitable given the lack of institutional structure in the Asia Pacific region as compared with Europe, a situation which is likely to continue for some time (see the papers in Soesastro and Bergin 1996).

11 Note the contrast with the global attempts to write rules for the 'new measure' areas under the auspices of the WTO, within a treaty-based non-political framework. These global attempts are immeasurably more difficult, not just because they are global, but because of the form that they are taking.

12 Related pressure also emerged for association agreements with those who may not be on the list for ultimate integration, such as Turkey.

13 This had become all the more urgent with the European plans under way to form the Single European Market.

14 It was extraordinary on two counts. First, it forced the EFTAns to accept future EC legislation without formal participation in the formation of these laws; and second, it created a good deal of supra-nationality amongst the EFTAns (the EEA Council).

15 A comparison with the Closer Economic Relationship between Australia and New Zealand makes this point; a considerable part of the recent re-industrialisation of the New Zealand economy has involved the production of white goods for the still-protected Australian market, rather than reintegration into the wider Asia Pacific and world markets. We owe this point of comparison to Ron Duncan; too little is known in detail about the empirical significance of this point in that case.

16 By way of comparison, the other items in the EU budget for that year were: research and development, energy and technology (3.3 per cent), administration (4.7 per cent), foreign aid (3.5 per cent) and other (1.3 per cent). The total size of the EU budget is small — between 1.2 and 1.3 per cent of the member countries' total GDP. The sources of EU budgetary revenue are as follows (proportions correspond to 1992 figures): a proportion (capped at 1.4 per cent) of member countries' value-added tax (VAT) receipts (58 per cent); all of member countries' tariff revenue (18.9 per cent); agricultural levies (3.3 per cent); the 'fourth resource', a levy based on GNP (13.9 per cent); other (5.8 per cent).

17 'Many commentators view this fund as a "sweetener" to persuade the poor EU states to agree to the tighter integration implied by the Maastricht treaty. As such, it is an excellent example of the EU's rich-North/poor-South politics. When the rich EU nations want something that does not directly benefit the poorer states, the poorer states demand generous transfers in exchange for acquiescence' (Baldwin 1994: 165).

18 It reflects the view that a widening of the European Union is important in the locking in of democracy in the East.

19 For a thorough and revealing discussion of the problems of rules of origin, see Krueger (1995). One reading of that paper is sufficient to overturn the normal presumption that free trade areas (FTAs) are better than customs unions. That presumption says that, because trade restrictions in FTAs are not set collectively, this makes it harder for an FTA bloc to exercise market power in the setting of restrictions, and makes it likely, other things being equal, that an FTA will be less protectionist than a customs union. But an FTA will have rules of origin in a way in which a customs union will not. In the presence of trade in vertically integrated products, it appears relatively easy for these rules to be tuned so as to create massive trade diversion. Consider the case of a highly developed country in the 'core' of an FTA which imports a finished product from its less developed partner in the periphery of the FTA, where it is assembled from imported components. All that is required is that the core country insist on a rule of origin which requires that its peripheral partner produce domestically a higher proportion of the product-plus-components than is possible. That rule will cause the partner country to source components not from the rest of the world — which might have been the cheapest approach in the past — but from the core country.

20 Until recently, it used also to be thought that integrating these countries into the European Union under existing rules would be prohibitively expensive. There are two components of cost: the CAP and the structural funds. Taken together, all ten of the CEEC countries would add another 104 million of population, with low per capita income, giving rise to an entitlement to structural fund support, and with a high proportion of GDP devoted to agriculture (and a strongly agricultural population) giving rise to an entitlement to CAP funds. However, a recent study by Baldwin, François, and Portes (1997) puts the likely net budgetary cost for the Visegrad four (Czech Republic, Slovak Republic, Hungary, Poland) at no more than ECU 19 billion, only 19 per cent of what the EU budget is projected to be without enlargement. There are two reasons for the lower figures. First, structural fund payments are likely to be limited to a politically realistic level (no more than 5 per cent of GDP), a constraint which was not properly recognised previously. Second, CAP payments are likely to be more limited than had been realised, as a result of (i) the low productivity of CEEC farming, (ii) the extent to which the MacSharry reforms have already been implemented, (iii) internal EU budget constraints on the CAP, and (iv) the fact that CEEC bindings on tariffs and subsidies which were given during the last Uruguay Round (which are not likely to be broken) would prevent CEEC countries from availing themselves of the levels of support which currently prevail within the European Union. Moreover, as Baldwin et al. (1997) point out, there will be economic benefits as well as budgetary costs.

21 For example Bayoumi and Eichengreen (1992), Eichengreen (1990a; b; c; 1994; 1996a; b), Feldstein (1997).

22 There is a problem with timing in this interpretation of the German position; it is an explanation which seems more powerful when applied to the behaviour of Chancellor Kohl after 1989.

23 The problem is that a belief that monetary policy will be used independently can set up expectations that the exchange rate peg will be abandoned; those expectations can induce additional capital flows, and that can make the expectation that the peg will be abandoned self-fulfilling. A stylised description of the United Kingdom's position during the EMS crisis of 1992 helps to make this point. The United Kingdom was in recession. It was committed not to change its parity within the EMS, which meant that it could not lower interest rates relative to those elsewhere, particularly in Germany. Since German interest rates had risen during 1991 and 1992 (because of the need to damp the demand effects coming from German re-unification), the United Kingdom was committed to the continued acceptance of high interest rates. But there came a point at which markets believed the government would risk depreciation in order to get interest rates down. This provoked the fear of a depreciation. To compensate portfolio holders in such circumstances would have required higher interest rates; these were not forthcoming, and thus the currency crisis occurred. This is a story of a fear of a depreciation provoking an actual depreciation. Such fears can be self-fulfilling in the sense that they can provoke the depreciation which is feared, even if the beliefs about the government on which they are based are not true. Without the fears the peg can be sustained; with them it becomes too costly.

24 Note a paradox. Fernandez (1997) argues that the main benefit of the North American Free Trade Area (NAFTA) is that it gives Mexico a guarantee that the United States will not be protectionist against Mexico if Mexico uses devaluation to solve external adjustment problems. That is, she suggests, an argument for trade integration whose purpose is to preserve the room for macroeconomic manoeuvre. How can we believe this, and at the same time believe that one needs to commit to macroeconomic rigidity in order to maximise the benefits of trade integration? Is the difference that Mexico is small and so effectively unimportant for the United States?

25 This was agreed at Dublin in December 1996 and finalised at the Amsterdam European Council in mid-1997.

26 Estimates of the (large) size of the required responses are given in Allsopp et al. (1995). In particular, a fiscal consolidation equal to 2 per cent of GDP may require a fall in the value of the euro of over 12 per cent. Actual falls in interest rates may not need to be very large, perhaps no more than 100 basis points, if investment and consumption are responsive enough.

References

All Souls College (1997) 'Report of proceedings of a conference on monetary union' held on January 15–16, Oxford.

Allsopp, C., G. Davies and D. Vines (1995) 'Fiscal policy in a European monetary union', *Oxford Review of Economic Policy,* Summer.

—— and D. Vines (1996) 'Fiscal policy in a European monetary union', *National Institute Economic Review.*

——, W. McKibbin and D. Vines (1997) 'Fiscal consolidation in Europe: Is the Stability and Growth Pact the easy solution to a prisoner's dilemma?', mimeo, Oxford: Institute of Economics and Statistics.

Alogoskoufis, G. and R. Portes (1997) 'The euro and the international monetary system', in P. Masson et al., eds, *EMU and the International Monetary System*, Washington DC: IMF.

——, R. Portes and H. Rey (1997) 'The emergence of the euro as an international currency', Discussion Paper No. 1741, CEPR, London.

APEC (1994) 'Achieving the APEC vision: free and open trade in the Pacific', Second Report of the Eminent Persons' Group, mimeo, August.

Artis, M.J. (1997) 'The Stability Pact: safeguarding the credibility of the ECB', mimeo, Florence: European University.

Baldwin, R. (1993) 'A domino theory of regionalism', Discussion Paper No. 857, CEPR, London, November.

—— (1994) *Towards an Integrated Europe*, London: CEPR.

——, J. François and R. Portes (1997) 'The costs and benefits of eastern enlargement: the impact on the EU and on Central Europe', *Economic Policy* 24, Basil Blackwell.

Bayoumi, T. and B. Eichengreen (1992) 'Shocking aspects of European Monetary Unification', Discussion Paper No. 643, CEPR, London.

—— (1995) 'Is regionalism simply a diversion? evidence from the evolution of the EEC and from NAFTA', Discussion Paper No. 1294, CEPR, London.

Bhagwati, J. and A. Panagariya (1996) 'The theory of preferential trade agreements: historical evolution and current trends', *American Economic Review*, Papers and Proceedings, 1996.

Centre for Economic Policy Research (CEPR) (1993) *Making Sense of Subsidiarity*, London: CEPR.

Cobham, D. (1994) *European Monetary Upheavals*, Manchester: Manchester University Press.

Croome, J. (1995) *Reshaping the World Trading System: A History of the Uruguay Round of Trade Negotiations*, Geneva: World Trade Organization.

Currie, D. (1997) 'The pros and cons of EMU', EIU Research Report, London: Economist Intelligence Unit.

Eichengreen, B. (1990a) 'One money for Europe? lessons from the US Currency Union', *Economic Policy* 10, pp. 117–87.

—— (1990b) 'Costs and benefits of European Monetary Unification', Discussion Paper No. 453, CEPR, London.

—— (1990c) 'Is Europe an optimal currency area?', Discussion Paper No. 478, CEPR, London.

—— (1994) *Monetary Arrangements for the 21st Century*, Washington: Brookings Institution.

—— (1996a) *Globalising Capital — a History of the International Monetary System*, Princeton: Princeton University Press.

—— (1996b) 'A more perfect union? On the logic of economic integration', Frank D. Graham Lecture, Princeton University.

—— (1997) *European Monetary Unification: Theory, Practice and Analysis*, Cambridge MASS: MIT Press.

European Commission (1996) 'Report on the Single Market Programme', *European Economy* No. 4.

Feldstein, M. (1997) paper forthcoming in *Journal of Economic Perspectives*, Fall.

Fernandez, R. (1997) 'Returns to regionalism: an evaluation of the non-traditional gains from RTAs', Discussion Paper No. 1634, CEPR, London.

Garnaut, R. (1997) *Open Regionalism and Trade Liberalisation*, Sydney: Allen and Unwin.

Garton Ash, T. (1993) *In Europe's Name: Germany and the Divided Continent*, Vintage.

Higgott, R. (1995) 'Beyond embedded liberalism: governing the international trade regime in an era of nationalism', paper presented to the Annual Conference of the British International Studies Association, Southampton, December.

Hirst, P. and G. Thompson (1996) *Globalisation in Question*, Cambridge: Polity Press.

Holmes, P. (1995) 'Competition policy and the WTO', Newsletter of the Global Economic Institutions Research Programme, London: CEPR, Issue 2.

Inman, R. (1997) 'Do balanced budget rules work? the US experience and possible lessons for EMU', Working Paper No. 5838, National Bureau of Economic Research (NBER), Cambridge, MASS.

Kenen, P. (1995) *European Monetary Union: Moving Beyond Maastricht*, Cambridge: Cambridge University Press.

Keynes, J.M. (1971) *The Collected Writings of John Maynard Keynes*, edited by Donald Moggridge and Elizabeth Johnson, vols 25 and 26, London: Macmillan.

Krueger, A. (1995) 'Free trade agreements versus customs unions', Working Paper No. 5084, National Bureau of Economic Research (NBER).

Lamers, K. (1996) 'Beyond the nation state: a German vision of Europe', *Times*, 27 April, p. 18.

Mélitz, J. (1994) 'French monetary policy and recent speculative attacks on the franc', in D. Cobham, ed., *European Monetary Upheavals*, Manchester: Manchester University Press, pp. 61–77.

Messerlin, M.J. (1996) 'Monetary union and preferential trade policies of the CCCs: Singapore and Geneva are the shortest route to Brussels', mimeo.

Neumann, M.J. (1995) 'Monetary union in the absence of political union', Yrjo Jahnsson European Integration Lecture No. 6, Helsinki, October.

Nurkse, R. (1945) 'Conditions of international monetary equilibrium', Princeton Essays in International Finance No. 4, International Finance Section, Department of Economics, Princeton University.

Obstfeld, M. (1986) 'Rational and self-fulfilling balance of payments crises', *American Economic Review*, vol. 76, pp. 72–81.

—— (1991) 'The destabilising effects of exchange rate escape clauses', Working Paper No. 3603, NBER.

—— (1994) 'The logic of currency crises', Working Paper No. 4640, NBER.

—— (1996) 'Models of currency crises with self-fulfilling features', Working Paper No. 5285, NBER.

Portes, R. (1993) 'EMS and EMU after the fall', *The World Economy* 16(1), pp. 1–15.

—— (1997) 'The real exchange rate and capital inflows in transition economies', mimeo, London Business School.

Rollo, J. (1994) 'The EC, European integration, and the world trading system', in V. Cable and D. Henderson, eds, *Trade Blocs?*, London: Chatham House.

Sachs, J. and A. Warner (1995) 'Economic reform and the process of global integration', Brookings Papers on Economic Activity, I, pp. 1–95 and 108–118.

Sampson, G. (1996) 'Compatibility of regional and multilateral trading arrangements: reforming the WTO process', paper presented at the Annual Meeting of the American Economic Association, San Francisco, January 5–7.

Sapir, A. (1997) 'Domino effects in West European trade, 1960–1992', Discussion Paper No. 1576, CEPR, London.

Soesastro, H. and A. Bergin (1996) *The Role of Security and Economic Cooperation Structures in the Asia Pacific Region*, Jakarta: Institute of Strategic and International Studies.

Vines, D. (1995) 'Unfinished business: Australian protectionism, Australian trade liberalisation, and APEC', *Australian Economic Review*, April.

Winters, A. (1996) 'Regionalism versus multilateralism', Discussion Paper, CEPR, London.

Wyplosz, C. (1997) 'EMU: why and how it might happen', *Journal of Economic Perspectives*, Fall.

5   Open regionalism: the nature of Asia Pacific integration

PETER DRYSDALE, ANDREW ELEK AND
HADI SOESASTRO

Introduction

Open regionalism is the idea that has defined the approach to the development of Asia Pacific Economic Cooperation (APEC) and Asia Pacific economic integration from its beginning. It is an approach to regional economic cooperation which seeks to promote economic integration among participants without discrimination against other economies.

At the outset, the term was adopted to distinguish the Asia Pacific approach to cooperation from the style of 'regionalism' adopted by the European Union (EU) and the North American Free Trade Area (NAFTA), which are based on discriminatory free trade areas and customs unions. By their nature, such regional initiatives divert economic activity. They need to be based on formal, legally binding rules: partly because any market-distorting arrangements need to be shored up by regulations and partly because preferential arrangements for trade in goods are not permitted under the General Agreement on Tariffs and Trade/World Trade Organization (GATT/WTO) in the absence of a formal agreement which meets (at least in broad terms) the provisions of Article XXIV. In contrast, Asia Pacific governments have embraced an evolutionary and voluntary approach to promote mutually beneficial economic integration.

Open regionalism has been given progressively clearer operational meaning over time as the process of cooperation has evolved and as its goals have been defined in greater detail. This chapter explains the evolution of the concept of open regionalism, the reasons for its adoption by APEC and how it has made it possible for APEC to make very rapid progress. The principles set out in the 1995 Osaka Action Agenda are designed to guide the liberalisation and facilitation of trade and investment by APEC governments towards the agreed objective of free and open trade and investment by 2020, consistent with the objective of promoting global as well as regional welfare. Practical cooperation has already begun and, as explained below, APEC governments are on a trajectory of trade liberalisation which is consistent with the achievement of this vision as well as with the concept of voluntary non-discriminatory dismantling of obstacles to economic integration.

The concept of open regionalism has been challenged in the past, most forcefully by those who believe that regional economic cooperation only makes sense, and can only work, if it discriminates against outsiders. These challenges will continue. But these challenges are not founded on economic logic, nor on the political realities of the Asia Pacific region, so they are not likely to prevail. However, they will need to be answered by continuing the steady progress Asia Pacific governments are making towards eliminating border barriers, based on their perception of the benefits of non-discriminatory liberalisation.

There is now another set of challenges as governments begin to implement the Manila Action Plan for APEC (MAPA). Up to this point, open regionalism has been used to distinguish between most favoured nation (MFN) and preferential liberalisation of border barriers to trade. As APEC governments develop concrete proposals to facilitate trade and investment, more precise guiding principles will be needed to ensure that cooperative arrangements are consistent with the basic objective of reducing impediments to trade and investment without detriment to other economies.

To promote rapid progress, APEC participants have agreed that those who are ready to implement initiatives for closer cooperation can do so, with others to join later. This makes it imperative to ensure that cooperative arrangements pioneered by some APEC economies are 'open clubs' which take full account of the interests of other economies and encourage them to join.

As APEC gathers momentum, participants will become increasingly aware of the need to ensure that cooperative arrangements among some participants are indeed capable of subsequent region-wide application. They will also need to ensure that new arrangements do not create new sources of discrimination, thereby fragmenting, rather than integrating, regional markets. That is likely to lead to the adoption of principles for the design of cooperative arrangements involving APEC economies which build on the guiding principles already agreed in APEC. Such principles are needed to generalise the fundamental GATT/WTO principles of transparency, non-discrimination and national treatment in order to apply them to new issues in international economic cooperation.

Such principles can also serve as a useful framework for managing relations between APEC economies and others. They can help APEC to admit new participants without damage to the prospects for free and open trade and investment. They can also help to promote mutually beneficial practical cooperation with non-participants, including European economies, without the need for elaborate formal structures.

If the Asia Pacific region and Europe could cooperate on a gradually wider range of issues, through cooperative arrangements which are 'open clubs', then their experience could also lead to the acceptance of new guiding principles for an international economic system designed to manage the emergence of complex cooperative arrangements covering many new forms of international economic transactions.

The prospects for such positive developments depend, vitally, on the European Union's response to trade liberalisation by APEC governments as they implement their Bogor commitments. Therefore, it is useful to begin to think about the evolution of relations and the potential for mutually beneficial cooperation between Asia Pacific and European economies.

APEC — its foundations

Origins of the idea

Regionalism in the Asia Pacific region is characterised by market-driven integration, rather than institutional integration; involves economies at different stages of economic development, rather than economies with similar income levels; and is outwardly oriented, rather than inward looking. These are also elements of open regionalism, the defining feature of Asia Pacific regionalism.

APEC adopted the principle of open regionalism formally in its Seoul APEC Declaration in 1991. But the concept was critical to APEC from its inception in 1989. It had its roots in the deep concern in the Western Pacific economies about the fate of the global, multilateral trade regime and the slow progress of multilateral trade negotiations in the Uruguay Round through the 1980s. East Asian economies understood their stake in the strength and continuity of an open trading system. Hence, open regionalism incorporates commitments to outward-looking trade and development policies, trade and investment liberalisation and GATT consistency.

The idea of keeping regionalism open in the Asia Pacific crystallised into policy commitments in the late 1980s, but it had its origins in much earlier dialogue that laid the intellectual foundations for the development of APEC. It was an approach dictated by the practical necessities of community building in a region of great economic, cultural, political and ethnic diversity, not merely a response to developments in the international economic policy environment. Regional community building in East Asia and the Pacific, it was argued (Drysdale 1988), had to be guided by three important principles: openness, equality and evolution.

Openness required non-discrimination and transparency in trade and economic policy, as well as in diplomatic stance in the last years of the Cold War.

Equality implied that activities needed to be of mutual benefit to all participants and recognised the rapid transformation in the structure of economic and political power taking place in the region.

Evolution of the process of regional cooperation recognised the importance to success of a gradual, step-by-step, pragmatic and sustained approach to economic cooperation based on consensus building and voluntary participation (Drysdale 1988: Chapter 10; PECC 1995).

The elements of open regionalism were set out for the first time at the Pacific Community Seminar held in Canberra in September 1980 at the initiative of then Prime Ministers Ohira of Japan and Fraser of Australia. This seminar was convened to explore the interest in Asia Pacific economic cooperation and launched the non-governmental, tripartite process that became the Pacific Economic Cooperation Council (PECC). Its recommendations encompassed the following principles for cooperation (Crawford and Seow 1980):

- the need to avoid military and security issues so as to create a sense of community without a sense of threat;

- the inappropriateness of a European Economic Community-type discriminatory trading arrangement in the Pacific;

- the need to 'hasten slowly' and proceed towards long-term goals step by step;

- the need to ensure that existing bilateral, regional and global mechanisms for cooperation were not undermined by any new, more comprehensive regional arrangement and that it be complementary with them;

- the need to ensure that it was an outward-looking arrangement;

- the need for an 'organic approach' building upon private arrangements and exchanges which already existed in the Pacific;

- the need to involve academics, businesspeople and governments jointly in cooperative endeavours;

- the need to avoid unnecessary bureaucratic structures;

- the need for a loose and, as far as possible, non-institutionalised structure;

- the need for all members to be placed on an equal footing;
- the need to concentrate efforts on areas of mutual regional interest.

The Canberra meeting coined the term 'open regionalism' to define its strategy for advancing Asia Pacific economic cooperation and thus set its stamp upon every major step in the process that emerged over the following two decades.

Main elements of open regionalism

There are three main reasons why the Asia Pacific region has eschewed discrimination in its approach to regional economic cooperation (Garnaut 1996).

First, it would be quite impracticable to undertake regional trade liberalisation by means of a conventional discriminatory free trade area of the kind sanctioned by the GATT/WTO. The substantial elimination of trade barriers through the negotiation of a free trade area within a reasonable period of time is not attainable within the Asia Pacific region. Negotiating such an arrangement would be highly divisive and delay the process of liberalisation it was supposed to promote (Elek 1995). It would corrode the objective of community building and lead to the exclusion of major players inside the region (such as China and Vietnam) as well as outside. Hence APEC opted for an alternative, new approach — setting targets for trade and investment liberalisation, rather than negotiating 'free and open trade and investment in the region'.

Second, the trading interests of East Asian and the Pacific economies extend beyond APEC, including to Europe. A conventional free trade area strategy towards trade liberalisation would deter internationally-oriented reform in the region's developing economies and introduce tensions into relations with major partners outside the region.

Third, trade discrimination involves the unnecessary costs of trade diversion, complicated in the Asia Pacific region by the likelihood of high associated political costs both within and outside the region (Garnaut and Drysdale 1994: Chapter 5).

APEC's agenda has evolved around giving progressively more precise expression and effect to the idea of open regionalism. At times the idea of non-discrimination has been challenged or blurred — in the recommendations of the APEC Eminent Persons Group (APEC EPG 1994) leading up to the Bogor Leaders' Meeting in Indonesia — but it has survived as an APEC imperative. Division over this issue remains in debate between those in East

Asia and Australia who have articulated Asia Pacific interests in terms of open regionalism and those in North America conscious of the political attractiveness of reciprocity, narrowly defined, in US trade policy dealings.

APEC formally espoused open regionalism at its Osaka meetings in 1995 and the Osaka Action Agenda was premised on the *voluntary* nature of the APEC process; an essential corollary to the idea of open regionalism. Commitment to unilateral liberalisation of barriers to trade and investment by APEC members, in their own self interest, is a necessary condition of progress on the basis of open regionalism. Such commitments are not seen as concessions for exchange in a negotiating process but their collective outcome (concerted unilateral liberalisation) is mutually re-enforcing of regional trade liberalisation, which is consistent with Article 1 of the GATT/WTO and does not require a formal Article XXIV style discriminatory agreement.

Equally important, in the context of Asia Pacific community building, is the sense of comfort that this modality provides to APEC member economies, by allowing flexibility in the implementation of liberalisation commitments not based on binding, negotiated schedules. APEC's trade liberalisation and facilitation agenda is adopted and implemented by the decisions of individual governments. Each member's liberalisation program is entered into voluntarily, in accordance with common guidelines for APEC cooperation adopted by consensus within the APEC process. Unilateral efforts are reviewed and monitored within APEC. As agreed in Osaka, members' Individual Action Plans (IAPs) cover trade liberalisation and trade and investment facilitation measures. In addition, Collective Action Plans (CAPs) open the possibility of non-discriminatory sectoral liberalisation in sectors of special interest to APEC members.

In Manila, in 1996, APEC members also laid the basis for adoption of the Information Technology Agreement (ITA) at the ministerial meetings of the WTO in Singapore late 1996. The ITA initiative is an example of the multilateral focus in APEC's liberalisation agenda, and the way in which open regionalism is meant to work.

Progress in APEC

The inaugural ministerial meeting in Canberra in 1989 was attended by 26 ministers from 12 economies, namely the six ASEAN (Association of Southeast Asian Nations) countries, South Korea, Japan, Australia, New Zealand, Canada and the United States. They agreed on the basic principles which would guide APEC. APEC's objective was to sustain growth and development in the region and to contribute to the growth of the world economy.

APEC should seek to strengthen the multilateral trading system and not be directed towards the formation of a regional trading bloc. APEC should focus on economic issues to advance common interests and foster constructive interdependence by encouraging the flow of goods, services, capital and technology.

The following meeting, in Singapore in 1990, established seven work projects. They were designed to foster the habit of cooperation and to demonstrate the benefits of economic cooperation through such activities as improving regional data on the flow of goods, services and investment, enhancing technology transfer and human resource development, promoting cooperation in energy, and in marine resources, as well as in telecommunications. Later three additional work projects were added: transportation, tourism and fisheries. The establishment of these ten work projects was a significant development in APEC as it promoted the initiation of regional networks among various governmental agencies. APEC ministers in Singapore issued a declaration underlining their commitment to a timely and successful completion of the Uruguay Round as a demonstration of APEC's support for a strong, open multilateral system. They also agreed that following the completion of the Uruguay Round, APEC would explore the scope for non-discriminatory regional trade liberalisation.

The third meeting, held in Seoul in 1991, adopted the Seoul APEC Declaration which set out the scope of activity, mode of operation of, and the principles for participation in APEC. APEC's scope includes: exchange of information and consultation on relevant economic policies; development of strategies to reduce impediments to trade and investment; and promotion of economic and technical cooperation. The Declaration explicitly stated that APEC's mode of operation is based on mutual benefit, a commitment to open dialogue and consensus building and cooperation through consultation and exchange of views. In addition, APEC welcomes the participation of the private sector in appropriate APEC activities. Following intensive diplomatic efforts by the host government, the meeting agreed to admit China, Hong Kong and Taiwan (Chinese Taipei) as members. This was another hugely significant development in APEC.

The following meeting, in Bangkok in 1992, marked the beginning of an institutionalisation of the process. The meeting agreed to set up a permanent international secretariat, located in Singapore, and an APEC Central Fund to finance APEC activities. The APEC process gained further momentum at the fifth meeting, in Seattle in 1993, when APEC admitted Mexico and Papua New Guinea as members. A decision was made to admit Chile in 1994 but to defer consideration of additional members for three years to allow the organisation sufficient time for consolidation.

The meeting in Seattle elevated the process of cooperation to the highest level of government. At the initiative of US President Clinton, an APEC informal leaders meeting was held in conjunction with the ministerial meeting. The leaders issued an Economic Vision Statement (APEC 1993) which contained three main elements. The first was an affirmation of the importance of an open multilateral trading system and the determination of Asia Pacific leaders to lead the way in taking concrete steps to produce the strongest possible outcome from the Uruguay Round.

The second was a vision of a community of Asia Pacific economies. This vision is of a community based on a spirit of openness and partnership, whose dynamic economic growth contributes to an expanding world economy and supports an open international trading system; where trade and investment barriers continue to be reduced; where the benefits of economic growth are shared by the people; where education and training are improved; where goods and people move quickly and efficiently because of advances in transportation and telecommunications; and where environmental protection is improved to ensure sustainable growth and to provide a more secure future for its people.

The third element was a list of initiatives which included, among others, the convening of meetings of APEC finance ministers, of APEC ministers involved with small and medium-sized business enterprises, the establishment of a Pacific Business Forum (now the Asia Pacific Business Advisory Council [ABAC]), and the development of a non-binding code of principles covering investment issues.

The APEC leaders' meeting the following year, held in Bogor (Indonesia), produced the Bogor Declaration of Common Resolve which set the goal of free and open trade and investment in the region by no later than 2010 for industrialised economies, and no later than 2020 for developing APEC economies. The commitment by leaders to achieve free and open trade by an agreed deadline was an important milestone in APEC's development. The Bogor Declaration stressed that these targets were to be achieved in a GATT-consistent manner, emphasising that APEC opposes the creation of an inward-looking trading bloc that would divert it from the pursuit of global free trade and that the APEC goal would be pursued in a manner that encourages and strengthens trade and investment liberalisation globally. Specifically, the outcome of APEC liberalisation will be the actual reduction of barriers not only among APEC economies but also between APEC economies and non-APEC economies.

In spite of these principles set out in the Bogor Declaration, some ambiguity remained about the means for achieving the APEC goal of free and open trade and investment in the region. These arose in proposals, including those put forward by the APEC Eminent Persons Group, which amounted to advocacy of a process of negotiated liberalisation among APEC members along the lines of a conventional free trade area. The benefits of such liberalisation could be extended only to non-members on a mutually reciprocated basis and in a way which would eliminate the problem of 'free riding', either within APEC itself or by non-members, notably Europe.

The task of clarifying these issues rested with Japan, the chair of APEC in 1995. There were concerns that Japan would not be able to provide the leadership necessary to craft the road map for implementing the Bogor Declaration. However, Japan successfully led the group to a consensus by producing an Action Agenda and 'brought the APEC process back on track' (Sopiee 1995).

APEC has taken a broad view of the nature of free and open trade and investment. The 1995 Osaka Action Agenda indicates that this will involve the elimination of all border barriers to trade and investment and the reduction of all other impediments to international economic transactions. The 15 areas of cooperation contained in the Agenda include the removal of tariff and non-tariff barriers to trade in goods and services and reducing the costs and risks of international commerce caused by inadequate communications, partly due to infrastructure constraints, inadequate information about opportunities for exchange, and uncertainty about future policies, as well as divergent approaches to many domestic economic policies.

APEC members have not ceded powers of regulation or enforcement to any supra-national regional authority. Consequently, there are no 'APEC decisions', as such. Since cooperation is voluntary, the many reforms that will be needed to reach the APEC goal will depend on policy decisions of individual governments. APEC's flexible approach makes it possible for Asia Pacific governments to set their own priorities and schedules for liberalisation, allowing the process as a whole to make early headway.

The Osaka Action Agenda is designed to maximise the potential advantages of flexible and voluntary cooperation, setting out ten agreed principles to guide implementation of the agenda: comprehensiveness; WTO consistency; comparability; non-discrimination; transparency; standstill; simultaneous start; continuous process and differentiated timetables; flexibility; and cooperation.

The principle of *comprehensiveness* combined with the principle of *flexibility* confirm that while members can determine the sequence of policy adjustments, 'sensitive' sectors and policy issues will not be excluded from the agreed target dates for free and open trade and investment. The principle of *cooperation* reflects the reality that economic and technical cooperation to pool information, experience, expertise and technology will be vital to achieving region-wide participation in many opportunities for facilitation of trade and investment. In turn, it will help strengthen the capacities of developing member economies to meet APEC's goals.

The principles of *comparability, standstill, simultaneous start, continuous process and differentiated timetables* and *flexibility* reflect political realities. While the dismantling of impediments to economic transactions among Asia Pacific economies is to be comprehensive, it is expected that most governments will leave what they perceive to be the most difficult political decisions to the later stages of the transition to free and open trade and investment. At the same time, for APEC to be credible, it is essential that all participants begin and sustain steady progress towards the agreed 2010 and 2020 targets. Hence the principles of *simultaneous start* and *standstill*, the latter ensuring that the dismantling of some obstacles to economic integration will not be accompanied by raising any others. In fact, the record of East Asian economies in this regard is good (PECC 1996).

The principle of *comparability,* viewed positively, reflects the intention of each APEC government to use the evidence of liberalisation and facilitation by other APEC economies as an argument to counter vested interests against reforms which increase competition. Such domestic political debates will be easier to manage if governments can point out that all APEC governments are taking political decisions of comparable difficulty in their shared interest as they move towards free and open trade and investment. On the other hand, too much emphasis on the 'comparability' of IAPs could divert members into time-wasting surrogate negotiations and become divisive. At worst, discussions among representatives of APEC governments could degenerate into GATT-style negotiations, where actions which benefit an economy come to be regarded as costs.

The principles of *transparency, WTO consistency* and *non-discrimination* are designed to maximise the benefits of cooperation as well as to ensure that cooperative arrangements among APEC economies take account of the interests of other economies. The principle of *non-discrimination* has been described as follows:

APEC economies will apply or endeavour to apply the principle of non-discrimination between and among them in the process of liberalisation and facilitation of trade and investment.

The outcome of trade and investment liberalisation in the Asia Pacific region will be the actual reduction of barriers not only among APEC economies but also between APEC economies and non-APEC economies.

The first part of the principle of non-discrimination recognises that community building in the region and the cohesion of APEC depend on avoiding, as far as possible, the creation of new sources of discrimination among APEC economies. The second underlines APEC's commitment to open regionalism. Both represent pragmatic compromises. The first recognises that some APEC economies belong to preferential sub-regional trading arrangements and that, under current legislation, the United States cannot guarantee unconditional MFN treatment of trade with China. Consistent with the concept of open regionalism, the second part of the non-discrimination principle confirms that APEC economies will reduce impediments to trade and investment with respect to non-participants. It also reflects the concern of some participants that if APEC market opening were extended equally to all other economies without some response on their part, it could encourage perceptions of free riding, particularly on the part of European economies.

These guiding principles have proved adequate to initiate substantive, practical cooperation among member economies. In Manila, at the seventh APEC meeting, in 1996, all members submitted their IAPs and agreed on a series of CAPs. The IAPs and CAPs were examined and discussed by APEC officials throughout 1996 under the chairmanship of the Philippines. Although there were no negotiations, there was extensive 'peer pressure' on all governments to make greater commitments in order to boost confidence in the capacity of the voluntary process of cooperation, or *concerted unilateralism*.

The individual and collective actions that form the MAPA are related to the three pillars of APEC: trade and investment liberalisation; facilitation; and economic and technical cooperation. An independent assessment undertaken by PECC in cooperation with the Philippine Institute for Development Studies, the Australia–Japan Research Centre and the Asia Foundation's Center for Asian–Pacific Affairs concluded that individual APEC economies are all well on track towards the Bogor goal and that their tariff reductions are mostly faster and deeper than their commitments under the Uruguay Round (AJRC 1995). As can be seen in Figure 5.1, the IAPs have further contributed to a lowering of tariffs in the region. The average (unweighted) tariff level was lowered from 15 per cent in 1988 to 9 per cent in 1996. By the year 2000, most APEC economies will be ahead of their Bogor target for tariff reduction. Some economies (Chile, China, Korea, Philippines and Thailand) have effected a dramatic reduction in their average tariff levels. Some (Chile, China, Indonesia and the Philippines) have made tariff reduction commitments, so that they are set to move ahead in achieving their Bogor target (PECC 1996).

The IAPs have also begun to address non-tariff measures. All APEC members outlined plans to reduce non-tariff barriers (NTBs) and most members have made a general commitment to review NTBs with a view to reduce or eliminate those NTBs that are not consistent with WTO measures. Some economies (Australia, China, Hong Kong, Indonesia, Japan, Korea, the Philippines and Papua New Guinea) have outlined detailed liberalisation measures.

Figure 5.1   *APEC and WTO tariff liberalisation, 1988–2000*

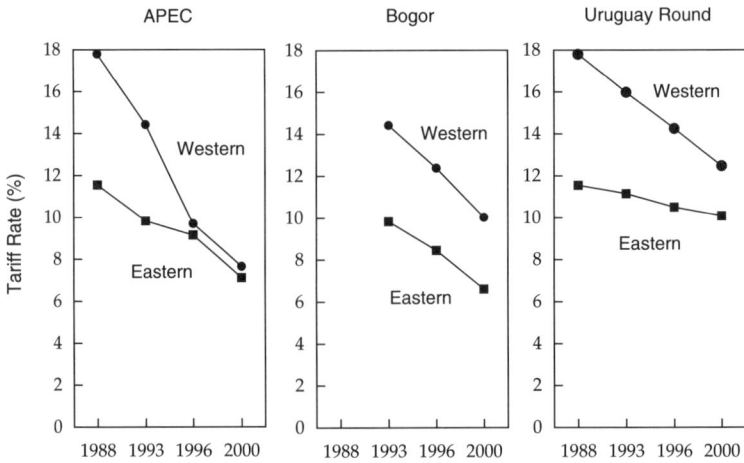

Note: Western includes East Asia and Australasia; Eastern includes North America.

Source: APEG, *Asia Pacific Profiles*, Financial Times Papers and Newsletters, Hong Kong, 1997.

In the area of trade in services, MAPA includes among other things: an explicit statement of support for the WTO negotiating process on services trade liberalisation; unilateral actions by some economies which go beyond their WTO schedules, especially with respect to the offshore establishment of service firms; commitments to collective APEC action to support WTO negotiations on professional services and on telecommunications; and the adoption of sets of APEC principles for the development of open markets for energy services and telecommunications.

In the area of investment, almost half of APEC members committed to undertake specific liberalisation measures. Commitments by other APEC members include continued improvement in facilitation and transparency measures; MFN treatment; and a recognition of the national treatment principle. Many other commitments were made, including in the area of facilitation and economic and technical cooperation.

Table 5.1   *Unweighted average tariffs of APEC economies, 1988–96*

	1988	1993	1996
Australia	15.6	9.0	6.1
Brunei	3.9	3.9	2.0
Canada	9.1	8.8	6.7
Chile	19.9	14.9	10.9
China	40.3	37.5	23.0
Hong Kong	0.0	0.0	0.0
Indonesia	20.3	17.0	13.1
Japan	7.2	6.5	9.0
Korea	19.2	11.6	7.9
Malaysia	13.0	12.8	9.0
Mexico	10.6	12.8	12.5
New Zealand	15.0	8.0	7.0
Philippines	27.9	23.5	15.6
Singapore	0.4	0.4	0.0
Chinese Taipei	12.6	8.9	8.6
Thailand	40.8	37.8	17.0
United States	6.6	6.6	6.4
Average	15.4	12.9	9.1

Source: PECC (1996).

Challenges for open regionalism

With the Manila Action Plan, APEC has moved a long way towards the ambitious objectives set in the Bogor Declaration and now faces the challenge of sustaining this progress by means of voluntary and flexible cooperation.

Certainly, the voluntary and flexible nature of APEC carries some risks. While simultaneous action is not needed to liberalise traditional border barriers to trade or investment, some governments may be tempted to slow the pace of reform if others are holding back. In the area of facilitation, encouraging some to move ahead can set positive examples, but it could also sow the seeds of division and confusion if cooperative arrangements among some APEC economies neglect or damage the interests of others.

Whether or not voluntary cooperation will be adequate to deal with 'sensitive' sectors has yet to be tested. Will it be possible to achieve deep liberalisation of agriculture trade in northeast Asia, for example, without the pressure of hard negotiation and reciprocated exchange of concessions?

The answer to this question may well be 'no'. But, consistent with the objectives and character of Asia Pacific economic cooperation, it should be possible to plan ahead and deal with the liberalisation of some 'sensitive' sectors within the WTO after digesting the commitments made in the Uruguay Round and before the APEC industrial country free trade deadline of 2010. This strategy also presents a way of dealing with the US concern about European 'free riding' and offers the opportunity to lock Europe into liberalisation of border barriers comparable to that taking place within APEC.

There is a further question — whether the APEC formula can manage the American lust for reciprocity, both from other APEC economies and from non-APEC members.

Over the next five years or so, this will not be a major problem. In practice, the United States will itself largely 'free ride' within APEC as the major action on liberalisation and internationally oriented reform continues to be in East Asia and the Western Pacific (Garnaut 1996). This is reflected in the minimalist IAP the United States presented at Manila. The United States can liberalise its remaining border measures subsequently in the context of broader WTO negotiations.

These reservations do not, however, imply that APEC is simply a holding operation. Quite the reverse. They underline its importance in providing a vehicle for active trade and investment liberalisation when this is an urgent priority for the industrialising economies of East Asia and other economies in the Western Pacific. These important opportunities to enhance the prospects for growth and mutually beneficial closer integration are being seized now, rather than holding back until the next comprehensive WTO round of negotiations.

Another significant challenge is whether the idea of open regionalism can be applied effectively beyond trade in goods, to new areas for cooperation where there are few significant multilateral disciplines against discrimination.

APEC will need to refine its guiding principles to deal with the reality that, in these areas, most cooperative arrangements will be pioneered by a few, and to explore how such principles could apply to relations between APEC economies and the rest of the world.

We turn to this challenge in the remaining sections of the chapter.

APEC — coping with diversity, managing flexibility

Variable geometry

APEC's flexible approach to cooperation allows Asia Pacific governments to determine the sequence of unilateral liberalisation to dismantle border barriers to trade and investment. It also allows groups of APEC governments to implement cooperative arrangements to facilitate trade and investment at different speeds. However, they will need a strategy for managing such 'variable geometry'.

For most options to facilitate trade or investment, the more economies involved, the greater the benefits to all of them. Therefore, it makes sense to encourage region-wide involvement from the outset. However, it would be counter-productive to insist that all APEC participants be involved in every specific initiative for cooperation. The very different economic structures of the current 18 participants of APEC, combined with diverse cultures, political systems and decision-making procedures, can make it difficult to prioritise and act on shared economic interests. One or more APEC participants may resist, or wish to delay, any specific proposal for practical cooperation. Moreover, APEC does not have a voting procedure to compel economies to take part in arrangements which some do not perceive to be in their interest.

For these reasons, APEC's Osaka Action Agenda contained an explicit provision for some Asia Pacific economies to set examples of cooperative arrangements which can be applied region wide once their benefits become clear. This can promote rapid progress as long as the initiatives taken by some are positive examples which are designed to maintain the cohesion of APEC and to provide practical means, as well as incentives, to widen the coverage to include all of the region.

At the same time, as already remarked, initiatives by some APEC economies to facilitate trade or investment could sow the seeds of division and confusion if these arrangements neglected, or damaged, the interests of others. Instead of promoting further market-driven integration of Asia Pacific economies, they could lead to an inefficient and needless fragmentation of markets.

Partly for these reasons, the European Union has chosen to insist that all members are involved in all but a few arrangements for deeper economic integration in Europe. That option is not open in a process of voluntary cooperation. But it is possible, and indeed imperative, to find ways to ensure that cooperative arrangements involving some APEC economies take careful account of the interests of others and promote the smooth evolution of region-wide arrangements. In other words, it will be important to set guidelines which encourage the design of 'open clubs'.

Designing 'open clubs'

The main characteristics of 'open clubs' are that they:

* do not seek to disadvantage outsiders;
* have transparent 'rules', including transparent criteria for admitting new members; and
* actively promote wider membership.

Few clubs meet all of these conditions, but such criteria can distinguish those clubs which are genuinely seeking to meet high standards of 'openness'. Correspondingly, it is possible to set guidelines or criteria for cooperative arrangements which are designed to reduce impediments to trade or investment consistent with the concept of open regionalism.

Cooperative arrangements to facilitate economic transactions among groups of economies are typically implemented by adopting certain 'norms' for policies which influence such transactions. For example, the 'policy norms' to implement a recent decision by Australia, Korea and the Philippines to introduce a streamlined system for business travel are likely to include agreed and transparent procedures for the issue of visas and electronic processing of travellers with such visas. An arrangement for the mutual recognition of disclosure requirements and auditing standards for firms would need the economies involved to adopt some agreed norms, or minimum standards of accounting.

Cooperative arrangements can thus be described as 'open clubs' if the policy norms of the arrangement are transparent, do not contain provisions which discriminate against products or producers from other economies and all economies which adopt the relevant policy norms have the right to accede to the arrangement. It is not easy to meet all of these criteria.

It is technically possible to reduce border barriers to trade in ways which do not discriminate among products from any source; this is usually described as liberalisation on an MFN basis. For trade in goods, Article I of GATT/ WTO requires MFN treatment, at least of products from WTO members, except in some special circumstances, for example in the context of preferential trading arrangements which comply with Article XXIV.

Beyond trade in goods, there are fewer restrictions on discrimination. It is also more difficult to design cooperative arrangements which do not discriminate in some way against other economies, either by design or by default. For example, free and open trade in services as well as free and open investment require national treatment of producers as well as of products.

Arrangements to facilitate international economic transactions will tend to divert economic activities, even in the absence of any explicit provisions which discriminate against products or producers from other economies. Such arrangements typically involve agreements by a group of governments to adopt a certain set of more convergent, or more compatible, policies. Since these arrangements are designed to reduce the costs or risks of economic transactions among one group of economies, they will create an added incentive for transactions within the group as opposed to transactions with others.

In some cases, the resulting diversion of trade and investment may be unintended and insignificant. In other cases, diversion may be exacerbated and entrenched by explicit discrimination against products or producers from other economies. Those outside such cooperative arrangements can often reduce any disadvantage to them by adopting, voluntarily, the relevant policy norms. However, to avoid any diversion they usually need to be admitted to the arrangement.

For example, an agreed procedure for resolving disputes between governments and foreign investors can facilitate international investment among economies which agree to follow these procedures, tending to divert investment from elsewhere. Any other economy can take unilateral action to adopt dispute settlement procedures which make it equally attractive to inward investment. However, its firms will have access to the same means for settling disputes with other members of the dispute settlement arrangement, only if it can become a full member of that 'club'.

These examples illustrate that it is not an easy matter to design cooperative arrangements to reduce impediments to international economic transactions without any detriment to other economies. Therefore, it is not surprising that, in practice, markets are fragmented in various ways by many cooperative arrangements among groups of economies, not only by explicitly preferential trading arrangements.

All such arrangements create an incentive for others to join, in order to avoid any diversion of trade or investment from their economies. At the same time, any arrangements which divert economic activity create vested interests against widening by those who benefit from such diversion. That makes it difficult to keep these 'clubs' open, unless clear rules for accession are built in from the outset. Moreover, many cooperative arrangements to facilitate international economic transactions, such as double tax agreements or arrangements for mutual recognition of product and process standards, are technically complex to administer. Even if their policy norms are transparent, it is difficult for others to adopt them in order to join such arrangements, unless those already involved are willing to share the relevant expertise and technology.

These considerations suggest that some guidelines are needed if cooperative arrangements among any groups of economies are to be 'open clubs'. In particular, if APEC participants want to ensure that cooperative arrangements pioneered by some APEC economies set positive examples and take account of the interests of others, they will need to devise and adopt principles for practical cooperation which build on those in the Osaka Action Agenda.

Such principles or guidelines can be especially useful in adapting cooperative arrangements which have been implemented in other regions in order to make them consistent with the Asia Pacific model of open regionalism. Most of the options for facilitating or liberalising trade and investment which are under consideration in the Asia Pacific have already been implemented in other processes of regional economic cooperation. It would be unwise and inefficient for APEC economies to ignore this experience. On the other hand, such arrangements have not always been designed to be 'open clubs'. Most existing cooperative arrangements among groups of economies contain provisions which discriminate explicitly among products and/or producers, thereby creating new market distortions. Moreover, few existing arrangements have well-defined means of accession which can overcome short-term vested interests against wider participation.

The following examples seek to illustrate the practical issues involved in designing cooperative arrangements among APEC economies and identifying some useful criteria for encouraging the emergence of 'open clubs'.

Liberalising border barriers

Trade in goods

APEC governments have agreed to dismantle all barriers to trade in all goods in a WTO-consistent manner by 2010/2020. As explained above, each government will set its own schedule for unilateral elimination of tariffs and any other border barriers to trade in goods by their respective deadlines.

APEC participants have rejected the option of setting up a formal trading arrangement, so Article I of the GATT/WTO will ensure that unilateral liberalisation of border barriers does not discriminate against any member of the WTO. Therefore, as long as all APEC economies join the WTO in the near future, unilateral liberalisation will not lead to any new discrimination.

However, the majority of APEC participants also belong to formal sub-regional preferential trading arrangements, so such unilateral reductions of tariffs and non-tariff barriers to trade in goods will be accompanied by liberalisation within these arrangements. Article XXIV of the GATT/WTO permits liberalisation within these groups to be preferential, that is, to proceed faster than liberalisation with respect to other economies, raising the prospect of some new discrimination by some APEC participants. Fortunately, most Asia Pacific governments are aware of the relatively greater advantages of non-discriminatory liberalisation. In practice, liberalisation within sub-regional arrangements is being accompanied by unilateral, non-discriminatory reduction of border barriers to trade.[1]

Both Australia and New Zealand have lowered trade barriers against the rest of the world while eliminating barriers to bilateral trade. In the 1996 Manila Action Plan for APEC, ASEAN governments confirmed that, as well as liberalising trade within AFTA (ASEAN Free Trade Area), they will also continue to lower tariffs unilaterally against all trading partners. Some of them, including Indonesia and the Philippines, have indicated that they will extend the liberalisation committed within AFTA to all members of the WTO.

Members of NAFTA are not expected to extend the liberalisation within that preferential trading arrangement to other economies. In that case, there would be some short-term diversion of economic activity away from other APEC economies. The extent of new trade diversion could increase if, as planned, all North and South American economies form a preferential Free Trade Area of the Americas. However, members of NAFTA are committed to eliminate border barriers to trade and investment in the Asia Pacific by 2010.

For these reasons, the 'WTO consistency' principle of APEC provides an adequate, and also a critical, guideline for limiting discriminatory liberalisation of trade in goods on the way to meeting the agreed 2010/2020 targets.

Trade in services

Free and open trade in services requires more than the elimination of border barriers to the delivery of services. It will also be necessary to get rid of artificial distinctions in the way policies apply among services (for example on the basis of how they are delivered) or to 'domestic' and 'foreign' providers of services, leading towards the 'national treatment' of all firms.

At present, there are few multilateral restraints to prevent governments from discriminating between 'domestic' and 'foreign' firms, or among 'foreign' firms of different 'nationality'. In practice, most cooperative arrangements to liberalise trade in services extend a greater degree of national treatment only to service providers from the economies involved. Other things being equal, such arrangements will divert activity away from economies which are not parties to these arrangements.

The design of practical guidelines for liberalising trade in services among APEC economies needs to accept that it would be unrealistic to expect all arrangements to move from highly fragmented markets to automatic MFN treatment of all service providers. The practical challenge is to ensure that cooperative arrangements to liberalise trade in services among some APEC economies can serve as 'stepping stones' to wider arrangements.

For example, it would be counter-productive to expect to move from a system of bilateral agreements on international aviation (which are mostly designed to limit competition) to free and open trade in aviation. In practice, reform is likely to proceed by the liberalisation of existing bilateral arrangements towards 'open skies' agreements and the subsequent linking of such agreements to cover more and more of the region. In other service sectors, the liberalisation of trade in services may advance most rapidly within existing sub-regional arrangements. That will rely on the acceptance of guidelines for cooperative arrangements on services which can ensure that liberalisation among some groups of APEC economies will lead smoothly towards the Bogor vision of free and open trade in services.

In line with APEC's 'standstill' principle, such guidelines should rule out any arrangements that create *new* sources of discrimination either among services or among service providers on the basis of their 'nationality'. While it might be unrealistic to expect all new cooperative arrangements to avoid any preferential features, it will be important to anticipate that preferential arrangements tend to set up vested interests to resist the inclusion of additional economies. That suggests criteria to ensure that cooperative arrangements are transparent and provide for the unconditional accession of any economy whose government adopts the policy norms agreed amongst existing parties.

International investment

Many of the steps towards free and open international investment will involve improving the transparency of investment policies and liberalisation to promote 'national treatment'; in other words, by dismantling artificial distinctions among firms on the basis of their place of registration or the nationality of their owners. Accordingly, the criteria proposed above for liberalisation of trade in services could be readily adapted to serve as guidelines for cooperative arrangements to liberalise international investment.

Facilitating trade and investment

Cooperative arrangements to facilitate international economic transactions among some economies require collective actions by several governments. It is seldom possible to include every economy in such arrangements. As discussed above, these arrangements will result in some additional incentives to conduct business among parties to arrangements to facilitate trade or investment. The following examples indicate how arrangements for facilitating trade or investment can be designed to be 'open clubs' which avoid needless detriment to other economies while encouraging them to join.

Harmonising administrative procedures

APEC participants are already implementing a proposal for the electronic interchange of customs information and harmonised clearance procedures. This arrangement is likely to be an 'open club'. The arrangement is not designed to favour any particular sector or economy, but to reduce the costs, uncertainties and delays of customs processing. The resulting improvement in infrastructure efficiency will be maximised if more economies join the arrangement. Accordingly, all APEC economies are expected to take part in the new cooperative arrangement. They also have an incentive to pool the relevant expertise and technology needed to allow all of them to implement the new procedures quickly and smoothly. Moreover, the benefits will be increased if all exporters to, or importers from, APEC economies also adopt the same procedures for customs documentation and clearance. It makes sense to strive for transparency and to avoid discrimination against non-participants.

Mutual recognition of standards

The evolution of the European Union has demonstrated how a cooperative arrangement for the mutual recognition of product and process standards is an essential ingredient of any serious effort to create an integrated market. Experience in Europe, and elsewhere, has also demonstrated the potential for standards to become new means of protection.

By definition, only those economies which adopt and monitor adherence to comparable standards can be parties to mutual recognition arrangements. Since the relevant products can be traded more conveniently among the parties to the arrangements, there will be an incentive to divert some economic activities away from other economies. Once again, unintended diversion of activity can be minimised by setting up arrangements which are 'open clubs'.

If all the relevant standards are transparent, then producers from any economy can choose to conform to them. If the procedures for demonstrating compliance to these standards are also transparent and applied without discrimination, then products from any source could be marketed in all the economies within the mutual recognition arrangement after being tested in any one of them. Producers outside the arrangement would still be at some disadvantage compared to those within, since they would still need to have their product tested by agencies of one of the parties to the mutual recognition arrangement. However, such residual disadvantage could also be eliminated if their governments were able to become full parties to the arrangement.

Accession should be feasible if the arrangement makes it clear that any economy which adopts the policies required to implement the arrangement is automatically entitled to join. To join an arrangement for mutual recognition, prospective parties would not only need to adopt comparable standards, but also to demonstrate their willingness and ability to monitor their producers' compliance with such standards (with comparable certainty as for existing parties). That may require the strengthening of some institutions, which may in turn depend on the willingness of existing parties to share the necessary information and expertise.

Guiding principles for 'open clubs'

The preceding examples of options to liberalise and facilitate trade and investment are by no means exhaustive. However, they illustrate the nature of the criteria which will be needed to help ensure that initiatives by some APEC economies for reducing impediments to trade or investment are 'open clubs' which set positive examples for subsequent region-wide cooperation. The next challenge is to translate these concepts into clear and concise guidelines which build on APEC's current guiding principles as well as the fundamental GATT/WTO principles of transparency, non-discrimination and national treatment.

Transparency

Practical guiding principles for transparency could require that the policies and procedures adopted for these arrangements be set out explicitly, typically in their legislation or regulations. These should be freely accessible to all governments and producers — in practice that can be achieved by preparing (where applicable) an authoritative translation into English, which is the working language of APEC. The policy norms of 'open clubs' should be available to all those interested, free of charge, through one or more recognised channels. In 1997, one of those would probably be on a World Wide Web site accessible, among many other ways, through the APEC secretariat's home page.

A second important aspect of transparency is prior notice of new arrangements (or significant amendments to existing arrangements). This can enhance the prospects for more economies to join these new arrangements at the outset. Prior notice can also allow governments of other economies to comment on the terms of the proposed arrangements. Such comments could improve the effectiveness of these arrangements and help to make them as consistent as possible with APEC's guiding principles for trade and investment liberalisation and facilitation.

Non-discrimination

For trade in goods, the WTO has adopted the combination of 'standstill' and 'roll-back' to promote a gradual trend towards non-discriminatory free trade. The liberalisation of border barriers to trade in goods by individual governments or groups of governments is expected to reduce some barriers without raising existing ones or creating new obstacles. Such a strategy can be generalised to apply to all cooperative arrangements to reduce impediments to international economic transactions.

APEC's agreed principles of 'standstill' and the commitment to 'endeavour to apply the principle of non-discrimination' can be given effect by guidelines which stipulate that new cooperative arrangements involving APEC economies should not lead to new discrimination. It will also be necessary to generalise the concept of national treatment to deal with the issues involved in reducing impediments to trade in services as well as to international factor movements. Accordingly, new arrangements should not contain any provisions which create additional or new forms of discrimination among products or producers, either on the basis of the location of various stages of production or the 'nationality' of producers.

Accession

As shown by the preceding examples, cooperative arrangements to facilitate trade or investment will tend to divert economic activity to the economies involved. Moreover, those who benefit from the diversion of trade or investment, intended or unintended, will tend to resist accession by additional economies. Therefore, if cooperative arrangements involving APEC economies are to be genuinely open to accession, their design will need to anticipate and minimise such resistance.

To a large extent, this can be achieved if the arrangements are highly transparent and do not create new discrimination among products or producers. In addition, the arrangements should specify, at the outset, that the only condition for accession by additional economies is their demonstrated ability to follow policies consistent with the arrangements. Many arrangements to facilitate trade or investment are technically complex; they will be 'open clubs' only if existing members are willing to share the requisite information, experience, expertise and technology. The 1996 Ministerial Declaration on an Asia Pacific Economic Cooperation Framework for Strengthening Economic Cooperation and Development commits all APEC participants to such pooling of resources.

Review

The earlier examples have also shown that it is not easy to ensure that cooperative arrangements among some economies are genuinely open clubs. While they may be designed in good faith to meet APEC's agreed guiding principles for trade and investment liberalisation and facilitation, their implementation could cause unexpected problems for other economies. Therefore, those involved in these arrangements should be willing, once again in good faith, to respond to constructive suggestions from other economies on how to improve the consistency of these cooperative arrangements with agreed guiding principles.

Based on all of these considerations, the criteria needed to ensure that all cooperative activities by various sets of APEC participants are 'open clubs' are listed below.

APEC economies that are ready to initiate and implement cooperative arrangements to reduce impediments to economic transactions are encouraged to do so, while taking account of the interests of other economies as follows:

Transparency   (i) The policies adopted to implement these arrangements should be documented explicitly (typically expressed in legislation or regulations of those economies) and be freely available and accessible, through convenient channels of communication.

(ii) APEC economies should provide reasonable prior notice of the nature and objectives of proposed cooperative arrangements as well as the policies by which these are to be implemented.

Non-discrimination   The arrangements should not contain any provisions which result in new or additional discrimination, either against products on the basis of the location of production, or among producers on the basis of their place of registration or ownership.

Accession   (i) Any economy whose government accepts the responsibilities as well as the benefits of following policies compatible with any existing or proposed cooperative arrangements among some APEC economies should be able to, and encouraged to, become parties to these arrangements.

(ii) Existing parties to these cooperative arrangements should be willing to share the information, experience, expertise and technology needed to enable others to adopt the relevant policies.

Review   APEC economies should endeavour to respond positively to constructive suggestions from other economies for improving the consistency of existing or proposed cooperative arrangements with APEC's agreed guiding principles for liberalising and facilitating trade and investment.

Cooperative arrangements which met all of these criteria could be appropriately described as 'open clubs'. As APEC gathers momentum, participants will become increasingly aware of the need to ensure that cooperative arrangements among some participants are indeed capable of subsequent region-wide application, as well as to avoid the proliferation of arrangements which fragment, rather than integrate, regional markets. That awareness is likely to lead to the adoption of principles along these lines to promote the design of cooperative arrangements which are 'open clubs'. Once adopted, such principles will also serve as a useful framework for the design of cooperative arrangements involving both APEC and non-APEC economies.

APEC — relating to other economies

Deepening and widening

Many Asia Pacific economies have sought to become APEC participants. APEC is open to widening, in principle, but most participants are concerned that widening may lead to a loss of momentum. The proposed principles can deal with these concerns by allowing prospective participants to demonstrate their potential to make a positive contribution.

All Asia Pacific economies have an incentive to join arrangements to reduce impediments to trade or investment among APEC economies. Becoming parties to such arrangements would facilitate their economic transactions with APEC participants as well as eliminate any diversion of economic activity from non-participants to APEC economies. If the cooperative arrangements pioneered by APEC economies are 'open clubs', then non-participants can opt to join in order to obtain these benefits.

Joining is not a matter of 'free riding' by APEC's neighbours. In order to qualify for accession, non-participants need to be willing to adapt their policies to be compatible with the norms adopted by the APEC economies which designed the relevant arrangements. Moreover, their ability to join in particular cooperative arrangements does not diminish their incentive to become full participants of APEC. Only full participation in the APEC process allows them to have a say in shaping the broad principles and priorities of the process and in the design of new options for practical cooperation.

APEC's principles for participation require potential members to have close linkages with the Asia Pacific region and to accept the objectives and guiding principles which have been adopted by existing participants. Now that the 2010/2020 deadlines for free and open trade and investment have been adopted, any would-be member would also be expected to set out a credible initial commitment to policy decisions, comparable to those of current participants which are set out in the 1996 Manila Action Plan for APEC. Current participants will also want to assure themselves that potential participants not only make impressive statements of intent, but also prove their capacity to implement them.

If cooperative arrangements involving APEC economies were open to accession, potential participants could be compared, not only in terms of their track record of unilateral liberalisation of border barriers, but also by their demonstrated willingness and ability to adopt policies compatible with APEC economies and to become constructive partners in cooperative arrangements pioneered within APEC. This could ensure an objective assessment of would-be members and help to ease the trade-off between deepening and widening the APEC process.

Relations with European economies

Consistent with the spirit of open regionalism, APEC participants want to establish mutually beneficial relations with all other economies. The future of relations with European economies, and with the European Union itself, is particularly important and will need careful management.

For at least the next ten years, APEC participants will need to give the highest priority to sustaining and managing their movement towards free and open trade and investment in the Asia Pacific and to promoting parallel global moves through the WTO. The European Union will be preoccupied with consolidating its proposed single currency and trying to find ways to extend its membership to more of Europe. Neither group may have much time to be concerned about more intensive cooperation with the other. However, for several reasons, it would be useful to begin to think about a suitable framework for managing the growing economic links among EU and APEC economies.

Firstly, the combined membership and the strength of existing economic links between many of the economies involved in the European Union or APEC means that neither group can expect to achieve its long-term objectives in isolation. As the cost of communications continues to decline and information technology makes fine specialisation more feasible and capital more and more mobile, a progressively more intensive economic integration of the two groups is inevitable. Their actions and ambitions will impinge substantially on each other and, between them, they will determine the shape and future of the global system of international economic transactions.

Secondly, European and Asia Pacific economies could reap enormous benefits from the achievement of free and open trade and investment, not only in each region, but also between these two large groups of economies. Large gains could certainly be achieved by eliminating all traditional border barriers to trade among both groups. Moreover, the EU experience has demonstrated that very significant additional advantages can be gained by addressing the full range of impediments, not just to trade, but to all international commerce between the two regions.

At the same time, the very different styles of cooperation adopted by the European Union and APEC will make it difficult to devise a conceptual framework for an orderly evolution of closer economic relations, which is consistent with the global as well as the regional objectives of European and Asia Pacific economies.

Since APEC is not based on a formal structure, substantive cooperation between EU and APEC governments will not proceed along the lines of the European Union itself. Nor is there any prospect for formal treaties or agreements between APEC as a whole and the European Union. In practice, economic cooperation will evolve from the many links which have already been formed between European and Asia Pacific economies. These include the recent Asia–Europe Meeting (ASEM) process, which will facilitate exchanges of information, experience and expertise and is likely to lead to concrete arrangements for mutually beneficial economic cooperation. There are also many bilateral arrangements and agreements on a wide range of economic and commercial matters including trade promotion, investment and taxation as well as sectoral agreements, for example in aviation.

These existing links could become the basis for a growing network of mutually beneficial links among all Asia Pacific and European economies, reducing impediments to trade and investment between as well as within the two regions. A mutually beneficial evolution of closer cooperation is far from assured, however. As emphasised earlier, it depends on the response of the European Union to unilateral liberalisation of border barriers to trade by APEC economies as they implement their Bogor commitments.

The opportunity

A positive response to APEC's lead on trade liberalisation, leading to a parallel commitment by the European Union to eliminate all border barriers to trade and investment by 2020, would set the stage for effective cooperation among both groups to achieve free and open trade and investment between them as well as within each region. That would pave the way for fruitful WTO negotiations to set schedules for progress towards full liberalisation of border barriers as well as create conditions for progress on many new international economic issues.

There would be no need to resort to special arrangements between European and Asia Pacific economies for liberalising border barriers. These 'traditional' issues would be handled in the WTO, which has been designed specifically for that purpose (Bora and Findlay 1996). Working together on these matters in the WTO would also set the scene for cooperation to reduce many other impediments to international economic transactions which are not dealt with in existing multilateral forums. The principles proposed above provide a framework for designing cooperative arrangements between Asia Pacific and European economies as 'open clubs' which take account of the interests of all economies.

To maintain APEC's cohesion, its participants will need to ensure that initiatives by some of them to cooperate with the rest of the world do not create new sources of discrimination within APEC or new distortions which cut across the market-driven economic integration of Asia Pacific economies. The principles proposed above can help APEC to meet this challenge, giving practical effect to APEC's agreed principle that trade and investment liberalisation in the Asia Pacific will result in reduced barriers, not only among APEC economies, but also between APEC economies and all others.

Such guidelines can also avoid a proliferation of overlapping 'hub-and-spokes' arrangements which might facilitate transactions with the European Union or with the currently largest economies in the Asia Pacific, but do not lend themselves to becoming more efficient plurilateral arrangements. Instead, each cooperative arrangement involving APEC economies would form the core of an arrangement which could be joined by others who perceive the advantages of doing so.

The proposed principles would ensure that practical initiatives for cooperation which are likely to evolve from the ASEM dialogue will not be at the expense of APEC's transpacific links. On the contrary, by making provision for any APEC participant to be a constructive party to these arrangements, ASEM could become one of the foundations of gradually more effective and mutually beneficial cooperative arrangements involving more APEC and European economies.

Correspondingly, any new arrangements to facilitate trade and investment between members of NAFTA and the European Union would also take account of the interests of the rest of APEC. For example, all East Asian participants in APEC would be able to become parties to any new arrangements to facilitate trade or investment across the Atlantic, as long as they also adopted the norms of international economic policy making inherent in those arrangements. More generally, it would be possible for various processes of dialogue and cooperation among various groups of European and Asia Pacific economies to contribute to a mutually consistent set of practical arrangements to reduce impediments to international economic transactions among all of them.

Such an evolutionary process could lead to increasingly productive economic links among the economies of the European Union and APEC without the need for formal or elaborate structures. The proposed guiding principles could also provide a framework for both of them to deepen and broaden the scope of their economic cooperation with Russia — a potential economic giant, whose size and strong links with both the European Union and Asia Pacific make it difficult to accommodate exclusively in either process. The proposed principles would allow EU and APEC economies to engage Russia in economic cooperation without seeking to disadvantage either existing group and without forcing Russia to make needless choices to favour the strengthening of one set of economic links at the expense of the other.

Perhaps most importantly, a framework of principles which makes it possible for Asia Pacific and European economies to implement practical proposals for mutually beneficial cooperation would also foster a greater sense of shared interests in an orderly, open international economic system. A growing set of open cooperative arrangements and understandings to facilitate a wide range of transactions among members of these two significant groups could readily serve as models for subsequent, wider global cooperation to address the many new challenges facing the international economic system.

The risks

These opportunities for cooperation between European and Asia Pacific economies would be lost if the European Union chooses to try to 'free ride' on APEC's efforts, without making any substantial effort to liberalise its remaining border barriers.[2] Such free riding would be of any consequence only in agriculture, since EU border barriers are already quite low in other sectors.

If the European Union chooses to adopt such an unhelpful strategy, it would be the APEC economies' turn to respond. APEC participants could decide to ignore such free riding, since the bulk of the cost of EU protection would continue to be borne by EU economies. But such a response is unlikely to be permitted by political pressures. Protectionists in APEC economies would use any EU free riding as an argument against reform, joining with those who are concerned with exercising 'leverage' against the European Union to try to unravel APEC's commitment to free and open trade.

It is hard to predict the extent to which the prospects of achieving APEC's Bogor vision could be damaged. One possible outcome might be for APEC economies to continue with their facilitation agenda, but for some Asia Pacific governments to delay trade liberalisation until the European Union is prepared to reciprocate. There would certainly be enormous, renewed pressure to exempt agriculture from the vision of free trade. Even if it were possible to resist such pressure, it is very likely that the multilateral agreement reached in the Uruguay Round to bring agriculture under normal GATT disciplines would falter, opening the option for APEC economies to liberalise agriculture only among participants.

That would be a very undesirable outcome, but the damage would be unlikely to stop there. There would be little incentive for APEC economies to design cooperative arrangements to facilitate trade and investment beyond the Asia Pacific.

If the European Union chose to free ride on APEC's market-opening moves whenever GATT/WTO disciplines made that possible, then Asia Pacific governments would be very likely to ensure that European economies derived very little, if any, benefit from Asia Pacific cooperation in areas where there are no effective multilateral obligations to limit discrimination. In the absence of significant multilateral disciplines to discriminate among producers on the basis of 'nationality', APEC participants can design many arrangements to liberalise or facilitate trade in services or international investment in ways which restrict benefits to outsiders. Cooperative arrangements among APEC economies can easily be set up as clubs which are open only to members of APEC.[3]

APEC economies are not likely to abandon open regionalism altogether by deliberately designing cooperative arrangements to damage other economies. They may even agree to guidelines for avoiding any new sources of discrimination against non-participants. However, they would be much less likely to make their cooperative arrangements open to accession by economies outside APEC. In practice, that would divert economic activity away from the rest of the world, damaging the interests of all economies, including the long-term interests of Asia Pacific economies.

Many opportunities for practical cooperation among European and Asia Pacific economies would be lost, together with the opportunity to extend the coverage of sensible multilateral principles to a wider range of international economic transactions.

For all of these reasons, once APEC demonstrates its capacity to move rapidly towards free trade, the European Union will have strong incentives to respond positively, clearing the way for many options for mutually beneficial facilitation of trade and investment among economies of both regions.

Conclusion

Between them, APEC and EU economies dominate global production, trade and investment. The two groups are closely linked by historical, cultural and economic ties, so they cannot expect to achieve their ambitions for economic cooperation in isolation. The cost of communications is continuing to decline and capital is becoming more mobile, making the progressively more intensive economic integration of the two groups inevitable. This is reflected in the growth of inter-regional trade and investment and, at the government level, by the recent initiative for regular Asia–Europe Meetings among heads of government. That process will evolve in the context of APEC's drive towards free and open trade and investment, the potential enlargement of the European Union and the collective opportunity and responsibility of Asia Pacific and European economies to shape the inter-national economic system of the twenty-first century.

As APEC advances towards its vision of free and open trade and investment, its participants will need to define the concept of open regionalism with even greater precision in order to guide specific aspects of their economic cooperation. To cope with APEC's remarkable diversity and the steadily increasing scope and sophistication of international economic transactions, it will be necessary to build on the fundamental GATT/WTO principles of transparency, national treatment and non-discrimination. Clear, concise operational guiding principles will be needed to ensure that all cooperative arrangements among APEC economies are 'open clubs', whose provisions:

• are as transparent as practicable;

• avoid new sources of discrimination among products and producers; and

• encourage other economies to become parties to these arrangements.

Such principles can also help APEC participants to develop their relations with other economies. They can help ease the potential trade-offs between widening participation and maintaining the momentum of cooperation. The principles proposed in this chapter can also serve as a framework for a gradual development of cooperative arrangements for facilitating trade and investment involving both Asia Pacific and European economies, without requiring elaborate, formal institutional linkages.

This is an opportunity with significant potential benefits for both regions. If these two groups of economies could adopt principles which promoted practical cooperative arrangements between them, these could also serve as models for subsequent, wider global cooperation to address the many new challenges facing the international economic system. Seizing this opportunity will depend, vitally, on a positive EU response to APEC's dismantling of trade barriers.

Notes

1 Since no APEC participant belongs to any customs union (such as the European Union), nothing prevents them from lowering trade barriers to outsiders at any pace they choose.
2 Such a 'free rider' approach is possible for trade in goods, but less so in services. Since APEC is not a formal trading arrangement, Article I of the GATT/WTO means that any liberalisation of trade in goods extended to all developed APEC economies will also need to be extended to all members of the WTO. In theory, the European Union could retain its border barriers to trade in goods while taking advantage of APEC's liberalisation.
3 For example, since international aviation remains outside the scope of the WTO, any 'open skies' agreements among APEC economies could not only discriminate against outsiders, but could also preclude them from joining such agreements.

References

APEC (1991) *Seoul APEC Declaration,* Ministerial Declaration, November.
—— (1993) *Economic Vision Statement,* November.
—— (1994) *Bogor Declaration of Common Resolve*, Second APEC Economic Leaders' Meeting, Bogor, November.
—— (1995) *Osaka Action Agenda: Implementation of the Bogor Declaration*, Third APEC Economic Leaders' Meeting, Osaka, November.
—— (1996a) *Manila Action Plan for APEC*, Ministerial-level meeting, Manila, November.
—— (1996b) *Manila Declaration on an Asia Pacific Economic Cooperation Framework for Strengthening Economic Cooperation and Development,* Ministerial-level meeting, Manila, November.

APEC Eminent Persons' Group (1994) *Achieving the APEC Vision: Free and Open Trade in the Asia Pacific*, Second Report of the Eminent Persons' Group, APEC Secretariat, August.
—— (1995) *Implementing the APEC Vision*, Third report of the Eminent Persons' Group, APEC Secretariat, Singapore, August.
Asia–Pacific Economics Group (APEG) (1997) *Asia Pacific Profiles*, Financial Times Newsletters.
Australia–Japan Research Centre (AJRC) (1995) *Implementing the APEC Bogor Declaration*, a report by A. Elek, H. Soesastro and I. Yamazawa, Canberra, June.
Bora, B. and C. Findlay (1996) 'Introduction and overview', Chapter 1 in B. Bora and C. Findlay, eds, *Regional Integration and the Asia–Pacific*, Melbourne: Oxford University Press.
Crawford, Sir John and Greg Seow eds (1981) *Pacific Economic Cooperation: Suggestions for Action*, Petaling Jaba, Selangor, Malaysia: Heinemann Asia, for the Pacific Community Seminar.
Drysdale, Peter (1988) *International Economic Pluralism: Economic Policy in East Asia and the Pacific*, Sydney: Allen and Unwin in association with the Australia–Japan Research Centre.
Elek, A. (1995) 'APEC beyond Bogor: an open economic association in the Asian Pacific region', *Asian Pacific Economic Literature* 9(1) May.
Garnaut, Ross (1996) *Open Regionalism and Trade Liberalisation*, Singapore: Institute of Southeast Asian Studies.
—— and Peter Drysdale eds (1994) *Asia Pacific Regionalism: Readings in International Economic Relations*, Sydney: HarperCollins in association with the Australia–Japan Research Centre.
PECC (1996) *Perspectives on the Manila Action Plan for APEC*.
PECC Trade Policy Forum (1995) *Survey of Impediments to Trade and Investment in the APEC Region*, Singapore: PECC Secretariat.
—— (1996) *Evaluation of the Manila Action Plan for APEC*, Singapore: PECC Secretariat.
Sopiee, Noordin (1995) 'Getting APEC back on track', *Asian Wall Street Journal*, 14 November.

6 Beyond liberalisation of trade in goods: alternative strategies for regional trade and investment facilitation

PONCIANO S. INTAL, JR AND CHRISTOPHER FINDLAY

Trade liberalisation: unfinished business

One of the more important international trade policy developments in the world economy during the past decade has been the significant reduction of tariffs on trade in goods. Trade liberalisation has been more pronounced among the developing countries, especially in East Asia. For example, Thailand's average tariff rate declined from 40.8 per cent in 1988 to 17 per cent in 1996. Similarly, tariff rates in China and the Philippines decreased from 40.3 per cent and 27.9 per cent respectively in 1988 to 23 per cent and 15.6 per cent respectively in 1996. Among APEC's developed economy members, Australia made the largest tariff cut, from 15.6 per cent in 1988 to 6.1 per cent in 1996. The unweighted average of tariff rates for the whole Asia Pacific Economic Cooperation (APEC) region decreased from 15.4 per cent in 1988 to 9.1 per cent in 1996 (Pangestu, Findlay, Intal and Parker 1996). The significant decline in tariffs in recent years stems largely from unilateral trade liberalisation measures.

Tariffs can be expected to decline in the future because of the implementation of Uruguay Round commitments, further unilateral trade liberalisation measures and trade liberalisation and tariff reduction programs under regional trading arrangements. For APEC member economies, the Bogor Declaration has set a goal of free and open trade and investment in 2010 and 2020 for developed and developing economy members respectively. The initial submissions of the individual action plans of the APEC member economies indicate tariff reduction programs that are on track toward a possible zero-tariff target under the Bogor goal of free trade. (APEC member economies have not clearly defined the operational meaning of the Bogor goal of free and open trade and investment in the region.) Most noteworthy are the more aggressive tariff reduction programs of Chile, China, Indonesia and the Philippines.

Drawing on the APEC framework of 'open regionalism', the Bogor goal of free trade is defined in non-discriminatory, most favoured nation (MFN) terms. This contrasts with the European Union (EU) or other free trade areas or customs unions, where tariffs are imposed on trade with non-members.

Despite significant progress made by member economies, trade liberalisation in goods in the APEC region is not finished: there remain significant challenges before the Bogor goal is attained. For example, there are substantial tariff peaks, especially in industries like automotive and textiles and clothing. The tariff peaks tend to be concentrated in either vulnerable or 'pet or targeted' industries, reflecting the dynamic of political economy considerations in the trade and industrial policies of APEC member economies. Agriculture will pose a special problem because the historical experience is that agricultural protection increases with the industrialisation of economies. Moreover, the northeast Asian experience indicates that where economic growth and structural change is particularly fast, the demand for agricultural protection intensifies. Perhaps more than in any other sector, agricultural trade liberalisation will test severely APEC members' resolve to undertake trade liberalisation.

East Asian economies may still be able to maintain sufficient momentum from coordinated unilateral action to attract greater attention from and commitment by the United States (Elek 1996). The prospects for a non-discriminatory free trade regime including the United States are greater, however, if the European Union is also positively engaged in the process. The importance of this connection suggests the value of a new round of multilateral trade liberalisation programs under the World Trade Organization (WTO).

The Bogor goal of free and open trade and investment provides a continuing reference point to encourage APEC member economies to extend the liberalisation of trade in goods. Nevertheless, because APEC emphasises a concerted but voluntary liberalisation process, each member economy undertakes liberalisation efforts only if it views the benefits of liberalisation as greater than the costs. It is likely that as tariffs come closer and closer to zero, the benefits of further tariff reduction will decline significantly, while the benefits of addressing other trade and investment barriers become more salient. Thus the importance of trade and investment facilitation measures increases. Indeed, it is likely that completing the unfinished agenda of liberalisation of trade in goods will require a sharper focus on extending this liberalisation into strengthening trade and investment facilitation measures. As we argue below, an extension of the scope of APEC into these areas could help deal with some of the tariff peaks and resistant sectors.

Trade and investment facilitation as a complement to trade liberalisation

International trade and investment can be significantly hampered by the high cost of doing business, thereby hindering economic integration. For example, the 'Costs of Non-Europe' Project (Cecchini 1988: 8) shows that the cost of red tape and delays in customs procedures for intra-European Community (EC) trade amounts to about 2 per cent of total transborder sales. Respondents to a survey of 11,000 businesses as part of the 'Costs of Non-Europe' Project ranked divergences in technical regulations and standards within the European Community as the second most important market barrier they faced after administrative barriers. Similarly, differing government regulations, primarily for prudential purposes, as well as divergent fiscal regimes, especially with respect to indirect taxes, contributed to the segmentation of the European Community during the 1980s. This runs counter to the meaning of a common market. Reducing these barriers effectively increases economic integration in the European Community, with the expected beneficial effects as follows (Cecchini 1988: 73):

* substantial reduction in costs;

* improved efficiency within firms;

* new patterns of competition between industries; and

* increased innovation.

Cecchini's team estimates that the benefits of increased market integration occasioned by the reduction of the various barriers to trade and investment in the EC would amount to about 5.3 per cent of the European Community's gross domestic product.

There is no comparable project in APEC. Hence, there are no estimates of the costs of barriers like customs procedures and divergences of technical regulations and standards in the region. Nevertheless, businesspeople in APEC have emphasised the problems of customs procedures and divergent standards and regulations as important barriers to intra-APEC trade and investment (PBF 1994).

Indications of the likely benefits from both trade liberalisation and trade and investment facilitation in APEC are provided by a recent study by Petri (1997). Petri incorporated microeconomic distinctions between foreign direct investment (FDI) and domestic activities in terms of both demand and production characteristics into a Computable General Equilibrium model. He used his model to simulate APEC trade liberalisation with or without significant reductions in barriers to FDI. His initial estimates suggest that APEC gains from trade liberalisation without a reduction in investment barriers would be two-fifths less than APEC gains from trade liberalisation with significant reductions in barriers to FDI. His results indicate that the major beneficiaries of trade and investment liberalisation are the newly industrialising economies (NIEs), China and the ASEAN4 countries (Association of Southeast Asian Nations — Indonesia, Malaysia, Philippines, Thailand) because of their comparatively high initial trade barriers and their greater trade orientation. The major loser would be the non-APEC world as FDI is redirected to APEC economies because of their more congenial environment for FDI. Petri's paper shows that '...endogenous FDI tends to make policy more competitive; regions do not merely forego gains by not liberalising, but can also lose by failing to keep up with liberalising neighbours' (Petri 1997: 29).

The positive role of FDI in the process of economic restructuring arising from trade liberalisation is probably best illustrated by the recent experience of the successful ASEAN economies. In all of them FDI hastened and smoothed the adjustment towards greater export orientation. Thus, for example, the rise of the electronics export industry in the region was virtually the creation of multinational corporations. FDI also played an important role in the development and export growth of more traditional industries like textiles and clothing in Indonesia and Thailand. Clearly, without the infusion of capital and technology by foreign investors, industrial adjustment towards a more open economy induced by trade liberalisation would have been more contentious, as was demonstrated by the experience of the Philippines during the 1980s and the early 1990s.

Trade and investment facilitation enhances the benefits of trade liberalisation. For example, commercial presence of the provider in the country where the services are demanded is often a requirement for international transactions. Hence, investment liberalisation and facilitation contributes to the liberalisation and development of the services sector. At the same time, it is now widely recognised that an efficient, competitive and innovative services sector, especially in the financial and transport sub-sectors, has a far-reaching positive impact on the whole economy, including the international competitiveness of a country's industrial sector. Thus, complementary action to trade liberalisation via investment liberalisation or other facilitation measures can ease the adjustment of firms responding to trade liberalisation and thereby reduce resistance to liberalisation in all forms.

In sum, trade and investment facilitation is a valuable complement to trade liberalisation. The challenge is to strengthen trade and investment facilitation measures as the trade liberalisation process continues. This is especially important for the APEC economies as they move towards the Bogor goal of free and open trade and investment.

Three elements of a framework towards strengthening trade and investment facilitation

Three elements help shape the framework that can be applied in strengthening trade and investment facilitation in the region and the world. These are complementarity of regional and multilateral initiatives, using an integrated approach and acceptance of flexibility in the trajectory to long-run goals.

Complementarity

The first element is to seek complementarity in regional and multilateral initiatives. That is, regional facilitation and cooperative efforts need to be made consistent with, or build up from, and even grow into, multilateral initiatives or disciplines. In this case, regional initiatives can be 'multilateral plus' just as sub-regional initiatives can be 'regional plus'. By deepening and broadening cooperative efforts in trade and investment facilitation as membership of the 'cooperation or integration club' narrows, the world is afforded alternative experiments and approaches that lead to further improvements, deepening or refinement of the multilateral disciplines. It is apparent that the complementarity of regional and multilateral initiatives is strengthened if the regional initiatives are not inward looking or restrictive (raising barriers) to non-members but rather are conducive to expanding the number of subscribing or participating economies.

Snape (1996) stresses the importance of the membership rule as a test of the openness of regional arrangements which apply to 'deeper' forms of integration. He notes that regional arrangements may cover new measures not now covered by the General Agreement on Tariffs and Trade (GATT). Those parts of the agreements may not be inconsistent with GATT principles even if only sub-groups of the signatories to the regional agreement take action of this type. But this is the case, he argues, as long as the other signatories to the regional agreement can join on similar terms (Snape 1996: 52). Snape argues that there is a precedent for this principle in the General Agreement on Trade in Services (GATS), Article VII, which applies to recognition of education achievements or other standards. It says that

> a Member may recognise the education or experience obtained, requirements met, or licenses or certifications granted in a particular country [through] harmonisation or otherwise...A Member which is party to [such] an agreement shall afford adequate opportunity for other interested Members to negotiate their accession to such an agreement or arrangement [and a] Member shall not accord recognition in a manner which would constitute a means of discrimination between countries in the application of its standards or criteria...Recognition should be based on multilaterally agreed criteria.

Snape goes on to argue that it might be easier to extend this type of harmonisation arrangement on a piecemeal basis. This is because harmonisation leads to greater export opportunities while at the same time providing better prospects for import penetration within the same industry. In other areas of liberalisation, there is greater resistance from industries which fear more rapid import penetration and, in such cases, a multi-sectoral approach is more valuable as a way of mobilising countervailing political support for liberalisation.

Snape does express some concern, however, about industry-specific approaches to harmonisation. Such arrangements, he argues, run the risk of regulatory capture by sectoral producer interests seeking to use the standards adopted to protect themselves against competition from the rest of the world. Snape observes, however, that openness to new members of this harmonisation arrangement is a safeguard against this occurrence.

Integrated approach

The second element of the framework is an 'integrated approach' to trade and investment liberalisation and facilitation. Specifically, agreements on certain regional or multilateral disciplines may require a greater emphasis on cooperative efforts to build the institutional capacities of member economies, especially developing economies, in implementing the spirit of the trade and investment facilitation or liberalisation agreements. For example, harmonisation of standards and mutual recognition of certification necessitate that participating economies have the laboratories and other facilities as well as the appropriate skills to undertake credible certification. This means that trade and investment facilitation initiatives would have to be interwoven with economic and technical cooperation initiatives among the participating economies. The same 'integrated approach' can be invoked for trade liberalisation initiatives, especially in contentious sectors: in these cases, liberalisation initiatives can be packaged with facilitation initiatives and economic and technical cooperation initiatives so that liberalisation efforts can be more ambitious in terms of pace and scope.[1] The element of 'integrated approach' is consistent with the analysis of the 'new regionalism' by de Melo, Panagariya and Rodrick, which states that '...the most important potential dynamic benefit for developing regional integration schemes comes from economic cooperation in areas where significant externalities and public goods (education, research and development, infrastructure and environment) exist' (1992: 185).

Evolutionary change

The third element of the framework is the bias towards evolutionary change which builds confidence in the face of wide differences in levels of development and institutional capacities of countries. An example is the initiative of adopting non-binding principles which in the future could be shaped into binding commitments, perhaps after an interim application of the principles in a well-defined and narrow set of (agreed) sectors or activities. The issue is that gradualism can become an excuse for inaction, but gradualism need not be a recipe for delay if there are agreed goals in terms of a target date. Its effect is instead to offer some flexibility in the trajectory on which members meet their commitments.

These three elements underpin a number of areas of trade and investment facilitation which are discussed in the rest of the chapter.

Facilitating cross-border investment flows

The sterling growth performance of a number of APEC member economies during the past decade owes much to the sharp rise in the investment rate in these economies. Although the investment surge has both domestic and foreign origins, FDI played a significant catalytic role in the investment surge in these economies, especially in ASEAN and China. FDI has brought funds, technology, market linkage and organisational know-how to the host economies. It is expected that foreign investment will continue to play an important role in maintaining the robust growth momentum in the region, especially in the developing APEC member economies. The World Bank, for example, estimates that the developing economies in the region need about US$1.5 trillion during the next decade just for infrastructure facilities to sustain their robust economic growth. In addition, of course, there are investment requirements for direct production activities.

The challenge of promoting cross-border investment flows hangs heaviest on the developing member economies because they are, by definition, capital-deficient economies. At the same time, it is in the developing economies that the benefits of investment liberalisation and facilitation are likely to be greatest because they tend to have the more distorted and inefficient investment regimes.

The survey of investment impediments in APEC economies undertaken by the Pacific Economic Cooperation Council (PECC) distinguishes four types of impediment to investment flows. These are:

- administrative procedures;

- operational restrictions;

- incentives; and

- market access and other standards of treatment.

The last of these includes rules on

- rights of establishment by foreign firms;

- whether, once established, foreign firms are treated in the same way as local firms in regard to matters such as local content rules or export requirements (the latter is sometimes summarised under the label of national treatment although it seems simpler to include both market access and conditions of operation under that category); and

- the equal treatment of investors from all home economies (the MFN principle).

Adding the issue of incentives to this list creates a group of issues to be dealt with under the heading of liberalisation.

Administrative impediments include lack of transparency, perhaps exaggerated by the large number of governments involved at each level (if there is the possibility of rejection at each level of government and even if this risk is low, the overall risk of rejection rises rapidly with the levels of government involved). Another source of lack of transparency might be the use of a positive list approach to policy making rather than a negative list.

Dealing with these matters can be summarised under the heading of facilitation, although they too could be classed as matters of national treatment (assuming the administrative processes are applied on an MFN basis).

PECC research indicates that the developing member economies tend to have greater foreign equity restrictions, more foreign investment restrictions, more performance requirements and rules and regulations which are less transparent (PECC 1995a: Table 6.5). Yet in the past decade or so, developing economy members have increasingly opened up to foreign investment. The substantial increase in the level of investment flows into the developing member economies during the period indicates that foreign investors respond well to improvements in investment regimes.

In recent years, many member economies have made significant efforts to facilitate investment liberalisation on a unilateral basis. Competition between them to attract foreign capital flows is a powerful force for reform. Unattractive regimes are more likely to be quickly revealed when aggregate FDI flows are growing rapidly. The costs of an inefficient investment policy regime are much more apparent and surface much more rapidly than those of an inefficient trade policy regime.

Despite these pressures from the market place, there remains much scope for further improvement in the investment regime through a package of investment liberalisation, facilitation and technical cooperation. There is also a qualification to the argument that market forces (reflected in FDI volumes, for instance) will signal the differences between efficient and inefficient regimes since inefficient investment policies can be offset by incentives or import protection. The PECC (1995b) has put forward some reasons why this investment policy reform should be undertaken more effectively in a cooperative way rather than via unilateral action. Some of the arguments are that

- international rules lock in unilateral reforms and make reversals more difficult;

- simultaneous action makes it easier to sell reform at home, and to mobilise sectors interested in outward investment to counteract pressure to retain restrictions in sensitive sectors;

- rules limit the extent to which governments can compete in the investment incentives 'game', with the result that everyone loses; and

- rent-seeking behaviour by 'policy shopping' investors and the scope for bureaucratic discretion is diminished by uniform rules.

Some more specific issues in the APEC process are examined below.

First and foremost is the need to define clearly and refine the concept of an open investment regime as enshrined in the Bogor Declaration. A clear target shapes the action program that needs to be undertaken in the interim to achieve the Bogor goal by the years 2010 and 2020, respectively, for the developed and developing member economies in APEC. The PECC's categorisation is a starting point in this search for a definition.

One operational example of a clear target for the APEC is also suggested by the case of the European Union; that is, virtually free flow of capital within the region. However, the European Union aims for a virtually integrated market within, but with barriers to investment from the outside. APEC, in contrast, is a looser form of economic integration than the European Union, without the particular political objectives that underpinned the economic integration program in the European Community. One way of characterising the challenge for APEC is to say it has to define how far to deviate from the EU model, for example, in terms of the right of establishment, while maintaining its adoption of the non-discriminatory MFN principle. In the process, APEC would decide which impediments to investment flows need to be eliminated or modified over a specific time frame.

The Non-binding Investment Principles endorsed by the APEC Ministers in 1994 represent a solid and substantial building block for an APEC collective action plan towards an open investment regime. The principles have contributed to confidence building and consultation among the APEC members towards further reform in their investment policies and regulatory practices. The Principles, however, include contentious issues that were deliberately weakly formulated or altogether omitted (Bora and Graham 1996) in order to bring on board all the APEC members despite wide variations in their investment regimes. Thus, the second important area for improvement in the investment policy regime in the region is the further refinement, definition and strengthening of the Non-binding Principles. There is scope for improvement in the following ways:

- set a target limit for exceptions to and exclusions from the right of establishment;
- agree on limits to coverage and the form of subsidies and incentives;
- agree on a target date for complete repatriation and convertibility of investments;
- agree to end performance requirements by a certain date; and
- include a standstill and roll-back provision.

These refinements and improvements are likely to give more teeth to the Non-binding Principles and improve the predictability and transparency of the investment policy regime in the region. Because the APEC Non-binding Principles include a strong statement for a non-discriminatory MFN provision, the APEC principles could be a prototype for a multilateral agreement under the WTO.

Sub-regional arrangements like North American Free Trade Association (NAFTA), Australia–New Zealand Closer Economic Relations (CER) and ASEAN can provide the mechanism for pro-active programs for further deepening and broadening of the investment liberalisation and facilitation process. This can be achieved through more ambitious time schedules for the implementation of investment liberalisation measures, deeper economic integration objectives, and closer technical cooperation in institution capacity building on investment promotion and regulation. The success of such pro-active programs at the sub-regional level makes it easier to encourage all members of regional arrangements to sign on to a stronger set of Investment Principles.

The papers by the ASEAN Working Group on Investment Cooperation and Promotion and by the ASEAN heads of investment agencies on realising an ASEAN Investment Area (AIA) provide a possible model for strengthening the investment and facilitation process in the APEC region (ASEAN Secretariat 1996). Some features are set out below.

- The AIA aims at enhancing ASEAN's attractiveness as an investment area for both ASEAN and non-ASEAN investors by ensuring a more liberal and transparent investment regime.

- All industries, with limited exceptions, would be open to foreign investment. The exceptions, to be kept to a minimum, relate to national security, protection of public morals and the protection of articles of artistic, historic and archaeological value.

- Following the mode of liberalisation in the ASEAN Free Trade Area (AFTA), economic activities are categorised into fast track, normal track, a temporary exclusion list and a general exception list. Within each list, investment impediments will be progressively phased out according to varying timetables. Fast track activities are areas where investment liberalisation and facilitation programs are carried out more rapidly than normal track activities. The general exception list consists of areas that are not to be included in the AIA.

- A Framework Agreement on the AIA would be formulated stipulating, among other things, the start and completion dates for the realisation of the

AIA as well as an indication of activities and industries that will be liberalised, along with a specific time frame according to the respective tracks and lists.

The APEC Business Advisory Council (ABAC) proposes a similar but less comprehensive approach to investment liberalisation and facilitation than the proposed ASEAN approach of categorising activities into tracks and lists. Specifically, ABAC proposes the identification of demonstration projects called APEC Voluntary Investment Projects (AVIP) which are accorded strong investment protection, especially in terms of national treatment, MFN treatment, access to domestic markets and resources, capital mobility, mobility of senior management, elimination of performance requirements, freedom from expropriation and adherence to international arbitration (ABAC 1996: 16–18). These are standards above and beyond those in the Non-binding Principles. As demonstration projects, the AVIPs, it is argued, would show the benefits to the host economies of strong investment protection through a positive investment response and lower financing costs. However the AVIP strategy has been strongly criticised by Bora and Graham (1997). They argue that its effect is to add another layer of discrimination into the policy mix, since it permits governments to discriminate not only among investors but also among projects. A preferable strategy would be to find a path for strengthening the application of the Principles across all projects without deviating along the way into further discrimination.

The current APEC Non-binding Investment Principles have been criticised for being weak and non-binding (see, for example, Lloyd 1997; Messing 1994). It is apparent, however, that enforceable legal investment codes enshrining liberalised investment rules at the regional level are an ultimate goal. The approach could be through a progressive process of refinement, clarification and ever-widening bindings on the various elements of the APEC investment principles. A complementary approach is through the possible accession of more and more of the APEC member economies into the OECD (Organisation for Economic Cooperation and Development). This means that they will be subject to the legally binding Codes of Liberalisation of Capital Movements and of Current Invisible Operations and will have to sign on to the 1976 Declaration and Decisions on International Investment and Multinational Enterprises that includes the National Treatment Instrument. The Codes and National Treatment Instrument are underpinned by two fundamental principles: right of establishment and national treatment (Houde 1995). This is a feasible route. Among the APEC developing economy members, Mexico and Korea are already members of the OECD while Malaysia, Thailand, Singapore, the Philippines and Chile are OECD's 'dynamic partners' and therefore are future candidates for OECD membership. (Indonesia would have been an OECD 'dynamic partner' also but for strong political and diplomatic objections for reasons related to the East Timor issue.)

Joint investment facilitation and technical cooperation activities contribute to improving the policy and institutional environment for investment liberalisation. Among the facilitation initiatives being undertaken or proposed are the holding of continuing dialogues and symposia with the business sector on investment issues, establishment of 'one stop' investment shops based on the best regional practice, continuing exchange on innovations on investment facilitation and regulatory reform such as build–operate–transfer models, joint publication of 'investment guides', and regular monitoring of progress on investment liberalisation, facilitation and technical cooperation (see, for example, ABAC 1996; APEC 1996; Pangestu et al. 1996).

Customs procedures and rules of origin

Customs procedures

Paperwork, administrative transactions and delays in customs procedures contribute significantly to the cost of doing business internationally. The 'Cost of Non-Europe' Project conducted one of the most detailed estimations of the direct and indirect costs of customs procedures. The direct costs included the internal administrative costs of exporting and importing firms, external costs of exporters and importers associated with customs clearance (for example, customs agents), costs of delays in terms of inventory and transport costs, and the cost of government personnel and material needed to staff customs posts and associated services. The indirect costs arise from reduced competition in the domestic economy from foreign suppliers due to customs impediments. It is estimated that direct administrative costs accounted for about 1.5 per cent of total intra-European Community trade during the late 1980s while the grand total of direct customs-related costs (that is administrative expenses, delays and costs of government personnel and material) reached about 1.9 per cent of total intra-EC trade (see Cecchini 1988; Emerson et al. 1988).

It is likely that the costs of customs procedures are higher in developing countries because of tariff and non-tariff barriers and other rules and regulations in addition to the general inefficiency of customs agencies in these countries. One estimate by de Rivera in *Asia Computer Weekly* suggests that the costs of paperwork amount to 7 per cent of the value of a product; another estimate by Price and Waterhouse/J. Cunanan suggests the average cost of processing export documents is US$110 (EDC n.d.). According to the ABAC, to complete an average international trade transaction at present involves 27–30 different parties, 40 documents, 200 data elements (30 of which are repeated at least 30 times) and re-keying of 60–70 per cent of the data at least once (ABAC 1996: 13). It is not surprising therefore that APEC businesspeople have emphasised the importance of streamlining customs procedures as an important trade facilitation measure on which APEC member economies should focus.

Recognising the importance of reducing the cost of customs procedures, the APEC member economies intend to '...move to a paperless system, and to operate simplified, harmonised, efficient and transparent customs rules and procedures throughout the region' (APEC 1996 Vol. 1: 17). The specific courses of action as agreed upon in the Manila Action Plan for APEC include the following:

- harmonisation of tariff nomenclature up to at least the six-digit level by adopting the 1996 version of the WCO harmonised system;

- accession to or simplification on the basis of the Kyoto Convention on simplification and harmonisation of customs procedures by 1998;

- adoption of the WTO Agreement on Customs Valuation principles by 2000;

- implementation of the UN/EDIFACT in automated customs clearance systems by 1999;

- publication of information on administrative guidelines, procedures and rulings in addition to customs laws and regulations by 1998. Related to this is the ongoing program of providing a database on tariffs and later on non-tariff barriers to the public through the Internet and other information media; and

- introduction of clear appeal provisions by 2000.

Technology and skills play an important role in the implementation of a stream-lined, transparent, paperless customs procedure. Specifically, it relies on electronic data interchange (EDI) that allows direct computer-to-computer exchange of standard documents among exporters/importers, banks, customs, government agencies and brokers/forwarders. Extensive use of electronic data interchange demands simplification of procedures in the relevant government agencies and customs, improves administrative efficiencies resulting in faster processing, enhances transparency of operations, allows better planning for production schedules, export shipments and deliveries, allows access to relevant information from concerned government agencies and customs, reduces clerical errors and the cost of messenger/courier services, and avoids the cost of delays.

Intensive use of EDI necessitates acquiring or updating skills in the relevant government agencies, especially in developing countries. Technical cooperation arrangements on skills development would help in hastening the implementation of streamlined customs procedures. Of course, minimisation of licensing requirements from, as well as simplification of procedures in, government regulatory agencies would be needed to benefit significantly from the streamlining of customs procedures through extensive use of electronic data interchange. Thus, simplification of customs procedures would also benefit from the parallel effort to minimise non-tariff barriers.

Rules of origin

The APEC region has a number of sub-regional free trade arrangements including NAFTA, CER, ASEAN, and Mercosur. Taking into consideration the various rules of origin governing regional, preferential and non-preferential trading arrangements among the APEC members, Stephenson (1996) estimates that there are nearly 60 different sets of rules of origin when adjustment is made for the members of the same groupings. This is a complex web of rules of origin, with attendant potentially high administrative and economic costs for the region's firms and economies. Administrative costs bear on both the firms and the government. There are no estimates for the administrative costs of rules of origin in the APEC. However, drawing from the median estimate of the cost of customs and paper work for European Free Trade Area (EFTA) firms in their trade with the European Community in the 1980s, which is 3 per cent of the value of finished products, Stephenson (1996) estimates that the cost of administering the rules of origin in preferential trading arrangements in the APEC could have been about US$70 billion in 1995.

Precisely because of the high transactions cost of meeting the requirements for a preferential tariff, a large percentage of export firms do not use preferential tariffs. In the case of EFTA exporters, about 25 per cent did not use the tariff preferences with the European Community (Stephenson 1996:9[n]). The historical experience in ASEAN during the 1980s and early 1990s indicates an extremely low availment rate of the ASEAN Preferential Trade Arrangement, suggesting that the benefits from that Trade Arrangement were not commensurate with the high administrative costs of meeting the rules of origin requirements.

The efficiency costs of restrictive rules of origin can also be significant and, perhaps more important, insidious. This is because restrictive rules of origin can become an instrument for industrial protection. For EFTA, the total administrative and efficiency costs of restrictive rules of origin ranged between 3 per cent and 5 per cent of the total value of traded products (Stephenson 1996: 9).

Given the potentially high cost of rules of origin, the challenge is to simplify the rule of origin requirement by narrowing the category required for the transformation under the 'change of heading requirement' or lowering the regional content requirement under the 'value-added approach', or reducing the stages needed to qualify as an originating product under the 'specific process' approach. An even simpler rule is that where the difference between the preferential tariff and the non-preferential MFN tariff is small (say, two percentage points), the preferential rules of origin are waived in favour of the non-preferential rules of origin (Stephenson 1996). The last suggestion significantly reduces the administrative and efficiency costs of rules of origin because WTO members, including the APEC member economies, are in the process of harmonising non-preferential rules of origin under the WTO and the WCO.

It is likely that the problem related to preferential rules of origin is transitory. As the MFN rates decline because of unilateral liberalisation as well as WTO-linked tariff reductions, the benefit and value of the preferential tariff privilege under a preferential trade arrangement erodes progressively. In the process, preferential trade declines in importance and, in the end, possibly disappears. The administrative and efficiency costs of restrictive rules of origin would then die away.

Technical regulations, standards and conformance

Survey respondents in the Cecchini study of European businesses identified standards and technical regulations as among the more important barriers to a unified market, especially in the more technology-intensive industries (Cecchini 1988; Emerson et al. 1988). The experience of the European Community shows that despite the elimination of tariffs, a bewildering array of standards and technical regulations can contribute to a segmentation of the common market and to the cost of international trading. Where such standards or technical regulations are primarily national standards and are rather idiosyncratic (for example, Italian pasta and German beer), they force firms to aim for national markets rather than international or regional markets, which results in higher prices to consumers in industries with the potential to achieve economies of scale. APEC businesspeople and governments have also acknowledged the role of technical regulations and standards as a potential market barrier to greater economic interchange and integration in the region.

The question is how to deal with these issues of different standards. One solution is to apply the principles of the 'open club', that is, negotiate a set of standards (or agree to the adoption of a set of standards) which is not deliberately designed to discriminate against others and which those not originally members of the negotiating group are encouraged to adopt. A criticism of this approach is that the very absence of the future members from the initial negotiations is likely to reduce the chances of their benefiting from future membership.

Furthermore, it is particularly difficult to choose an appropriate standard when 'industry standards' change over time as a result of competitive behaviour among firms. The adoption of any particular standard might then simply have the effect of protecting a particular group of incumbent service suppliers and inhibiting the entry of others offering differing standards. A further risk is that standard-setting organisations (professional bodies from which advice might be taken by officials seeking to deal with these issues) might be captured by particular groups of firms who have common interests in seeing a particular set of standards adopted. These issues are discussed in more detail by David and Shaiman (1997) in a review of a series of papers which suggest that the APEC process will have to apply a high level of vigilance to defend its openness as it considers standard-setting issues. Some features of current proposals for action in APEC are noted in the next few paragraphs, in particular the reference to international standards as a benchmark and the stress put on mutual recognition.

ABAC has proposed:

- alignment of each member economy's standards in priority sectors with international standards by 1998;

- adoption of mutual recognition agreements in priority areas by 1998; and

- establishment of an internationally recognised testing authority (ABAC 1996: 13).

The collective action plan of the APEC member economies on standards and conformance is broadly similar to the recommendations of APEC businesspeople; that is, alignment of national with international standards, mutual recognition in the voluntary and regulated sectors, technical infrastructure development and transparency of activity (Boxall 1996). The approach used by APEC follows the 'new approach' used by the European Union, rather than the European Union's 'old approach' which emphasised excessive harmonisation (see Pelkmans 1989). The use of mutual recognition agreements is a key feature.

The APEC proposal to align national standards with international standards instead of creating APEC standards is noteworthy because it indicates that the outward orientation of APEC member economies is consistent with the APEC's framework of open regionalism. Standards adopted, at least within APEC, are then less likely to be used as a potential trade barrier between APEC economies and the rest of the world. The alignment of national standards with international standards is also worth noting because it implies the 'maturation' of international standardisation bodies. These bodies, primarily the International Organisation for Standardisation (ISO) and the International Electrochemical Commission (IEC), were established principally to bring together and harmonise existing national standards, whereas today they are increasingly used as a basis for regional and international standards (Quinn 1996).

Standards are not likely be internationally uniform, because of the unique circumstances of each country. One example is the requirement for country-specific standards for reasons of safety, health, and so on. Countries which sit on the earth's earthquake belt are likely to have different standards for construction materials and building codes than countries far from the earthquake belt. Precisely because of this country specificity of standards and technical regulations in certain areas, standards and regulations can potentially be used for industrial protection. Nevertheless, the WTO TBT and SPSS agreements provide a good counter-balance to the potential abuse of standards and technical regulations for industrial protection.

Mutual recognition arrangements are an important component of an APEC standards and conformance strategy since they prevent the high cost of multiple testing which would effectively exact a heavy burden on exporters. However, mutual recognition arrangements can be implemented only if there is a credible technical infrastructure for conformity assessment. Achieving agreement on certification bodies is likely to be easier than agreeing across countries on the standards themselves. Conformity assessment consists of inspection and laboratory testing and calibration, product certification and quality management systems certification. The building blocks of the technical infrastructure include national standards for physical measurement, accredited calibration laboratories, a network of accredited testing laboratories, documentary standards, and legal metrology (Boxall 1996). Thus, ultimately, implementing the action plan for standards and conformance in APEC involves an investment in the development of the technical infrastructure and a demand for human skills for conformity assessment. It is apparent that the challenge is greatest for the developing countries because of their inadequate technical infrastructure and relatively scarce skilled labour. Technical cooperation in the area of standards and conformance can partly address the problems facing developing countries. Given the limited resources of the developing countries, the ABAC proposal for focusing standards and conformance activities and investments in APEC on priority sectors is sensible.

Conclusion

We have argued for the complementarity of regional trade, investment facilitation and the liberalisation of trade in goods. The gains from the latter will be greater and meet with less resistance in the presence of the former. And the liberalisation of trade in goods, including a commitment to avoid backsliding on commitments to free trade, focuses attention on other barriers to international commerce, especially those which might otherwise constrain the adjustment strategies of the business sector as it responds to reform.

Within the APEC region we have argued for the application of a number of principles in the facilitation program. These include the importance of maintaining its consistency with multilateral initiatives, and the value of an integrated approach to liberalisation, facilitation and economic and technical cooperation. A third principle is the advantage of choosing a well-defined target but permitting flexibility in the choice of path in reaching that target. The extra gains from cooperative action over unilateral action were also noted.

We then illustrated the application of these ideas to investment liberalisation and facilitation, to reform of customs systems, to changing rules of origin and to standards-setting. A theme of these remarks has been the importance of adopting procedures which avoid discriminatory outcomes. This can be achieved in a number of ways, quite often involving the application of a membership rule which permits newcomers to join on the same terms as establishment members of the 'liberalisation and facilitation club'.

One of the most difficult areas is the application of these ideas to standards-setting, especially in fields where new products are continually emerging and where technological change is rapid. There is a risk that systems of standard-setting may become a source of discrimination. The commitment in the short run to aligning APEC initiatives with global rules, systems or standards and to putting a stress on mutual recognition helps deal with the potential problems that might arise. However, the resolution of the tensions between competitive processes, and the shifts in technologies, products and therefore standards that follow, and the desirability of maintaining non-discriminatory market access is an important area of research.

Note

1 This idea was broached by Mr Edsel Custodio, head of the Philippine delegation, during the first APEC Senior Officials Meeting for 1997 in Victoria, British Columbia.

References

APEC (1996) *Manila Action Plan for APEC.*

APEC Business Advisory Council (ABAC) (1996) *APEC Means Business: Building Prosperity for our Community*, Report for the APEC Economic Leaders' Summit.

ASEAN Secretariat (1996) 'A comparison between the ASEAN Heads of Investment Agencies (AHIA) and the ASEAN Working Group on Investment Cooperation and Promotion (WGICP)', *Papers on Realising the ASEAN Investment Area*, Manila, mimeo.

Bora, B. and Edward M. Graham (1996) 'Non-binding investment principles in APEC', in B. Bora and M. Pangestu, eds, *Priority Issues in Trade and Investment Liberalisation: Implications for the Asia Pacific Region*, Singapore: PECC.

—— (1997) 'Can APEC deliver on investment?', forthcoming in F. Bergsten, ed., *Whither APEC? Progress to Date and Agenda for the Future*, Washington DC: Institute for International Economics.

Boxall, G. (1996) 'APEC Standards and Conformance Sub-Committee (SCSC) and the Specialist Regional Bodies', paper presented during the 1st APEC Conference on Standards and Conformance, Manila, Philippines, 9–11 October 1996.

Cecchini, P. (1988) *The European Challenge 1995: the Benefits of a Single Market*, Aldershot, England: Wildwood House.

David, Paul A. and T. Shaiman (1997) 'Standards setting and the global information infrastructure', Newsletter, Global Economic Institutions Research Programme, No. 4, CEPR, London, February, pp. 2–7.

de Melo, J., A. Panagariya and D. Rodrick (1992) 'The new regionalism: a country perspective', in J. de Melo and A. Panagariya, eds, *New Dimensions in Regional Integration*, Cambridge University Press for the CEPR.

EDC (n.d.) 'Electronic Data Interchange (EDI): Networking trade for Philippines 2000', Manila, mimeo.

Elek, Andrew (1996) *Europe, East Asia and APEC, Initial Report*, Australia–Japan Research Centre, ANU.

Emerson, M. et al. (1988) *The Economics of 1992*, Oxford University Press.

Houde, M.F. (1995) *OECD Instruments for Promoting the Liberalisation of Foreign Direct Investment*, OECD Working Paper No. 24.

Lloyd, P. (1997) 'An APEC or multilateral investment code', in B. Bora and M. Pangestu, eds, *Priority Issues in Trade and Investment Liberalisation: Implications for the Asia Pacific Region*, Singapore: PECC.

Messing, J. (1994) 'Toward a modern investment policy', in B. Bora and M. Pangestu, eds, *Priority Issues in Trade and Investment Liberalisation*, Singapore: PECC.

Pacific Business Forum (PBF) (1994) *A Business Blueprint for APEC: Strategies for Growth and Common Prosperity*, Report to APEC, October.

Pangestu, M., C. Findlay, P. Intal and S. Parker (1996) *Perspectives on the Manila Action Plan for APEC*, Manila: PECC, PIDS and the Asia Foundation.

PECC (1995a) *Milestones in APEC Liberalisation: A Map of Market Opening Measures by APEC Economies*, Singapore: PECC Secretariat.

—— (1995b) *Survey of Impediments to Trade and Investments in APEC Region*, Singapore: PECC Secretariat.

Pelkmans, J. (1989) 'Preventing a trench war: removing technical barriers in Europe and lessons for ASEAN', in N. Sopiee, C.L. See and L.M. Jin, eds, *ASEAN at the Crossroads: Obstacles, Options and Opportunities in Economic Cooperation*, Kuala Lumpur: ISIS.

Petri, P. (1997) 'Foreign direct investment in a Computable General Equilibrium framework', paper presented at the conference on Making APEC Work: Economic Challenges and Policy Alternatives, Keio University, Tokyo, March.

Quinn, T.J. (1996) 'A global standards and conformance system — a challenge at the dawn of the 21st century', paper presented during the 1st APEC Conference on Standards and Conformance, Manila, Philippines, 9–11 October.

Snape, R. (1996) 'Which regional trade arrangement?' in B. Bora and C. Findlay, eds, *Regional Integration and the Asia-Pacific*, Oxford: Oxford University Press.

Stephenson, S. (1996) 'The economic impact of rules of origin in the Asia–Pacific region', paper presented to PECC TPF IX, Seoul.

Part III

Modelling the regional integration process

7 Trade liberalisation in the European Union and APEC: What if the approaches were exchanged?

YONGZHENG YANG, RON DUNCAN AND
TONY LAWSON

Introduction

The group of countries which have joined what is known as Asia Pacific Economic Cooperation (APEC) have agreed to phase out their trade barriers on a unilateral basis by the year 2010 in the case of the developed countries and by 2020 in the case of developing countries. The agreed process of APEC trade liberalisation is that countries liberalise on a most favoured nation (MFN) basis, that is trade barriers are reduced on the same basis for countries outside the APEC group as for other APEC countries. Given the coverage of countries which have joined APEC, this decision will mean adoption of free trade over a substantial proportion of trade within the Asia Pacific region and free entry for the rest of the world to a large trading bloc.

Within Europe, economic integration is being undertaken in a different manner. The countries of Western Europe have formed a customs union which mainly links the industrialised countries but has included less developed countries such as Greece, Portugal and Spain. The developing trade relationship with the Central and Eastern European countries (CEECs) of the defunct Comecon bloc has been an *ad hoc* process of bilateral market access arrangements (the Association Agreements). These separate agreements, negotiated between the European Union (EU) and several CEECs, establish market access on a product basis. They are, in general, most restrictive towards the products in which the former centrally planned economies would appear to have a comparative advantage: agricultural products, basic metal manufactures, and clothing and textiles. Besides these agreements, the European Union maintains a maze of trade agreements, with different product coverage and no links between them, such as the Lome Convention with the ACP (African, Caribbean and Pacific) countries, and the European Free Trade Area (now comprising only Iceland, Norway and Switzerland).

This chapter looks at the implications for the respective regions and for global trade more generally of the European Union adopting the APEC form of liberalisation and the APEC grouping adopting the EU form of liberalisation. The increasing openness of the APEC grouping is seen as a key to the success of future economic developments in the region. What difference would an APEC-type trade liberalisation make to trade and development in Europe? Alternatively, there is a view, largely coming from the United States, that the APEC's MFN approach will be to the disadvantage of the Asia Pacific region because of Europe's free riding. Hence, another question is: what would be the impact on the APEC countries and the rest of the world of the adoption of preferential trade liberalisation by Asia Pacific countries?

The study uses the latest version of the Global Trade Analysis Project (GTAP) model and its latest release of data.[1] The latest database allows the CEECs and the former Soviet Union (FSU) to be separated out in the model. The chapter is organised as follows. In the next section, we briefly review the trade flows among the European Union, CEECs and the APEC economies and their trade barriers against each other. The GTAP model is then used in section 3 to examine trade liberalisation in Europe, followed by an assessment of APEC trade reform in section 4. Throughout the analysis, the contrast between MFN and free trade area (FTA) approaches to trade liberalisation is highlighted, and the role of agriculture is emphasised. The chapter concludes with a brief summary of the main findings.

Trade flows and protection

In this section, we briefly outline the trade flows and protection barriers among various regions as a background for European integration and APEC trade liberalisation. This enables us to see which commodities are important in various bilateral trade flows and where trade liberalisation is going to have the strongest impact. Table 7.1 reports the bilateral trade between the European Union and the CEECs.[2] Machinery and equipment and basic manufactures are shown as the most important products traded between the European Union and CEECs. This is, of course, largely due to the aggregation chosen in this study, as these two product categories comprise most manufactures. Tariffs on these commodities are relatively low compared with other manufactures (see Table 7.5). Not surprisingly, textile exports are more important than clothing for the European Union, while clothing is a more important export for the CEECs. Despite the relatively small trade volumes of these two commodities, European integration is likely to have a significant impact on the textile and clothing sector because of the existence of the Multi-fibre

Table 7.1   *Trade between the EU and CEECs, 1992, US$ million*

	EU exports to CEECs		CEEC exports to EU	
	($million)	(% of total)	($million)	(% of total)
Crops	994	2	725	2
Livestock products	430	1	1611	4
Natural resources	780	2	1831	5
Processed food	1793	4	1154	3
Textiles	3635	9	2181	6
Clothing	838	2	3834	11
Machinery & equipment	15941	39	5976	16
Basic manufactures	10539	26	12290	34
Services	6238	15	6890	19
Total	41188	100	36492	100

Source: GTAP database, Version 3.

Arrangement (MFA) and the relatively high tariffs prevailing in this sector. Agricultural trade is not particularly important in the bilateral trade. The European Union enjoys a moderate surplus in crops while the CEECs have a substantial trade surplus in livestock products. Given the high trade barriers in the European Union for livestock products (Table 7.5), economic integration will substantially boost CEECs' agricultural exports to the European Union.

Table 7.2 presents the various regions' exports to the European Union for 1992. Australasia (Australia and New Zealand) had a substantial interest in agricultural exports to the European Union, especially livestock products, while its manufactured exports were small. Exports of natural resources also featured prominently in Australasia's exports to the European Union. North America (the United States and Canada) had large exports of crops and processed food to the European Union. As expected, manufactured and services exports dominated North America's exports to the European Union. Japan's exports to the European Union were largely concentrated in machinery and equipment, of which automobiles were the most important. Clothing, textiles and other labour-intensive manufactures accounted for a large proportion of Asian developing economies' exports to the European Union. Machinery and equipment were also important. The Association of Southeast Asian Nations (ASEAN) is the largest agricultural exporter among these economies. Overall, the newly industrialising economies (NIEs), ASEAN and China had quite

Table 7.2 *Exports to the EU, 1992, US$ million*

	AUS	NAM	EU	JPN	NIE	ASN	CHN	SAS	LTN	CEA	FSU	ROW	TOTALS
Crops	647	4495	1689	49	177	1928	448	659	7055	725	624	6803	25299
Livestock products	2533	837	1172	14	26	106	388	34	1482	1611	200	1584	9987
Natural resources	2680	6034	3337	233	257	817	321	1225	6914	1831	10706	69229	103585
Processed food	248	5005	3421	136	337	2283	462	483	5677	1154	180	6298	25684
Textiles	203	2118	6636	940	3180	2319	2942	3769	1568	2181	190	6431	32478
Clothing	36	640	4370	193	5268	2948	3592	2849	363	3834	167	10607	34867
Machinery & equipment	988	68370	64870	60812	27104	7175	4196	737	2983	5976	1025	30393	274629
Basic manufactures	1135	29631	67005	7269	5562	3571	2436	866	7422	12290	8528	40092	185806
Services	1133	60911	50256	10718	9575	8249	7341	3169	8903	6890	2430	38295	207869
Total	9604	178042	202755	80363	51485	29398	22127	13789	42366	36492	24051	209732	900203

Acronyms: **AUS**: Australasia; **NAM**: North America; **EU**: European Union; **JPN**: Japan; **NIE**: NIEs; **ASN**: ASEAN; **CHN**: China; **SAS**: South Asia; **LTN**: Latin America; **CEA**: Central European Associates; **FSU**: Former Soviet Union; **ROW**: Rest of the world.

Source: GTAP database, Version 3.

diverse exports of manufactures. In contrast, South Asia's exports were dominated by clothing and textiles. Agricultural and processed food products were Latin America's most important exports to the European Union, while the FSU and the rest of the world are the major suppliers of natural resources to the European Union.

The CEECs are a small market (Table 7.3). Their imports from the APEC economies comprise mostly crops, clothing, machinery and equipment. While machinery and equipment imports are largely from North America, Japan and the NIEs, imports of clothing are predominantly supplied by the ASEAN economies, China and South Asia. Given the relatively weak trade links between the CEECs and the APEC economies, the impact of European integration on the APEC region will largely come from trade diversion in the EU market, rather than directly from the EEC markets.

Table 7.4 summarises the exports of the European Union and CEECs to the APEC region. The European Union's exports are predominantly manufactures, but agricultural and processed food exports are also significant. While the European Union is a major clothing market for the APEC region, its textile exports to the region are substantial, reflecting the relatively capital-intensive nature of these commodities compared with clothing. The CEECs' total exports to the APEC region are less than US$9 billion, or less than 3 per cent of the European Union's exports to the region. Services are the largest export of the CEECs to the APEC region, accounting for nearly 60 per cent of their total APEC exports.

As indicated earlier, the impact of trade liberalisation depends not only on the magnitude of trade flows but also on the present levels of barriers to these flows. Table 7.5 summarises the estimates of trade barriers and their production subsidies for the regions in the version of the GTAP model used in this study. The patterns of these distortions are well known and need little elaboration. It should be noted, however, that in the GTAP model, trade barriers are bilateral, hence these summary statistics may not accurately reflect the extent of trade restrictions on individual economies. The trade barriers include not only tariffs and export subsidies/taxes, but also their equivalents of other forms of restrictions, such as import quotas, anti-dumping duties, voluntary export restraints (VERs), and price undertakings. Export taxes on clothing and textiles shown in the table are predominantly the export tax equivalents of MFA quotas.

Table 7.3   *Exports to CEECs, 1992, US$ million*

	AUS	NAM	EU	JPN	NIE	ASN	CHN	SAS	LTN	CEA	FSU	ROW	TOTALS
Crops	7	117	994	0	9	100	64	75	168	92	200	326	2150
Livestock products	20	110	430	1	0	0	2	0	2	109	80	50	804
Natural resources	69	125	780	39	19	16	23	12	122	290	3421	2011	6927
Processed food	1	74	1793	6	5	35	43	59	341	187	50	481	3075
Textiles	9	56	3635	12	75	22	58	65	43	88	60	286	4409
Clothing	0	7	838	1	31	354	142	40	1	18	5	195	1632
Machinery & equipment	9	1100	15941	676	509	38	84	22	15	614	455	1099	20563
Basic manufactures	8	278	10539	94	51	19	55	17	35	1111	800	1541	14548
Services	57	1732	6238	477	646	46	23	52	428	45	211	575	10530
Total	181	3599	41188	1306	1344	630	494	342	1154	2554	5284	6562	64638

Acronyms: See Table 7.2.
Source: GTAP database, Version 3.

Table 7.4   *EU and CEEC exports to the APEC region, 1992, US$ million*

Commodity	From EU	From CEECs
Crops	1576	71
Livestock products	3172	240
Natural resources	7040	57
Processed food	11046	182
Textiles	10404	258
Clothing	3658	198
Machinery & equipment	114432	897
Basic manufactures	63980	1862
Services	100828	5150
Total	316135	8915

Source: GTAP database, Version 3.

Integration and liberalisation in Europe

An FTA in Europe

In this section, we examine the impact of forming a free trade area between the European Union and the CEECs. An FTA is what the Association Agreements were intended to achieve before full economic integration in Europe. As a large part of the Association Agreements has already been implemented, their effects on the world economy may have already worked through to a considerable degree (European Commission 1994). The Association Agreements deal with non-agricultural trade between the European Union and CEECs. There is considerable uncertainty over when full European integration will eventuate, but it will take at least several years. By the time full integration occurs, the structure of the global economy will be quite different from what it is today. In particular, as the CEECs recover from the economic down-turns following the collapse of the former Soviet bloc and, one hopes, enjoy rapid economic growth, their economies will experience considerable structural change.

To capture the impact of European integration, the world economy is first projected to the year 2005. The projected 2005 equilibrium provides a baseline for subsequent comparative static simulations of European integration. Thus,

Table 7.5   Pre-Uruguay Round distortions, per cent

	AUS	NAM	EU	JPN	NIE	ASN	CHN	SAS	LTN	CEA	FSU	ROW
Production subsidies												
Crops	2	16	36	20	19	1	-3	2	0	0	-1	0
Livestock products	0	3	4	1	3	-1	-1	-1	0	3	2	-1
Import tariffs												
Crops	3	40	53	127	104	95	-11	8	3	9	-2	28
Livestock products	4	19	44	231	48	108	-1	14	10	14	21	35
Natural resources	0	1	0	2	3	13	6	9	6	2	0	13
Processed food	4	5	14	13	21	25	52	32	19	22	0	32
Textiles	23	9	7	11	5	36	59	57	20	11	0	37
Clothing	53	21	12	12	5	43	80	49	32	16	0	23
Machinery & equipment	13	10	6	1	6	22	34	34	19	10	0	17
Basic manufactures	9	5	5	3	6	17	21	47	12	8	0	15
Average	9	8	6	14	9	21	29	28	13	8	1	15
Export subsidies												
Crops	-1	5	91	0	0	-2	0	0	-1	0	-2	-6
Livestock products	-1	5	64	0	0	-4	0	0	-1	0	3	-2
Natural resources	-1	0	-3	0	0	-4	0	0	-1	0	-38	-2
Processed food	0	0	-6	0	0	-4	0	0	-1	0	-5	-6
Textiles	0	0	0	0	-1	-3	-2	-6	-4	-3	-2	-2
Clothing	-1	0	0	0	-13	-20	-12	-21	-15	-10	-4	-6
Machinery & equipment	1	0	0	-4	-2	-8	0	0	-1	-1	-1	-1
Basic manufactures	-1	0	-1	-1	0	-5	-1	-1	-2	-2	-8	-3
Services	0	0	-1	0	0	-4	0	0	0	0	-1	-1

Acronyms: See Table 7.2. *Source:* GTAP database, Version 3.

we examine the question: what difference would European integration make to the world economy in the year 2005? Such a projection could involve forecasts of the growth of primary factor accumulation and technological change over the period 1995–2005. Alternatively, one can forecast real gross domestic product (GDP) growth and primary factor accumulation and deduce technological change. The latter approach is followed in this study. Table 7.6 summarises our projections of major macroeconomic variables for various regions over the period 1992–2005. We based our projections of GDP growth and primary factor uses on Hertel et al. (1997) and the World Bank (1995). Because only economy-wide GDP forecasts are available, we can only deduce technological change at the economy-wide level.[3] It should be noted, however, that sectoral GDP does not grow at the same rate in the projection even though only the economy-wide GDP growth rate is projected. Because of variations in factor intensity among sectors, different rates of factor accumulation mean that GDP growth will differ among sectors — the Rybczynski effect. In addition, consumer preferences are non-homothetic, so that the growth of demand for various products differs as income rises.

In the projection, all prices and sectoral quantities endogenously adjust to the exogenous changes in macroeconomic variables. Labour and capital are perfectly mobile across sectors while land is partially mobile. Trade deficits are balanced by capital inflows in the form of savings, which are driven by the rate of return to investment. No policy change is implemented in the projection. Based on the evidence provided by Gehlhar (1997), the trade elasticities in the GTAP model are doubled in the projection and subsequent central scenarios of comparative static simulations.[4]

Many Association Agreements will be implemented in parallel with the Uruguay Round reforms. The benchmark against which the impact of these agreements on the world economy is measured is therefore important. The impact of integration would be greater if it occurs before the Uruguay Round reforms, and the impact diminishes if integration begins from post-Uruguay Round trade distortions. Because of this overlapping, two sets of experiments are carried out. In the first set, we simulate the integration from a pre-Uruguay Round equilibrium in 2005, which is the projected baseline without policy change. In the second set, integration simulations are carried out from a post-Uruguay Round 2005 equilibrium. These two sets of experiments will provide the upper and lower bounds of the effects of the agreements.

The post-Uruguay Round equilibrium of the world economy is created by simulating the Uruguay Round reforms at the projected baseline in 2005. Our estimates of tariff cuts and agricultural liberalisation are based on GATT (1993 and 1994) and UNCTAD (1995). Essentially, domestic support for agriculture is reduced by 20 per cent, and export subsidies and tariffs

Table 7.6   *Projected annual average growth of macroeconomic variables, 1992–*
             2005, per cent

	Population	Labour	Capital	Real GDP
Australasia	0.7	0.6	2.1	2.5
North America	0.7	0.9	2.8	2.7
EU12	0.2	0.2	1.3	2.2
Japan	0.3	-0.2	3.3	2.6
NIEs	0.9	0.9	6.3	6.3
ASEAN	1.6	2.2	6.8	6.8
China	1.3	2.4	9.3	8.9
South Asia	1.8	2.4	7.1	5.2
Latin America	1.7	2.2	1.2	3.6
Central and Eastern Europe	0.9	0.9	6.0	6.0
Former Soviet Union	0.0	0.0	4.4	4.4
Rest of the world	1.3	2.4	2.5	2.5

Source: Hertel *et al.* (1995), World Bank (1995) and Yang and Zhong (1996).

(including their equivalents of quantitative restrictions) by 36 per cent. Tariffs on textiles and clothing are reduced by 18 per cent in North America, 16 per cent in the European Union (15 per cent for imports from developing economies), and 33 per cent in Japan. For developing countries, domestic support for agriculture is cut by 15 per cent, export subsidies by 24 per cent, and tariffs by 26 per cent. Tariff reductions in developing countries are two-thirds of those of the industrial countries.

The standard GTAP closure is used in the Uruguay Round reform experiment and all other comparative static simulations.[5] In particular, all prices and quantities are endogenously determined except for the numeraire — the price of savings. Land, labour, capital stock and technology are all fixed. Similar to the projection simulation, however, labour and capital are perfectly mobile across sectors, while land is only partially mobile. Because GTAP is a one-period model, investment does not augment capital stock in the next period, although it affects final demand in the current period. The trade balance is endogenous, and savings are allowed to cross national borders in response to the level of return to investment. However, all capital returns are intra-regional.

In implementing free trade between the European Union and the CEECs, all border barriers, except those to agricultural trade between the two regions, are eliminated in accordance with the Association Agreements.

(Agricultural issues will be dealt with separately in the following section.) On the import side, these barriers include tariffs, quotas, variable import levies and any other import restrictions. On the export side, export subsidies, taxes and MFA quotas (which are modelled as export taxes) are abolished altogether. However, output subsidies in both the European Union and CEECs are retained. All bilateral barriers on trade between Europe and the rest of the world remain unchanged. The results of the simulated effects of such free trade between the European Union and the CEECs are reported in Table 7.7.

Both the European Union and CEECs benefit from free trade with each other, as measured by equivalent variation.[6] The gain to the CEECs is, however, much larger, in either absolute or relative terms. While real GDP growth in the European Union is negligible, it amounts to 1 per cent in the CEECs in the first experiment, and 0.14 per cent in the second. Note that welfare gains do not change proportionately with real GDP, because of the considerable terms-of-trade effects resulting from trade liberalisation. Substantial improvements in the termsof trade for the CEECs lead to more significant welfare equivalent variation gains than GDP growth suggests. In contrast, a deterioration in the terms of trade for the European Union reduces the welfare gain that might be implied by GDP growth.

In a neoclassical model like GTAP, welfare change arising from policy changes comprises two components: allocative efficiency and the terms-of-trade effects. The change in allocative efficiency for the European Union and CEECs from European free trade depends on the level of trade barriers and possible second-best outcomes arising from the continuation of particular distortions during the process of liberalisation. An important second-best outcome is the expansion of agriculture in the European Union as a result of free trade with the CEECs in non-agricultural commodities. Severe distortions in EU agriculture mean that the more the sector produces and exports, the more the European Union loses.

Theoretically, a unilateral tariff reduction by a member of an FTA improves the terms of trade of the partner country. However, if all members reciprocate, then the terms-of-trade effect for any particular member depends primarily on its size. In the standard Armington (1969) framework of production differentiation, all countries are 'large' in a sense that they all produce unique products. Given that the Armington elasticities of substitution are identical across all regions in GTAP, the size of a country is the single most important factor determining the change in its terms of trade. Another factor is the structure of trade, as the substitution elasticities do vary from commodity to commodity.

As the small party to the European Free Trade Area, the CEECs enjoy a favourable terms-of-trade effect of bilateral free trade. The overall terms of

Table 7.7   *Macroeconomic effects of the Association Agreements, 2005*

	Pre-Uruguay Round			Post-Uruguay Round		
	Equivalent variation (US$b)	GDP (%)	Terms of trade (%)	Equivalent variation (US$b)	GDP (%)	Terms of trade (%)
Australasia	-0.03	0.00	-0.03	-0.03	0.00	-0.02
North America	-0.09	0.00	-0.01	-0.24	0.00	-0.01
EU12	2.18	0.00	0.09	2.63	0.01	0.09
Japan	-0.67	0.00	-0.04	-0.40	0.00	-0.02
NIEs	-1.70	-0.06	-0.10	-0.37	-0.01	-0.03
ASEAN	-2.22	-0.19	-0.16	-0.79	-0.02	-0.12
China	-2.40	-0.14	-0.18	-0.68	-0.02	-0.09
South Asia	-1.94	-0.20	-0.49	-0.36	-0.02	-0.15
Latin America	-0.36	-0.01	-0.05	-0.19	0.00	-0.03
Central and Eastern Europe	7.82	1.02	2.60	1.46	0.14	0.66
Former Soviet Union	0.23	0.03	-0.03	0.01	0.01	-0.08
Rest of the world	-4.37	-0.12	-0.20	-0.95	-0.02	-0.06
World	-3.56		0.0	0.08		0.0

Source: Simulations of the GTAP model.

trade for the European Union also improve slightly. This, however, is unlikely to result from an improvement in its terms of trade against the CEECs, as the latter are a very small market for the European Union. Increased imports from the CEECs raise import prices, while increased exports lead to declines in export prices. However, trade diversion resulting from the European Free Trade Area improves the European Union's terms of trade *vis à vis* the rest of the world, which is a much larger market than the CEECs.

Free trade between the European Union and the CEECs results in welfare losses to the rest of the world. These losses are substantial if free trade reform is implemented on the basis of pre-Uruguay Round distortions, while the losses are significantly smaller if free trade starts from the post-Uruguay Round situation. The largest losses are seen in the Asian economies. China and the ASEAN economies are most affected. This largely results from trade diversion in the textile and clothing sector. As the CEECs gain free access to the EU textile and clothing market, Asian textile and clothing exports become less competitive in price terms. This also explains the difference in welfare losses for these economies between the two experiments. Once the MFA is eliminated as part of Uruguay Round reform, trade diversion in the textile and clothing sector becomes much smaller despite relatively high tariffs on these commodities in the European Union.

The world as a whole loses considerably from free trade between the European Union and the CEECs if the bilateral liberalisation is carried out on the basis of pre-Uruguay Round trade distortions, but gains marginally if the post-Uruguay Round distortions are the starting point of liberalisation. Again, trade diversion in the textile and clothing sector plays an important role in this respect. The abolition of the MFA for the CEECs alone increases distortions in the world textile and clothing market, and hence may reduce world welfare. In other words, the removal of MFA quotas under the Uruguay Round agreements would avoid trade diversion arising from European integration.

Incorporating the CEECs into the CAP

The agricultural sector in the European Union and CEECs is the most diffi-cult to integrate because of the Common Agricultural Policy (CAP) in the European Union. High distortions in the EU market mean that more substan-tial adjustment has to be made if agriculture becomes part of the FTA in Europe. Should the CEECs have free access to the EU agricultural market, their exports would increase. So would their domestic prices. This would lead to increased imports into the CEECs from the rest of the world and undermine the effectiveness of the CAP. Without rules of origin constraints, the CEECs would serve as an entry point for farm exports from the rest of the world to the European Union. In the long run, even with rules of origin, free access to the EU market could induce higher productivity in CEEC agriculture and make it difficult to sustain the CAP.

The CAP would be under even greater strain if the European Union were to maintain domestic market prices following integration, let alone if it were to maintain producer prices. To maintain domestic market prices, the Euro-pean Union could reduce imports from third regions by raising its variable import levy. It could also increase export subsidies to dispose of its farm products in the world market. Finally, it could reduce production subsidies to induce lower farm output, which would result in higher market prices but lower producer prices. The first two options would violate the European Union's World Trade Organization (WTO) commitments, and the last option would face political opposition from EU farmers unless they were adequately compensated (Tangermann 1996). Even in the last scenario, the European Union may not be able to fulfil its Uruguay Round obligations in terms of reductions in domestic support and export subsidies, depending on the extent to which domestic output declines in the wake of integration. It is not clear whether and how reduced interventions in the EU market as a result of European integration might be counted as part of its Uruguay Round commitments.

If the CEECs were to impose higher restrictions on imports from the rest of the world in order to maintain the existing CAP, their Uruguay Round commitments would also be in doubt. However, in the process of integration, higher import restrictions may be allowed for the CEECs if a customs union were formed between the European Union and the CEECs. In that case, agricultural protection in the CEECs may be raised to the level of the average of existing EU and CEEC protection. Such an averaging formula was used in the initial formation of the European Economic Community (Winters 1993). Indeed, there would be political pressure to treat CEEC farmers on an equal basis with their EU counterparts in a fully integrated Europe. In this case, to maintain the CAP, not only would import protection in the CEECs have to increase, but also their export and production subsidies may have to rise. To what extent agricultural protection in the CEECs would have to rise without violating their and the European Union's Uruguay Round commitments is a difficult issue requiring further analysis and will not be pursued here. Instead, we will evaluate the economic consequences of such policy options for the European Union and CEECs.

The economic consequences will not only involve economic efficiency in Europe and its commitments to the Uruguay Round and the General Agreement on Tariffs and Trade (GATT), but also the budgetary implications for Europe. If interventions in CEEC agriculture increase, who will finance the export and production subsidies? In addition, the European Union will probably have to compensate for the losses its farmers suffer from integration. Should the CEECs pay the bill, their benefits from integration would be substantially curtailed. They could even lose in principle, as deadweight losses from increased distortions may outweigh the gains resulting from increased market access to the European Union.

In the following, two scenarios for integrating the CEECs into the CAP are explored. In both scenarios, all post-Uruguay Round border distortions (import restrictions and export subsidies), including those in agriculture, in the trade between the European Union and CEECs are eliminated, while *ad valorem* output subsidies remain unchanged.[7] In the first scenario, we assume that the CEECs raise their subsidies on production and exports to the post-Uruguay Round levels in the European Union (exports to the European Union are of course exempted). We further assume that the European Union is to finance the subsidies by way of income transfers to the CEECs. This extra-budgetary revenue is raised by increasing income taxes on the factors of production in the European Union. Compensation for EU farmers, which is

Table 7.8   *Macroeconomic effects of a full European FTA, 2005*

	Export subsidies and domestic support with transfers			Export subsidies and domestic support without transfers		
	EV (US$b)	GDP of trade (%)	Terms (US$b) (%)	EV (%)	GDP of trade	Terms (%)
Australasia	-0.26	0.00	-0.20	-0.30	0.00	-0.23
North America	-0.18	0.00	-0.04	-0.30	0.00	-0.05
EU12	-27.42	0.02	-0.11	5.14	0.05	0.01
Japan	0.34	0.01	-0.01	0.42	0.01	0.00
NIEs	-0.03	0.00	-0.01	-0.05	0.00	-0.01
ASEAN	-0.40	0.00	-0.08	-0.50	0.00	-0.10
China	-0.37	-0.01	-0.05	-0.45	-0.01	-0.06
South Asia	0.01	0.02	-0.05	-0.02	0.02	-0.08
Latin America	-0.48	0.00	-0.11	-0.55	0.00	-0.13
Central and Eastern Europe	23.90	-1.55	3.26	-4.37	-1.69	1.71
Former Soviet Union	1.12	0.07	0.40	0.98	0.06	0.35
Rest of the world	-0.14	0.01	-0.05	-0.06	0.02	-0.07
World	-3.91			-0.08		

Source: Simulations of the GTAP model.

to keep factor incomes unchanged following trade liberalisation, is also paid out of the increased income taxes. It is assumed that the total transfer required is the net increase in agricultural spending by the governments in the CEECs.[8] In the CEECs a variable import levy against third countries is introduced to maintain the current level of imports. No other policy changes are implemented. The second scenario simulates the same set of policy changes as the first scenario, but with no income transfers from the European Union to the CEECs. Instead, the CEECs have to finance their production and export subsidies by increasing their own income taxes. The results for the two scenarios are presented in Table 7.8.

The welfare implications of including agriculture in the European Union– CEEC free trade area are very significant. The European Union would suffer a massive US$27 billion welfare loss, and the CEECs would benefit by about US$24 billion if the European Union were to finance increased farm subsidies in the CEECs. Europe as a whole would be worse off by US$3.5 billion, and the world by US$4 billion. The income transfer required to finance the expansion of agriculture in the CEECs would be over US$28 billion, and EU farmers would need compensation of US$8 billion.[9] To finance this huge transfer and provide compensation for its farmers, the European Union would have to increase its income taxes by 0.4 per cent on all factors. To prevent any increases in imports, the CEECs would have to raise their import tariffs on crops and livestock products by 21 and 38 per cent, respectively.

What would happen if the European Union did not offer any transfers to the CEECs? In this case, the European Union would gain, while the CEECs would lose. Thus, the CEECs' welfare gain from free access to the EU market is more than offset by the efficiency losses resulting from heavy farm subsidies. To finance increased subsidies, the CEECs would need to increase their income taxes by 14 per cent. Although the CEECs would be worse off, integration would bring nearly US$1 billion benefit to Europe as a whole, compared with a US$3.5 billion loss in the case of income transfers, and the world as a whole would be only marginally worse off.

When the CEECs impose a uniform income tax on all factors of production to finance increased farm subsidies, it tends to make CEEC agricultural exports more competitive than they would be in the case of income transfers. Thus, the European Union's agricultural imports from the CEECs increase more when no transfer occurs, reducing the welfare losses in the European Union. The resulting efficiency gain is further strengthened by more significant reductions in farm exports from the European Union. As the CEECs' agriculture is less distorted than that in the European Union, any expansion of CEEC agriculture at the expense of EU agriculture would improve the combined welfare of the two regions.

In both cases, the overall welfare effect on the rest of the world of full European integration is negative but quite small (US$0.4–0.9 billion). This is partly because we have assumed that MFA reform under the Uruguay Round agreements is completed before full European integration. Most economies in the rest of the world suffer an adverse terms-of-trade effect, but Japan and the FSU gain. Japan benefits from its export expansion in manufactured goods, especially machinery and equipment, while the FSU benefits from increases in its exports of national resources. Both commodities become relatively expensive in Europe as a result of free trade with the CEECs.

MFN liberalisation in Europe

In this sub-section, we focus on the alternative MFN approach to trade liberalisation in Europe. Under this approach, bilaterally negotiated trade liberalisation is unconditionally extended to the rest of the world, without reciprocity. This is equivalent to concerted unilateral trade liberalisation by the European Union and the CEECs. Two experiments are carried out. In the first, trade liberalisation is confined to non-agricultural sectors — an analogy to the European FTA excluding agriculture. In the second experiment, all barriers to import and export flows between the European Union and CEECs, including those to their agricultural trade, are eliminated. Unlike in the FTA experiments including agriculture, output subsidies on agriculture in the European Union and CEECs are also eliminated. Trade policies in third countries remain unchanged. Both experiments are carried out on the basis of the post-Uruguay Round world economy in 2005.

The most salient outcome of MFN trade liberalisation in Europe is a much greater global gain compared with the FTA approach (Table 7.9). Even without agricultural liberalisation, the world benefits as much as US$24 billion (this result can be compared with the post-Uruguay Round results in Table 7.7). When agriculture is included in concerted trade liberalisation, the global gain increases by US$63 billion.[10]

Both the European Union and the CEECs suffer an adverse terms-of-trade effect arising from trade liberalisation. If agriculture is excluded, this effect is so large that the European Union is substantially worse off measured in equivalent variation, despite an increase in real GDP. The loss is offset only when agricultural reform is included as part of the concerted trade liberalisation. In this case welfare improves along with an increase in real GDP. Agricultural liberalisation brings as much as US$30 billion, making the European Union US$2.5 billion better off, in contrast to the US$27.5 billion loss resulting from non-agricultural liberalisation alone.

Two factors underlie the agricultural liberalisation result. First, unlike the manufacturing sector which is primarily protected by import restrictions, agriculture in the European Union is distorted by output and export subsidies, as well as by import barriers. When all these distortions are eliminated, the resulting allocative efficiency gain tends to be larger than when only border restrictions are removed. In addition, reduced farm exports following the removal of output and export subsidies lead to increases in export prices, which offset part of the adverse terms-of-trade effect resulting from import liberalisation. This is reflected in the relatively small welfare gain to the rest of the world (US$8 billion) resulting from agricultural liberalisation in Europe. Second, the simultaneous elimination of all agricultural distortions also avoids the costly second-best welfare losses associated with non-agricultural liberalisation. When non-agricultural sectors are liberalised while agricultural distortions remain, resources shift to the inefficient agricultural sector. Given the high distortions in EU agriculture, welfare losses from this increased misallocation of resources can be large.

Table 7.9   *Impact of MFN liberalisation in Europe, 2005*

	Excluding agriculture			Including agriculture		
	Equivalent variation (US$b)	Real GDP (%)	Terms of trade (%)	Equivalent variation (US$ b)	Real GDP (%)	Terms of trade (%)
Australasia	0.2	0.0	0.2	1.4	0.0	1.1
North America	0.2	0.0	0.1	2.9	0.0	0.3
EU12	-27.5	0.1	-1.5	2.5	0.5	-2.2
Japan	35.8	0.2	1.4	33.5	0.2	1.4
NIEs	3.9	0.1	0.3	2.9	0.0	0.2
ASEAN	4.1	0.2	0.5	4.3	0.1	0.6
China	3.2	0.1	0.4	2.9	0.1	0.4
South Asia	1.5	0.1	0.6	1.3	0.0	0.7
Latin America	1.2	0.0	0.2	5.5	0.0	1.2
Central and Eastern Europe	0.0	0.3	-0.9	1.0	0.3	-0.3
Former Soviet Union	0.0	0.0	0.2	-0.4	-0.1	0.2
Rest of the world	1.7	0.0	0.2	5.6	-0.1	0.8
World	24.2	n.a.	0.0	63.4	n.a.	0.0

Source: Simulations of the GTAP model.

All third economies except the FSU gain from unilateral trade liberalisation in Europe. Japan is by far the largest beneficiary. This stems from the elimination of the extensive EU non-tariff barriers against Japanese automobiles and other manufactures. Other Asian economies also gain substantially, both as a result of increased exports to Europe and of their improved terms of trade.

While Asia's increases in exports to Europe mostly occur in manufactured commodities, Australasia benefits largely from increases in demand for its agricultural commodities. Without agricultural liberalisation, Australasia's exports would actually decline. Agricultural reform also substantially boosts exports from Latin America, which is less competitive in manufactured exports than the Asian economies.

APEC trade liberalisation

MFN versus FTA approaches

As APEC trade liberalisation will not be fully accomplished until the year 2020, we have projected the world economy to that year in order to assess its impacts, following the same procedures as those used for the projection to 2005. We did this from the 2005 post-Uruguay Round database by accumulating factors of production and increasing real GDP across the regions consistent with the forecasts. In most cases, this amounts to extrapolating the trend forecasts of the period 1992–2005 to the year 2020. In the case of China, we have projected a slowing down of GDP growth for the period 2005–2020 (to 7.3 per cent per year). Unlike in the period 1992–2005, when the labour force grows much more rapidly than population, we have assumed that over the period 2006–2020, labour force growth is the sum of population growth, which is based on the State Statistical Bureau (1996) projection, and any unemployment left over from the period 1992–2005 (Yang and Zhong 1996). Again, no policy changes are implemented in the projection.

Once a 2020 equilibrium of the world economy is established, two sets of comparative-static experiments on trade liberalisation in the APEC region are carried out: one set includes agricultural liberalisation and the other excludes agricultural liberalisation. Both MFN and FTA liberalisations are carried out in each set.

If agriculture is included in APEC liberalisation, MFN trade liberalisation improves world welfare by as much as US$326 billion (Table 7.10). All economies except South Asia benefit from the reform. Japan is again the largest beneficiary, followed by the NIEs, the European Union, the ASEAN economies and China. North America does not benefit as much as one might expect, largely due to an adverse terms-of-trade effect. South Asia's loss also results from a slightly adverse terms-of-trade effect.

The results for the terms-of-trade effects on both the European Union and North America are not surprising in view of their size. However, one would not have expected such strong effects given that the APEC region is projected to produce 55 per cent of world output and 64 per cent of world trade by 2020.[11] Theoretically, if unilateral MFN liberalisation involves a large enough portion of the world trade, then the adverse terms-of-trade effect on liberalising countries would be muted, although large countries would still enjoy a less favourable terms-of-trade effect than small countries. Our results show that, given the substitution elasticities assumed, for a region as large as APEC the adverse terms of effect on liberalising countries can still be large and the free

Table 7.10   *APEC trade liberalisation including agriculture: FTA versus MFN approach, 2020*

	Excluding agriculture			Including agriculture		
	Equivalent variation (US$b)	Real GDP (%)	Terms of trade (%)	Equivalent variation (US$ b)	Real GDP (%)	Terms of trade (%)
Australasia	4.0	0.3	0.7	5.8	0.3	1.7
North America	13.7	0.2	-0.4	33.2	0.1	0.5
EU12	45.0	0.0	1.1	-3.2	0.0	-0.1
Japan	106.1	0.7	1.5	121.4	0.7	2.1
NIEs	70.6	1.5	1.0	83.7	1.5	1.6
ASEAN	28.6	3.5	-3.1	26.4	3.0	-2.6
China	23.9	2.9	-4.1	25.5	2.6	-3.5
South Asia	-0.9	-0.1	0.0	-8.5	-0.3	-1.2
Latin America	5.0	0.0	0.6	-8.5	-0.1	-0.9
Central and Eastern Europe	1.3	0.0	0.4	-0.3	0.0	-0.1
Former Soviet Union	4.7	0.1	1.6	0.1	0.1	-0.5
Rest of the world	23.9	0.2	1.2	7.1	0.1	0.3
APEC	246.9	n.a.	n.a.	296.1	n.a.	n.a.
Non-APEC	79.0	n.a.	n.a.	-13.3	n.a.	n.a.
World	325.9	n.a.	0.0	282.8	n.a.	0.0

Source: Simulations of the GTAP model.

riding equally significant, as indicated by the European Union's large terms-of-trade gain. After all, non-APEC regions are collectively an important trading partner of APEC countries. Despite the increased trade among themselves following their concerted liberalisation, APEC countries collectively bid up the prices of their imports from the rest of the world and drive down the prices of their exports to the rest of the world.

An FTA approach to full trade liberalisation in the APEC region would reduce the global welfare gain by US$43 billion compared with the MFN approach (Table 7.10). Under the FTA approach, all APEC economies except ASEAN gain more than under the MFN approach, but the additional gain to North America is especially significant. At the same time, major non-APEC regions lose from APEC FTA liberalisation. Both results are due to the terms-of-trade effect.

When agriculture is excluded from APEC liberalisation, there are dramatic changes in the outcome of the reforms. North America could lose as

Table 7.11   *APEC trade liberalisation excluding agriculture: FTA versus MFN approach, 2020*

	Excluding agriculture			Including agriculture		
	Equivalent variation (US$b)	Real GDP (%)	Terms of trade (%)	Equivalent variation (US$ b)	Real GDP (%)	Terms of trade (%)
Australasia	0.0	0.3	-1.0	0.6	0.2	-0.6
North America	-25.7	0.1	-1.4	-16.5	0.1	-1.0
EU12	55.7	0.1	1.0	-5.3	0.0	-0.2
Japan	65.0	0.1	2.1	84.2	0.1	2.7
NIEs	41.3	0.2	1.7	59.1	0.3	2.4
ASEAN	14.9	2.1	-2.3	18.5	1.9	-1.7
China	16.2	2.7	-4.2	18.8	2.4	-3.5
South Asia	-4.5	-0.2	-0.3	-11.5	-0.5	-1.4
Latin America	1.1	0.0	0.1	-7.4	-0.1	-0.8
Central and Eastern Europe	1.5	0.0	0.5	-0.2	0.0	0.0
Former Soviet Union	4.6	0.1	1.5	0.0	0.1	-0.5
Rest of the world	15.8	0.1	0.8	3.3	0.0	0.2
APEC	111.8	n.a.	n.a.	164.6	n.a.	n.a.
Non-APEC	74.2	n.a.	n.a.	-21.2	n.a.	n.a.
World	186.0	n.a.	0.0	143.5	n.a.	0.0

Source: Simulations of the GTAP model.

much as US$26 billion under the MFN approach and US$17 billion under the FTA approach (Table 7.11). Again, this results from a substantial deterioration in the terms of trade for North America — more so under the MFN approach than the FTA approach. All other APEC countries gain less from APEC reforms if agriculture is excluded from their reforms; and this is especially significant for Japan and the NIEs, where the agricultural sector is severely distorted and its liberalisation would bring large benefits. China and ASEAN lose from the exclusion of agriculture partly because they also have considerable trade distortions in agriculture and partly because their exports would not expand as much if agriculture were not part of APEC reform.

It seems paradoxical that the European Union gains from the exclusion of agriculture from APEC MFN liberalisation (to see this, compare the MFN results in Tables 7.10 and 7.11). This is probably a second-best outcome for the European Union. As agriculture in the European Union is highly distorted, any reductions in the European Union's agricultural exports as a result of the absence of agricultural reform in APEC would improve economic welfare for the European Union. More specifically, the exclusion of agriculture in APEC liberalisation reduces the European Union's subsidised agricultural production and exports and hence by comparison with the situation including agricultural liberalisation, its economic efficiency is greater. This conclusion is supported by the fact that the terms-of-trade effect for the European Union is less favourable when agriculture is excluded from APEC reforms than when it is included.

The world as a whole gains much less if agriculture is not included in APEC liberalisation. Under both the MFN and FTA approaches, the global welfare gain is about US$140 billion lower, and for the APEC region, US$130 billion lower. Thus, the main impact of excluding agriculture from APEC reform would be on APEC members themselves.

FTA liberalisation by the APEC economies not only reduces the welfare of the European Union, but also that of most other non-APEC economies (Tables 7.10 and 7.11). South Asia and Latin America suffer the most. Such an adverse impact on non-APEC members could have two effects on the political economy of world trade liberalisation. For small economies such as those in South Asia and Latin America, there would be a strong incentive for them to join APEC. For the European Union and the CEECs, they could be either induced to negotiate with the APEC for inter-regional MFN trade liberalisation or to seek to deepen European integration to offset the losses from a discriminatory APEC. Clearly, the gain to the world economy from the first option will be greater than from the second, as shown in our next experiment.

In this experiment, MFN liberalisation (including agriculture) is carried out in both the APEC region and Europe. As expected, most economies benefit more from this much broader liberalisation (Table 7.12). In addition, no economy loses from this reform. Although North America does not gain as much as under the FTA approach to APEC liberalisation, its welfare gain is substantial and is only 17 per cent lower than its benefit from the FTA among the APEC economies.

The results of this experiment also suggest that much of the terms-of-trade effect on North America is in agricultural trade. The difference in the terms-of-trade effect between APEC MFN liberalisation alone and combined APEC–EU MFN liberalisation is half a percentage point (to see this, compare the MFN terms-of-trade result for North America in Table 7.10 with that in Table 7.12), whereas whether or not agriculture is included in APEC MFN liberalisation makes a difference of a full percentage point (compare the MFN terms-of-trade results for North America in Tables 7.10 and 7.11). This latter difference can also be compared with the difference that the two liberalisation approaches make in APEC liberalisation (0.9 of a percentage point, see

Table 7.12   *MFN trade liberalisation in the APEC region and Europe (including agriculture), 2020*

	Equivalent variation (US$b)	Real GDP (%)	Terms of trade (%)
Australasia	6.5	0.3	1.8
North America	27.4	0.2	0.1
EU12	47.4	0.6	-1.2
Japan	139.9	0.8	2.4
NIEs	80.2	1.5	1.3
ASEAN	41.9	3.7	-2.6
China	33.8	3.0	-3.8
South Asia	0.2	0.0	0.2
Latin America	14.6	0.0	2.0
Central and Eastern Europe	2.0	0.3	-0.3
Former Soviet Union	3.6	0.0	1.8
Rest of the world	28.5	0.1	1.8
APEC	329.6	n.a.	n.a.
Non-APEC	96.2	n.a.	n.a.
World	425.8	n.a.	0.0

Source: Simulations of the GTAP model.

Table 7.10). Agriculture in some of the APEC economies, namely Japan, South Korea and Taiwan, is among the most restricted in the world. Agricultural liberalisation in the APEC region can therefore improve North America's terms of trade just as much as trade liberalisation in the European Union.

Sensitivity analysis

The above experiments have shown that the terms-of-trade effect is crucial in determining the welfare effects of trade liberalisation on individual economies. The terms-of-trade effect, in turn, depends on the magnitude of the elasticities of substitution, as well as country size. There is considerable uncertainty about the magnitude of these elasticities in Computable General Equilibrium (CGE) models. Their values are typically based on estimates that are not always obtained consistently for any particular CGE model.

In the following, we undertake two sensitivity analyses of APEC trade liberalisation. The Armington elasticities of substitution between domestically produced and imported goods and those among sources of supply by country are first doubled and then halved. The results of these two experiments are reported in Table 7.13. These results are comparable with those in Table 7.10.

When the elasticities are doubled, the estimated global welfare gains from trade liberalisation increase. No economy loses. However, even with doubled elasticities, which tend to moderate the terms-of-trade effect of trade liberalisation, the free riding problem of MFN remains — as shown in the European Union's substantial gain. In addition, North America still gains less under the MFN approach than it would under the FTA approach, although its gain under higher elasticities is more than doubled. With lower elasticities, the contrast between MFN and FTA approaches is not only more pronounced for North America, but also for other APEC economies. Both ASEAN and China suffer large losses from APEC liberalisation, rather than reap the huge benefits that accompany higher elasticities.

The sensitivity of the simulation results to the elasticities of substitution suggests that the results should be treated with caution. In the real world, terms-of-trade effects do occur as a response to natural or policy shocks, and it is essential that they are taken into account in the evaluation of welfare change. However, the sensitivity analyses also highlight the importance of the adjustment of the world economy to changes in trade policy. The responsiveness of the world economy to shocks as reflected in the elasticities is not only determined by the physical substitutability between commodities, but also by economic policies. In other words, these elasticities are not entirely exogenous to the policy environment. For example, a world trading system stricken with quantitative restrictions will respond less to trade policy changes, while a system governed by tariffs will be more responsive. Thus, trade liberalisation and willingness to adjust can reduce the terms-of-trade effects and increase the global welfare gains from trade liberalisation.

Conclusion

The debate on regionalism is fought on two fronts. One concerns whether preferential trade arrangements improve the welfare of member countries and the world as a whole, and the other concerns whether the proliferation of preferential trade areas will accelerate or retard the process of global trade liberalisation. While Bhagwati (1993) and Krueger (1993), among many others, argue that the spread of preferential trade areas poses a threat to the world trading system, both through their adverse welfare effects on certain member countries and through slowing global trade liberalisation, others (for

Table 7.13   *Sensitivity analyses of the welfare effects of APEC trade liberalisation (agriculture included), 2020, equivalent variation in US$billion*

	Higher elasticities		Lower elasticities	
	MFN approach	FTA approach	MFN approach	FTA approach
Australasia	3.1	4.8	4.5	6.9
North America	28.5	35.6	2.9	28.5
EU12	69.5	18.0	40.9	-9.8
Japan	173.0	190.7	60.3	78.1
NIEs	112.1	125.2	49.3	63.1
ASEAN	96.2	89.6	-3.0	-1.3
China	112.8	110.0	-20.5	-14.0
South Asia	4.1	-6.1	-1.2	-8.8
Latin America	4.9	-9.8	5.2	-8.9
Central and Eastern Europe	2.1	-0.1	1.2	-0.4
Former Soviet Union	7.4	1.9	3.5	-1.1
Rest of the world	37.7	17.0	20.1	1.9
APEC	525.7	555.9	93.4	161.3
Non-APEC	125.6	20.9	69.7	-27.1
World	651.3	576.8	163.0	134.3

Source: Simulations of the GTAP model.

example Summers 1991 and Krugman 1991) tend to believe that FTAs are likely to improve welfare and to serve as 'building blocs' for global trade liberalisation. This paper has so far focused on the first question. Nevertheless, our answer to the first question can have significant implications for the second.

Our simulation results on the first question can be summarised as follows. We note that whether and how much economic integration will benefit the world economy and the individual economies involved depends on how integration is achieved. In the case of ongoing European integration between the European Union and the CEECs, an agriculture-exclusive FTA comprising the two regions tends to benefit both parties. Given the existing instruments of protection in the two regions, the smaller party — the CEECs — tends to gain much more than the larger one, either in absolute terms or as a percentage of initial income. This is because the resulting terms-of-trade effects tend to favour the small party. The global welfare effect of such an FTA is ambiguous.

The outcome of full European integration is complicated by the CAP. Our simulation results show that an 'integration CAP' in the CEECs can more than offset the gains for Europe from bilateral free trade in non-agricultural commodities. In fact, a fully-fledged CAP in the CEECs can reduce Europe's economic welfare by as much as US$3.5 billion if the European Union finances the agricultural subsidies in the CEECs. The rest of the world also loses marginally.

The non-discriminatory MFN approach to trade liberalisation in Europe brings a much greater benefit to the world. However, the gains to the European Union and the CEECs depend critically on whether agriculture is included in trade liberalisation. The European Union would gain moderately if agriculture is included, but suffer substantially if agriculture is excluded. Unilateral liberalisation tends to result in deterioration of the terms of trade for the European Union and the CEECs. If agriculture is excluded from MFN trade liberalisation, the loss from the adverse terms-of-trade effect outweighs the efficiency gain.

The two approaches to trade liberalisation also make significant differences to the outcome of the APEC agreement. The agreed MFN approach benefits every economy in the region in the central simulation scenario, while the FTA approach tends to do so at the expense of non-APEC economies — a consequence similar to that of European integration. Also, like European integration, unilateral trade liberalisation tends to affect the terms of trade for the APEC economies adversely, even though APEC is projected to produce well over half of world GDP and trade by 2020. The MFN approach makes most APEC economies worse off in comparison with FTA liberalisation. The robustness of this result over a quite large range of Armington elasticities suggests that there may be a free riding problem with MFN liberalisation both in Europe and the APEC region. Also, as in Europe, agriculture plays a critical part in APEC trade liberalisation. Without agriculture, benefits from the APEC initiative would be substantially reduced. The United States may even be worse off from APEC liberalisation in such circumstances.

Strong as these results may seem to be, they must be treated with caution. The importance of the terms-of-trade effects in the results may say more about the parameters assumed in the model than about the real world. Most economists find it difficult to believe that monopoly power is as pervasive in world trade as assumed. In the absence of more reliable estimates of the substitution elasticities, a more extensive sensitivity analysis than that carried out in this paper is desirable.

The GTAP model does not take into account the short-term adjustment costs arising from trade liberalisation. This tends to overestimate the benefits of trade liberalisation. There are, however, a number of factors which tend to lead to the underestimation of the benefits from trade liberalisation. The GTAP model is essentially designed for comparative static analysis. It does not take into account possible endogenous productivity improvement arising from trade liberalisation. If trade or openness also has a growth effect, as some have suggested (for example Feder 1982; Edwards 1992), the benefits from trade liberalisation could also be much larger than we have estimated (Yang 1997).

The model also assumes perfect competition and hence constant economies of size. The potential improvement in productivity and the pro-competition effect arising from trade liberalisation thus cannot be captured. Some studies have shown that these effects are important (François et al. 1997), although others (for example Harrison et al. 1996) have failed to show such significant effects.

Another factor which tends to lead to the underestimation of benefits from trade liberalisation is international re-allocation of capital. Although the GTAP model does allow some capital flow, it is limited to the global balancing of current year savings, and capital assets are not modelled, unlike models such as G-Cubed (McKibbin and Wilcoxen 1995). Without incorporation of full capital flows, results from static models essentially represent somewhat short- to medium-run outcomes of trade liberalisation. In addition, capital flows allow greater adjustment in the world economy and hence potentially greater benefits from trade liberalisation. Greater adjustment means larger price responses to policy changes (larger elasticities) and hence smaller terms-of-trade effects arising from trade liberalisation.

It is not clear, however, how these factors would affect these results on the merits of alternative approaches to trade liberalisation. For example, does productivity grow more rapidly in the process of multilateral trade liberalisation or regional free trade? Does imperfect competition imply that multilateral trade liberalisation is more beneficial than FTA arrangements? These questions are difficult to answer. However, we do know that FTAs entail some extra costs, such as those resulting from the extensive rules of origin associated with FTAs (Krueger 1993). Incentives to rent-seeking are probably also stronger under FTA arrangements.

As to whether FTAs are building blocks for global trade liberalisation, our results suggest that the free riding issue (real or perceived) with unilateral liberalisation is a critical factor in the political economy of world trade liberalisation. How governments respond to such a problem can have a profound impact on the process of global trade liberalisation. If APEC and Europe react to this problem by reciprocating each other's MFN liberalisation, it will result in a greater welfare improvement for both parties, as well as for the rest of the world. The question is: Can this be achieved? If it can, will it be more effectively done through multilateral negotiations or inter-regional negotiations? Or should we fight on both fronts?

Appendix 7A: The GTAP model

GTAP is a comparative-static, general equilibrium model of the global economy. Other models of this type include Whalley's (1985) model of world trade, the Michigan model of world production and trade (Deardorff and Stern 1986), the RUNS model (Goldin, Knudsen and van der Mensbrugghe 1993), the WALRAS model (Burniaux et al. 1990) and the SALTER model (Zeitsch et al. 1991). Like the GTAP model, these models include full general equilibrium features of individual economies and link these economies through international trade. Some (for example the latest version of SALTER) also have linkages through international capital markets.

In the GTAP model, the activities of economic agents (consumers, producers and governments) are modelled according to neoclassical economic theory. Consumers are assumed to maximise utility, and producers to maximise profits. The market is perfectly competitive and there are constant returns to scale.

On the demand side, each individual economy is represented by a single 'super-household'. This household disposes of total national income according to a Cobb-Douglas per capita utility function specified over three forms of final demand: private household expenditure, government expenditure, and savings. This means that national income is spent in fixed proportions in these three components. Government expenditure is also distributed on the basis of constant budget shares among composite goods and services, which are composed of domestically produced and imported goods and services. Domestic and imported goods and services are treated as distinctive products in the concept of the Armington product differentiation (Armington 1969). The demands for domestically produced and imported goods and services are determined by their relative prices and the level of the demand for the composite goods and services according to constant elasticity of substitution (CES) functions. Similarly, demand for imports from a particular foreign supplier is also determined in the CES fashion by the level of imports from all sources and the relative prices of the goods and services from this particular source. On the other hand, private households allocate expenditure on various composite commodities according to the so-called constant difference of elasticity (CDE) function. This functional form is used to capture the non-homothetic nature of private household demand because income elasticities for different commodities vary. Once the demand for composite goods and services is determined, CES functions are again used to determine import levels and their sourcing from individual foreign suppliers.

On the supply side, gross output is composed of value added and a composite intermediate input, and demand for both of them is proportional to output levels (Leontief technology). Value added is in turn composed of labour, capital and land (for agricultural use only), and demand for them is governed by CES functions. Similarly, the composite intermediate input consists of those produced domestically and imported, and their substitution is determined by CES functions. Demand for imports is sourced again according to CES functions. It should be noted that labour and capital are perfectly mobile across industries, while land is only partially mobile. This implies that wages and rental prices are equalised across industries, while land prices can vary from industry to industry.

Apart from goods and services sectors within national boundaries, there are two global sectors in the model. One is the global transport sector which provides services to individual countries. Transport costs make up the differences between the CIF (cost, insurance and freight) and FOB (free on board) prices of traded commodities. The other global sector is the banking sector. This sector intermediates between global savings and investment. The level of investment is determined by the expected rate of return to investment. The change in the expected rate can be assumed to be either equal or variable across countries, according to the economic circumstances being modelled.

Appendix 7B: Region and commodity descriptions

Table 7B.1 *Region descriptions*

Region	GTAP region descriptions
Australasia	Australia and New Zealand
North America	United States and Canada
EU12	Belgium, Denmark, France, Germany, Greece, Ireland, Italy, Luxembourg, Netherlands, Portugal, Spain, United Kingdom
Japan	Japan
NIEs	Hong Kong, Republic of Korea, Singapore, Taiwan
ASEAN	Indonesia, Malaysia, the Philippines, Thailand
China	China
South Asia	Bangladesh, Pakistan, India, Sri Lanka, rest of South Asia
Latin America	Mexico, Central America and the Caribbean, Argentina, Brazil, Chile, rest of South America
Central and Eastern Europe	Poland, Hungary, Czech Republic, Slovakia, Romania, Bulgaria
Former Soviet Union	Former Soviet Union
Rest of the world	Regions not included above

Table 7B.2 *Commodity descriptions*

Commodity	GTAP commodity descriptions
Crops	Paddy rice, wheat, other grains, non-grain crops and processed rice
Livestock products	Wool, other livestock, meat products and milk products
Natural resources	Forestry, fishery, coal, oil, gas and other minerals
Processed food	Other food products and beverages & tobacco
Textiles	Textiles and leather products
Clothing	Clothing
Machinery & equipment	Transport equipment, machinery and equipment, other manufactures
Basic manufactures	Lumber, pulp & paper etc., petroleum & coal, chemicals, rubber & plastics, non-metallic minerals, primary ferrous metals, non-ferrous metals and fabricated metal products
Services	Electricity water & gas, construction, trade & transport, other services (private), other services (government), and ownership of dwellings

Appendix 7C: Trade elasticities

Table 7C.1 *Central scenario trade elasticities used in this study*

	Elasticities of substitution between imports and domestic products	Elasticities of substitution among imports by place of production
Crops	4.4	8.8
Livestock products	4.9	9.3
Natural resources	5.6	11.2
Processed food	5.0	9.9
Textiles	5.3	11.6
Clothing	8.8	17.6
Machinery & equipment	7.1	13.7
Basic manufactures	4.5	9.0
Services	3.9	7.6

Notes

* An earlier version of this chapter was presented at the conference 'Europe, East Asia and APEC', held at the Australian National University, Canberra, 28–29 August 1996. The authors would like to thank David Vines as well as participants at the above conference for their comments.

1 The GTAP model was developed at the Global Trade Analysis Project led by Thomas Hertel of Purdue University and its initial database is closely related to the SALTER model developed by the Industry Commission on behalf of the Australian Government's Department of Foreign Affairs and Trade. Appendix 7A provides a brief introduction to the GTAP model. Interested readers are referred to Hertel (1997) for more details of the model and to McDougall (1997) for details of the database.

2 See Appendix 7B for details of commodities and regions identified in the version of the model used for this study.

3 This is necessary because the number of equations in the model must be equal to the number of endogenous variables. Since economy-wide GDP variables are normally endogenous, we need to exogenise them by making endogenous an equal number of economy-wide technological change variables.

4 See Appendix 7C for the magnitude of the trade elasticities used in this study.

5 See Hertel (1997) for possible closures in the GTAP model.

6 This is a measure of change in income (valued at initial prices) which would be equivalent to the utility change resulting from policy reforms. Utility in the GTAP model is a Cobb-Douglas function of household utility, government utility and national savings. Household utility is in turn modelled by the constant differences of elasticities (CDE) function, while government utility is a Cobb-Douglas function of government consumption. See Hertel (1997) for details.

7 Since output subsidies affect all bilateral trade flows, not just those between the European Union and CEECs, it does not make sense to remove them in FTA experiments.

8 In the GTAP model, there are no government budget constraints. This assumption therefore ignores the effects of integration on overall government budgets, although net increases in agricultural spending are covered by increased income taxes.

9 The combined extra expenditure for the EU budget is about US$36 billion, about US$11 billion smaller than the estimate by Anderson and Tyers (1993). Also see Tangermann (1996) for a survey of the range of estimates.

10 This number is not comparable with the numbers for the world in Table 7.8, as the results there do not include the effect of the removal of output subsidies. Also see Note 7.

11 These numbers omit the contribution of Mexico and Chile as they are included in Latin America, despite both being APEC members. In comparison, the European Union is projected to produce 28 per cent of world output and 18 per cent of world trade by 2020. Intra-regional trade is excluded in the calculations of these shares.

References

Anderson, K. and R. Tyers (1993) 'Implications of EC expansion for European agricultural policies, trade and welfare', Discussion Paper No. 829, CEPR, London.

Armington, P.S. (1969) 'A theory of demand for products distinguished by place of production', *IMF Staff Papers* 14, pp. 159–78.

Bhagwati, J. (1993) 'Regionalism and multilateralism: an overview', in J. de Melo and A. Panagariya, eds, *New Dimensions in Regional Integration*, Cambridge: Cambridge University Press.

Burniaux, J.M., F. Delorme, I. Lienert and J.P. Martin (1990) 'WALRAS — a multi-sector, multi-country applied general equilibrium model for quantifying the economy-wide effects of agricultural policies', *OECD Economic Studies*, No. 13: 69–102.

Deardorff, A.V. and R.M. Stern (1986) *The Michigan Model of World Production and Trade*, Cambridge: MIT Press.

Edwards, S. (1992) 'Trade orientation, distortions and growth in developing countries', *Journal of Development Economics* 39, pp. 31–57.

European Commission (1994) *European Economy*, Supplement A: Recent economic trends, No. 7, July.

Feder, G. (1982) 'On exports and economic growth', *Journal of Development Economics* 12, pp. 59–73.

François, J.F., B. McDonald and H. Nordstrom (1997) 'The Uruguay Round: a global general equilibrium assessment', in D. Robertson, ed., *East Asian Trade after the Uruguay Round*, Cambridge: Cambridge University Press.

GATT (1993) *An Analysis of the Proposed Uruguay Round Agreement, with Particular Emphasis on Aspects of Interest to Developing Economies*, Geneva: 29 November.

—— (1994) *News of the Uruguay Round of Multilateral Trade Negotiations*, Geneva, April.

Gehlhar, M. (1997) 'Historical analysis of growth and trade patterns in the Pacific Rim: an evaluation of the GTAP framework', in T. Hertel, ed., *Global Trade Analysis Using the GTAP Model*, Cambridge: Cambridge University Press.

Goldin, I., O. Knudsen and D. van der Mensbrugghe (1993) *Trade Liberalisation: Global Economic Implications*, Paris: OECD and World Bank.

Harrison, G.W., T.F. Rutherford and D. Tarr (1996) 'Quantifying the Uruguay Round', in W. Martin and A.L. Winters, eds, *The Uruguay Round and the Developing Countries*, Cambridge: Cambridge University Press.

Hertel, T. ed. (1997) *Global Trade Analysis Using the GTAP Model*, Cambridge: Cambridge University Press.

——, W. Martin, K. Yanagishma and B. Dimaranan (1995) 'Liberalising manufactures trade in a changing world economy', in W. Martin and A.L. Winters, eds, *The Uruguay Round and the Developing Countries*, Cambridge: Cambridge University Press.

Krueger, A.O. (1993) 'Free trade agreements as protectionist devices: rules of origin', Working Paper: No. 4352, National Bureau of Economic Research (NBER), April.

Krugman, P. (1991) 'Is bilateralism bad?', in E. Helpman and A. Razin, eds, *International Trade and Trade Policy*, Cambridge: MIT Press.

McDougall, R.A. ed. (1997) *Global Trade, Assistance, and Protection: The GTAP 3 Data Base*, Centre for Global Trade Analysis, Purdue University, West Lafayette, USA.

McKibbin, W.J. and P.J. Wilcoxen (1995) 'The theoretical and empirical structure of the G-Cubed model', Brookings Discussion Papers in International Economics No. 118, Washington, DC: Brookings Institute.

Sheehy, J. (1994) 'CEECs' growth prospects for GDP and manufacturing trade with the EC — a short literature survey', in Economic Commission, *European Economy* 6, pp. 7–16.

State Statistical Bureau (1994) *Xia shiji de zhongguo renkou* (China's population into the next century), Beijing: China Statistics Publishing House.

Summers, L. (1991) 'Regionalism and the world trading system', in Federal Reserve Bank of Kansas City, *Policy Implications of Trade and Currency Zones*, pp. 295–301.

Tangermann, S. (1996) 'Reforming the CAP: a prerequisite for eastern enlargement', paper presented at the Kiel Week Conference on 'Quo Vadis Europe?', Institut für Weltwirtschaft, Kiel, pp. 26–27, June.

UNCTAD (1995) *An Analysis of Trading Opportunities Resulting from the Uruguay Round in Selected Sectors: Agriculture, Textiles and Clothing, and Other Industrial Products*, Geneva: UNCTAD.

Whalley, J. (1985) *Trade Liberalization among Major Trading Areas*, Cambridge: MIT Press.

Winters, A. (1993) 'The European Community: a case of successful integration?', in J. de Melo and A. Panagariya, eds, *New Dimensions in Regional Integration*, Cambridge: Cambridge University Press.

World Bank (1994) *World Development Report*, New York: Oxford University Press.

—— (1995) *Global Economic Prospects and the Developing Countries*, Washington DC: World Bank.

Yang Y. and C. Zhong (1996) 'China's textile and clothing exports in a changing world economy', *Economic Division Working Papers*, East Asia, No. 96/1, Australian National University, Canberra.

Yang Y. (1997) 'A general equilibrium assessment of the Uruguay Round with trade-related externalities', in D. Roberton, ed., *East Asia after the Uruguay Round*, Cambridge: Cambridge University Press, pp. 131–51.

Zeitsch, J., R. McDougall, P. Jomini, A. Welsh, J. Hambley, S. Brown and J. Kelly (1991) 'SALTER: a general equilibrium model of the world economy', *SALTER Working Paper*, No. 4, Canberra: Industries Commission.

8 Regional and multilateral trade liberalisation: the effects on trade, investment and welfare

WARWICK J. MCKIBBIN

Introduction

When a country reduces barriers to international trade, a number of factors determines the nature of the resulting gains and losses in both the short run and the longer run. Some of the key mechanisms through which gains are realised are direct, but many others are indirect and require the use of an economy-wide model to capture these effects. In addition, the time profile of liberalisation as well as the fact that the restructuring of any economy does not come without cost complicate the analysis in the short run. Many studies, and the professional debate in general, tend to ignore the short-run adjustment issues of trade liberalisation. This complicates the political barriers to trade liberalisation once the liberalisation begins because the gains take a while to materialise and are widely dispersed, yet the costs are usually highly visible and incurred in the short term. This of course differs across economies and depends on whether liberalisation is being undertaken during a period of rapid or stagnant economic growth. With highly visible short-run job losses, the resolve of liberalisers is sorely tested. It is important to explore empirically these adjustment problems because it needs to be recognised in advance that some costs may be incurred to achieve more substantial medium- and long-term gains. However, an understanding of the likely adjustment path is also important for formulating appropriate macroeconomic policy responses to ease the transition. It is reassuring to know from many Computable General Equilibrium (CGE) studies that gains will be achieved in the long run from trade liberalisation, but it is possibly more important for policy makers to know what the road will look like during the adjustment process.

CGE models have become a popular tool for calculating the various direct and indirect effects of trade liberalisation and provide a range of useful insights. The sorts of mechanism that these models capture are clear. In the case of unilateral liberalisation, a reduction in trade barriers tends to reduce import prices which increases the purchasing power of consumers, thus making consumers directly better off. The change in relative prices induces firms to re-allocate resources away from protected sectors towards other more efficient activities, which tends to raise economic efficiency in the economy. CGE models are particularly useful for calculating how much the efficiency gains will be and how much consumption will rise as a result of these processes in the longer run.

However, there are other gains that many standard CGE models ignore. One aspect is if there is imperfect competition or increasing returns to scale (see François et al. 1995). Another occurs if the removal of distortions increases the return to capital and stimulates investment in the economy. These dynamic effects can be much larger than the efficiency triangles many CGE modellers calculate (see McKibbin and Salvatore 1995). Once allowance is made for the reality that financial capital is mobile internationally and these financial flows are related to the real returns to physical capital, then further complications arise. If domestic saving does not rise as the return to capital rises from trade liberalisation and these additional investments are made by foreign owners of capital, then additional GDP (gross domestic product) will be generated in the economy but this will not show up directly as a domestic consumption gain because the returns will be repatriated to foreign owners of capital (see Manchester and McKibbin 1995). Thus it is important to evaluate trade liberalisation in terms of income or consumption gains rather than changes in production or GDP (see McKibbin 1996). In all evaluations of trade liberalisation, understanding the dynamic path of adjustment is crucial.

The gains to an economy from the liberalisation of another economy are transmitted through a number of channels. Other things being equal, the reduction in trade barriers in foreign economies will stimulate the demand for exports, which will raise income in the home economy, although not by the full value of increased exports because these exports need to be produced with resources that otherwise would be domestically consumed. Secondly, owners of capital in the home economy may be able to invest in the liberalising economy, leading to additional income gains if those investments realise a higher rate of return than in the home economy.

The process becomes more complicated in the case where trade reform is phased in or where an economy exhibits short-term Keynesian features due either to wage stickiness or adjustment costs in allocating physical capital, or where asset prices adjust quickly in response to international financial capital flows yet other prices are more sticky. In this case, overshooting of the exchange rate (see, for example, Dornbusch 1976) during the adjustment process can complicate the standard insights.

This chapter has a number of goals, all of which are aimed at improving our understanding of the magnitude of the above factors. The first goal is to determine the extent to which longer-run gains from trade liberalisation in particular economies are due to domestic liberalisation versus gains from other countries' liberalising. This provides direct evidence for the arguments by economists such as Garnaut (1996) that trade liberalisation is a prisoner's delight (all participants gain) rather than a prisoner's dilemma (where a gain by one country is a loss for another). Trade liberalisation under four alternative trade groupings is considered in this chapter: unilateral liberalisation; ASEAN (Association of Southeast Asian Nations) liberalisation; APEC (Asia Pacific Economic Cooperation) liberalisation; and multilateral liberalisation involving APEC and European economies. In each case the trade liberalisation is phased in according to the timetable underlying the APEC Bogor declaration in which industrial economies committed to reduce barriers to trade to zero by 2010 and developing economies by 2020 (the exceptions are Taiwan, Korea and Singapore which follow the 2010 timetable).[1] This type of liberalisation assumes the concept of 'open regionalism' defined by Garnaut (1996) in which liberalisation is non-discriminatory. Thus the chapter does not focus on regional trading blocs *per se*. Discriminating and non-discriminating trade reform in ASEAN versus APEC regional groups using an earlier version of the same multi-country model is explored further in McKibbin (1996).

The second goal of the chapter is to show the difference between the allocation of production across economies as a result of trade liberalisation versus the gain in welfare which we measure by gains in real consumption per capita. It is quite possible for GDP to fall in a country but for consumption to rise because additional income is generated by shifting production overseas. In the model underlying this study, labour is assumed to be immobile across economies but there is a high degree of financial capital mobility (which, over time, implies mobility of physical capital in response to arbitrage between financial returns and the real rate of return to physical capital adjusted by the cost of moving physical capital). Therefore to the extent that trade liberalisation leads to a re-allocation of capital to take advantage of high rates of return from other countries' liberalisation, there can be a fall in GDP but higher income to domestically owned factors of production and therefore higher consumption generated.

The third goal is to explore the short-run adjustment process when there is allowance for Keynesian style rigidities in labour markets, the costs of adjusting physical capital stocks and exchange rate overshooting from a combination of sticky wages and flexible asset prices.

This study can be distinguished from other studies of trade liberalisation such as Dee and Welsh (1994), François et al. (1995), Goldin and van der Mensbrugghe (1995), Harrison et al. (1995), Hertel et al. (1995), Huff et al. (1995), Martin and Winters (1995) or Murtough et al. (1994) because the model used in this paper is not of the class of static or period-linked CGE models that have been used in these earlier studies. This study follows the alternative Dynamic Intertemporal General Equilibrium (DIGEM) approach focusing on the dynamic adjustment to trade reform as in Manchester and McKibbin (1995); McKibbin (1994) using the MSG2 model; McKibbin and Salvatore (1995) using the GCUBED model; and McKibbin, Pearce and Wong (1995) and McKibbin (1996) using the Asia Pacific G-Cubed Model.

The model used in this paper is derived from the G-CUBED model developed by McKibbin and Wilcoxen (1992; 1995). Because of this link, this model is named the Asia Pacific GCUBED model (AP-GCUBED). As with the GCUBED model, this new model captures simultaneously the macroeconomic and sectoral linkages in a global model with partially forward-looking asset market and spending decisions (assuming rational expectations). The AP-GCUBED model has country/regional disaggregation of: Korea, Japan, Thailand, Indonesia, China, Malaysia, Singapore, Taiwan, Hong Kong, the Philippines, Australia, the United States, India, the rest of the OECD (Organisation for Economic Cooperation and Development), oil exporting developing countries, Eastern Europe and the former Soviet Union and all other developing countries. Each country/region has an explicit internal macroeconomic and sectoral structure with sectoral disaggregation in production and trade into six sectors based on data from standardised input–output tables.

The following section gives a brief overview of the theoretical basis of the AP-GCUBED model. The alternative scenarios for trade liberalisation are analysed in the next section. The results are examined in two parts. The longer-term outcomes are examined first in order to determine for each economy whether the gains arise from a country's own liberalisation or various forms of coordinated liberalisation. The dynamic adjustment path is then explored for a sub-group of countries focusing on how economic activity, trade and capital flows adjust to trade liberalisation that is gradually phased in. Finally, a conclusion is presented.

The AP-GCUBED model

The AP-GCUBED multi-country model is based on the GCUBED model developed in McKibbin and Wilcoxen (1992; 1995). It combines the approach taken in the MSG2 model (McKibbin–Sachs Global model) of McKibbin and Sachs (1991) with the disaggregated, econometrically-estimated, intertemporal general equilibrium model of the US economy by Jorgenson and Wilcoxen (1990). The MSG2 model featured one sector per country. The Jorgenson–Wilcoxen model has 35 separate industries, each of which is represented by an econometrically estimated cost function. The AP-GCUBED model has six sectors in each of the 17 economies.

The GCUBED model was constructed to contribute to the current policy debate on global warming, trade policy and international capital flows, but it has many features that make it useful for addressing a range of issues in environmental regulation, as well as microeconomic and macroeconomic policy questions. It is a world model with substantial regional disaggregation and sectoral detail. In addition, countries and regions are linked both temporally and intertemporally through trade and financial markets. Like MSG2, GCUBED contains a strong foundation for analysis of both short-run macroeconomic policy analysis as well as long-run growth consideration of alternative macroeconomic policies. Intertemporal budget constraints on households, governments and nations (the latter through accumulations of foreign debt) are imposed. To accommodate these constraints, forward-looking behaviour is incorporated in consumption and investment decisions. Unlike MSG2, the GCUBED model also contains substantial sectoral detail. This permits analysis of environmental and trade policies which tend to have their largest effects on small segments of the economy. By integrating sectoral detail with the macroeconomic features of MSG2, GCUBED can be used to consider the long-run costs of alternative environmental regulations and trade policy changes, yet at the same time consider the macroeconomic implications of these policies over time. The response of monetary and fiscal authorities in different countries can have important effects in the short to medium run which, given the long lags in physical capital and other asset accumulation, can be a substantial period of time. Overall, the model is designed to provide a bridge between computable general equilibrium models and macroeconomic models by integrating the more desirable features of both approaches. The AP-GCUBED model differs from the GCUBED model because of the focus on the Asia Pacific region as well as having six sectors compared to the 12 used in GCUBED. The theoretical structure is essentially the same.

The key features of AP-GCUBED are summarised in Table 8.1. The country and sectoral breakdown of the model is summarised in Table 8.2. The model consists of 17 economic regions with six sectors in each region (there are two additional sectors in each region that produce the capital good for firms and the household capital good). The 17 regions in AP-GCUBED

Table 8.1   *Main features of AP-GCUBED*

- Specification of the demand and supply sides of economies.

- Integration of real and financial markets of these economies with explicit arbitrage linking real and financial rates of return.

- Intertemporal accounting of stocks and flows of real resources and financial assets.

- Imposition of intertemporal budget constraints so that agents and countries cannot forever borrow or lend without undertaking the required resource transfers necessary to service outstanding liabilities.

- Short-run behaviour is a weighted average of neoclassical optimising behaviour based on expected future income streams and Keynesian current income.

- The real side of the model is disaggregated to allow for production of multiple goods and services within economies.

- International trade in goods, services and financial assets.

- Full short-run and long-run macroeconomic closure with macro dynamics at an annual frequency around a long-run Solow/Swan/Ramsey neoclassical growth model.

- The model is solved for a full rational expectations equilibrium at an annual frequency from 1995 to 2070.

---

can be divided into two groups: 14 core countries/regions and three others. For the core regions, the internal macroeconomic structure as well as the external trade and financial linkages are completely specified in the model. Our approach for each country is first to model them assuming the theoretical structure we use for the 'generic' country but calibrating each country to actual country data. We then proceed country by country to impose institutional features, market structures, market failures or government regulations that cause certain aspects of these economies to differ from our generic country model. This chapter represents only the beginning of this process, therefore the countries in the region are endowed with resources, trading patterns, saving and investment patterns and so on that are based on actual data for these countries but which in many important ways may not be truly

Table 8.2   *Overview of the AP-GCUBED model*

Regions	Sectors
United States	Energy
Japan	Mining
Australia	Agriculture
Rest of the OECD (ROECD)	Non-durable manufacturing
India	Durable manufacturing
Korea	Services
Thailand	
Indonesia	
China	
Malaysia	
Singapore	
Taiwan	
Hong Kong	
Philippines	
Oil exporting developing countries	
Eastern Europe and the former Soviet Union	
Other developing countries	
Agents	**Markets**
Households	Final goods
Firms	Services
Governments	Factors of production
	Money
	Bonds
	Equities
	Foreign exchange

representative of these countries because of institutional factors that are still being incorporated into the model.

Each core economy or region in the model consists of several economic agents: households, the government, the financial sector and the six production sectors listed in Table 8.2. Each of these economic actors interact in a variety of markets, both domestic and international. Each of the six sectors within each country is represented by a single firm in each sector which chooses its flexible inputs (labour, energy, materials) and its level of investment in order to maximise its stock market value subject to a multiple-input production function (Capital–Labour–Energy–Materials [KLEM]), in the knowledge that physical capital is costly to adjust once it is in place, and subject to a vector of prices it takes to be exogenous. Energy and materials are an aggregate of inputs of intermediate goods. These intermediate goods are, in turn, aggregates of imported and domestic commodities which are taken to be imperfect substitutes. Due to data limitations, we assume that all agents in the economy have identical preferences over foreign and domestic varieties of each particular commodity. We represent these preferences by defining six composite commodities that are produced from imported and domestic goods.

Following the approach in the MSG2 model, we assume that the capital stock in each sector changes according to the rate of fixed capital formation and the rate of geometric depreciation. The investment process is assumed to be subject to rising marginal costs of installation, with total real investment expenditures in the sector equal to the value of direct purchases of investment plus the per unit costs of installation. These per unit costs, in turn, are assumed to be a linear function of the rate of investment. One advantage of using an adjustment cost approach is that the adjustment cost parameter can be varied for different sectors to capture the degree to which capital is sector specific.

The price of labour is determined by assuming that labour is mobile between sectors in each region, but is immobile between regions. Thus, wages will be equal across sectors. The wage is assumed to adjust to varying degrees based on labour market institutions in the different economies. In the long run, labour supply is given by the exogenous rate of population growth, but in the short run, the hours worked can fluctuate depending on the demand for labour. For a given nominal wage, the demand for labour will determine short-run unemployment in each industry. This will vary across industries, depending on the composition of demand for each sector's good.

The solution of the optimisation problem also gives that the rate of gross investment in sector h is a function of 'Tobin's q' for that sector. Following the MSG2 model, it is assumed that investment in each sector is a weighted average of forward-looking investment and investment out of current profits.

Households consume a basket of composite goods and services in every period and also demand labour and capital services. Household capital services consist of the service flows of consumer durables plus residential housing. Households receive income by providing labour services to firms and the government, and from holding financial assets. In addition, they also receive transfers from the government.

Aggregate consumption is chosen to maximise an intertemporal utility function subject to the constraint that the present value of consumption is equal to human wealth plus initial financial assets. Human wealth in real terms is defined as the expected present value of future stream of after tax labour income of households. Financial wealth is the sum of real money balance, real government bonds in the hand of the public, net holding of claims against foreign residents and the value of capital in each sector. The solution to this maximisation problem is the familiar result that aggregate consumption is equal to a constant proportion of private wealth, where private wealth is defined as financial wealth plus human wealth. However, based on the evidence cited by Campbell and Mankiw (1987) and Hayashi (1982), we follow the approach in the MSG2 model and assume that only a portion of consumption is determined by these intertemporally-optimising consumers and that the remainder is determined by after tax current income. This can be interpreted as liquidity constrained behaviour or a permanent income model in which household expectations regarding income are backward looking. Either way, we assume that total consumption is a weighted average of the forward-looking consumption and backward-looking consumption.

Once the level of overall consumption has been determined, spending is allocated among goods and services based on relative prices.

We take each region's real government spending on goods and services to be a fixed share of GDP and assume that it is allocated among final goods (consisting of both domestically produced and imported goods), services and labour in fixed proportions, which we set to 1992 values. Total government outlays include purchases of goods and services plus interest payments on government debt, investment tax credits and transfers to households. Government revenue is generated from sales tax, corporate income tax and personal income taxes, and by issuing government debt. We assume that agents will not hold government bonds unless they expect the bonds to be paid off eventually. This transversality condition implies that the current level of debt will be equal to the present value of future budget surpluses.[2]

The implication of these constraints is that a government running a budget deficit today must run an appropriate budget surplus at some point in the future. Otherwise, the government would be unable to pay interest on the debt and agents would not be willing to hold it. To ensure that the constraint holds at all points in time, we assume that the government levies a lump sum tax in each period equal to the value of interest payments on the outstanding debt.[3] In effect, therefore, any increase in government debt is financed by consols, and future taxes are raised sufficient to accommodate the increased interest costs. Thus, any increase in the debt will be matched by an equal present value increase in future budget surpluses. Other fiscal closure rules are possible, such as requiring the ratio of government debt to GDP to be unchanged in the long run. These closures have interesting implications but are beyond the scope of this chapter.

The 17 regions in the model are linked by flows of goods and assets. Flows of goods are determined by the import demands described above (based on demand for goods for consumption, investment and government uses).

Trade imbalances are financed by flows of financial assets between countries (except where capital controls are in place). We assume that existing wedges between rates of return in different economies are generated by various restrictions that generate a risk premium on country-denominated assets. These wedges are assumed to be exogenous during simulation. Thus when the model is simulated, the induced changes in expected rates of return in different countries generate flows of financial capital reacting to return differentials at the margin.

Determining initial net asset positions and hence base case international capital flows is non-trivial. We assume that capital flows are composed of portfolio investment, direct investment and other capital flows. These alternative forms of capital flows are perfectly substitutable *ex ante*, adjusting to the expected rates of return across economies and across sectors. Within an economy, the expected return to each type of asset (bonds of all maturities, equity for each sector and so on) are arbitraged, taking into account the costs of adjusting physical capital stock and allowing for exogenous risk premia. Because physical capital is costly to adjust, any inflow of financial capital that is invested in physical capital (direct investment) will also be costly to shift once it is in place. The decision to invest in physical assets is based on expected rates of return. However, if there is an unanticipated shock, then *ex post* returns could vary significantly. Total net capital flows for each economy in which there are open capital markets are equal to the current account position of that country. The global net flows of private capital are constrained to zero.

The data used in the AP-GCUBED model come from a number of sources. Unlike the GCUBED model, we have not yet estimated the CES (constant elasticity of substitution) production elasticities of substitution. We currently assume the production function is Cobb-Douglas.

The input–output tables for the Asia Pacific economies are from the Institute of Developing Economies. The Australian table is from the Australian Bureau of Statistics. In lieu of obtaining input–output tables for the aggregate ROECD (other OECD) region, we currently create the tables for this region based on the US table and adjusted for actual final demand components from aggregate ROECD macroeconomic data. In effect, we are assuming that all countries modelled share the same production technology but differ in their endowments of primary factors and patterns of final demands. This assumption is a temporary necessity while we complete construction of the AP-GCUBED database.

Trade shares are based on the United Nations SITC (Standard Industry Trade Classification) data for 1992 with sectors aggregated from 4 digit levels to map as closely as possible to the SIC (Standard Industry Classification) used in the US input–output data. These data are from the International Economic Databank at the Australian National University (ANU).

The parameters on shares of optimising versus backward-looking behaviour are taken from the MSG2 model. These are based on a range of empirical estimates (see Campbell and Mankiw 1987 and Hayashi 1982) as well as a tracking exercise used to calibrate the MSG2 model to the experience of the 1980s (see McKibbin and Sachs 1991). It is important to stress that the results in this paper are very sensitive to the range of parameters used in the model. In particular, the substitution possibilities in production are important. It is also worth stressing that the adjustment cost model of capital accumulation implies that short-run changes in inputs for a given relative price change will be lower than the long-run substitution possibilities (despite having the same partial substitution elasticities in the short and long runs) precisely because physical capital is fixed in the very short run and therefore substitution possibilities are reduced.

AP-GCUBED is solved using the same software as the MSG2 model. The model has approximately 7,400 equations in its current form with 140 jumping or forward-looking variables, and 263 state variables. For further details on the model, see McKibbin and Wilcoxen (1995) and McKibbin and Wong (1997).

Results for trade liberalisation

The results for trade liberalisation in each country under each regional grouping are presented in this section. Results are first presented for the longer-run outcomes focusing on the year 2020. Next the dynamics of adjustment for various countries are examined in some detail. Of the vast number of results, only a subset is presented to illustrate various key points in this section.

To generate the results, we first solve the model from 1996 to 2070 to generate a model baseline based on a range of assumptions. Table 8.3 contains the aggregated tariff rates for each sector and each region in the model based on a WTO (World Trade Organization) tariff database supplied by the Centre for International Economics. These tariff rates are assumed to be unchanged for the horizon of the baseline simulation. Other crucial assumptions needed for generating the baseline include assumptions about population growth and sectoral productivity growth by country as well as fiscal and monetary policy settings. The issue of projection using a model such as the AP-GCUBED model is discussed in detail in Bagnoli et al. (1996).

Once the baseline is generated, each simulation is run and results are reported as a percentage deviation from this baseline. For each tariff

Table 8.3   *Initial tariff rates, per cent*

	Agriculture	Energy	Mining	Durable manu-facturing	Non-durable manu-facturing
United States	6.7	0.5	0.0	8.5	26.2
Japan	148.8	1.1	0.6	4.9	59.4
Australia	1.9	0.7	0.7	13.9	15.2
Indonesia	11.0	1.5	2.4	16.4	11.4
Malaysia	104.0	2.5	3.5	13.7	57.4
Philippines	104.0	5.8	10.2	24.1	63.3
Singapore	9.9	2.1	0.0	0.2	9.6
Thailand	107.6	6.9	10.9	33.4	70.5
China	16.7	14.0	18.7	45.1	43.5
Taiwan	12.6	14.3	23.5	39.3	42.1
Korea	105.0	2.8	4.4	16.0	41.0
Hong Kong	0.0	0.0	0.0	0.0	0.0
India	24.0	0.9	3.2	15.7	20.7
ROECD	6.9	0.4	0.2	8.2	16.5

Source: Centre for International Economics aggregations based on WTO/World Bank data.

reduction simulation, countries are assumed to reduce tariff rates from the levels shown in Table 8.3 to zero over the period specified. In each case, industrial economies are assumed to reduce tariffs in equal increments from 1996 to 2010. Developing countries are assumed to reduce tariffs by 2020. Taiwan, Singapore and Korea are assumed to follow the timetable for non-developing economies.

It is important to stress that macroeconomic policy is assumed not to respond to undesirable fluctuations in short-run economic activity. Monetary policy is assumed to be targeting a stock of nominal money balances in each economy. Fiscal policy is defined as a set of fixed tax rates (apart from a lump sum tax on households that varies to satisfy the intertemporal budget constraints facing the government) and government spending constant relative to simulated GDP. With higher output, tax revenues rise, implying a move towards fiscal surplus in each economy. In McKibbin (1996), higher growth meant lower fiscal deficits. In this chapter, higher growth leads to higher government spending and therefore fiscal deficits are relatively constant.

Table 8.4   *Percentage change in real GDP in 2020 from trade liberalisation*

	Own	ASEAN	APEC	Multilateral
United States	-0.04	0.03	0.23	0.23
Japan	-0.95	-0.01	-0.87	0.86
Australia	0.62	0.01	0.77	0.82
Indonesia	1.58	1.99	6.19	6.93
Malaysia	1.09	1.44	1.77	1.84
Philippines	-0.28	-0.18	1.99	2.26
Singapore	0.64	0.79	0.91	1.09
Thailand	-1.42	-1.14	1.00	1.40
China	0.46	-0.01	0.91	1.01
India	0.24	0.00	0.12	0.49
Taiwan	0.96	0.05	1.80	1.92
Korea	-0.66	-0.04	0.08	0.17
Hong Kong	0.00	0.04	0.16	0.18
ROECD	0.05	0.00	0.07	0.12

Source: AP-GCUBED model simulation.

Longer-run results

Tables 8.4 to 8.7 show results for GDP, consumption, investment and exports under the four assumptions about the group of countries undertaking trade liberalisation. The results in each table are the percentage deviation from what otherwise would have occurred by 2020 relative to the baseline projection of the model without any trade liberalisation.

Table 8.4 provides the results for real GDP. The first column contains the country names. The second column shows that the percentage deviation in US GDP from own liberalisation is -0.04 per cent relative to the baseline by 2020. This compares to a gain in GDP of 0.23 per cent under both APEC (column 4) and multilateral (column 5) liberalisation. For each country, GDP is higher when liberalisation is undertaken with other countries in a group than when undertaken alone. The highest gains for GDP occur under multilateral liberalisation. For some countries (the United States, Japan, the Philippines, Thailand and Korea), own liberalisation leads to a reduction in GDP. This implies that capital flows out of the liberalising economy into other economies as a result of the trade reforms. This is not necessarily a negative outcome, as can be seen from the results in Table 8.5 for consumption in each economy. All countries have higher consumption by 2020 under

Table 8.5   *Percentage change in real consumption in 2020 from trade*
             liberalisation

	Own	ASEAN	APEC	Multilateral
United States	0.16	0.14	1.30	1.19
Japan	0.21	0.01	0.51	0.54
Australia	1.08	1.04	1.20	1.26
Indonesia	1.66	2.00	5.48	6.00
Malaysia	4.46	5.29	7.21	7.40
Philippines	2.95	3.19	5.28	5.50
Singapore	0.73	1.57	2.51	2.61
Thailand	2.05	2.37	3.91	4.14
China	1.22	0.03	2.03	2.15
India	0.66	0.02	-0.04	0.71
Taiwan	3.42	0.18	6.80	7.26
Korea	0.78	0.01	2.33	2.52
Hong Kong	0.00	0.40	0.08	0.00
ROECD	0.39	0.02	0.18	0.58

Note: Results for consumption and exports are now expressed as percentage
           deviation from the baseline. In earlier versions of this chapter they were
           expressed as the percentage of GDP deviation from the baseline.
Source: AP-GCUBED model simulation.

unilateral liberalisation despite the fact that GDP falls in some countries. This is because the return to capital that is freed up as a result of the liberalisation is higher than in the baseline case, but some of this higher return is being earned outside the domestic economy.

The consumption results follow the same pattern as the GDP results as you move across the table from left to right, in the sense that consumption is higher when liberalising with a group of countries than when liberalising alone. This suggests that trade liberalisation, at least in the longer run, should be a 'prisoner's delight' in the Garnaut (1996) sense. A country's own liberalisation raises consumption and the liberalisation of other countries raises the first country's consumption even more. One point to note from the comparison between consumption and GDP is that for some countries, the gains from one's own liberalisation more than outweigh the gains to the same country from other countries' liberalisation. For example, the gains to Australia from

APEC liberalisation increase Australia's gain from its own liberalisation by 11 per cent and multilateral liberalisation increases these gains by 17 per cent. In contrast, for the United States, own liberalisation gains are small and most of the gains come from other countries' liberalisation. These relative differences reflect a number of factors including the amount of liberalisation being undertaken domestically relative to the amount being undertaken overseas (that is the United States does not need to do much). It also reflects the degree to which other liberalising economies are markets for home country products, the composition of home country production relative to the extent of distortions being removed in similar sectors in foreign economies as well as each country's initial reliance on international trade for income generation. The asymmetries across economies in many of these factors underlies the dispersion of results in Tables 8.4 and 8.5.

Table 8.5 illustrates another important point. For members of APEC, liberalisation within this regional grouping captures most of the gains from multilateral liberalisation because APEC is so large. It should be stressed that many developing countries are not counted in the multilateral liberalisation exercise.

Table 8.6 shows the percentage change in real private investment by 2020 relative to what it otherwise would have been in 2020. As indicated in the results for GDP, physical investment in some economies falls as a result of trade liberalisation. This fall in domestic investment is more than offset by a rise in home investment in foreign economies. Overall world investment rises.

Table 8.7 shows the effect of own versus alternative group liberalisations on real exports of each economy by 2020. In each case for each country, international trade expands. When an individual economy reduces tariffs, the nominal exchange rate depreciates, which causes a real depreciation and stimulates demand for exports. This also reflects the falling input costs in export sectors from the reduction in tariffs. In the group liberalisations these exchange rate effects are diminished because as more countries liberalise, there are fewer countries to depreciate against. Nonetheless, the stimulus to world trade is reinforced by the demand spillover effects of foreign countries reducing their tariffs and raising their demand for home country exports. In each case a greater number of countries liberalising leads to a larger expansion of exports for each country.

The results for 2020 accord with results from many studies using CGE models apart from the impact of endogenous capital accumulation and savings behaviour incorporated in the AP-GCUBED model.

Table 8.6   *Percentage change in real investment in 2020 from trade liberalisation*

	Own	ASEAN	APEC	Multilateral
United States	-0.14	0.33	2.84	2.66
Japan	-1.92	-0.12	-1.78	-1.85
Australia	3.55	-0.05	4.39	4.51
Indonesia	3.16	3.37	7.01	7.63
Malaysia	0.47	1.26	2.79	3.00
Philippines	2.37	2.53	3.50	3.58
Singapore	-0.49	-0.22	0.73	0.88
Thailand	0.40	0.49	1.80	2.01
China	0.62	-0.08	0.75	0.80
India	0.80	-0.03	-0.21	0.73
Taiwan	2.94	-0.11	4.37	4.51
Korea	-0.55	-0.16	0.31	0.36
Hong Kong	0.00	0.00	0.52	0.48
ROECD	0.99	-0.01	1.06	2.06

Source: AP-GCUBED model simulation.

Table 8.7   *Percentage change in real exports in 2020 from trade liberalisation*

	Own	ASEAN	APEC	Multilateral
United States	14.49	0.16	14.63	21.90
Japan	10.08	0.66	13.28	15.24
Australia	8.51	1.36	18.76	21.77
Indonesia	3.00	4.76	13.20	15.78
Malaysia	12.57	15.33	19.92	22.13
Philippines	12.67	14.93	30.95	34.46
Singapore	1.88	3.66	10.97	13.25
Thailand	22.30	24.00	34.93	38.31
China	12.17	0.76	19.77	21.93
India	8.65	2.72	14.76	32.40
Taiwan	11.77	0.95	17.24	18.71
Korea	7.57	0.72	14.17	16.00
Hong Kong	0.00	0.90	8.91	10.85
ROECD	5.35	0.49	6.68	12.08

Note: Results for consumption and exports are now expressed as percentage
deviation from the baseline. In earlier versions of this chapter they were
expressed as the percentage of GDP deviation from the baseline.

Source: AP-GCUBED model simulation.

Dynamic adjustment

We now turn to the dynamic adjustment from the time the tariff reductions are announced until 2020. This yields a vast amount of results for each country. Rather than presenting pages of numbers, a few select results will be presented in order to draw out some key insights.

Figure 8.1 presents the time path of real GDP for four countries: Australia, Taiwan, China and Indonesia. These countries are selected to represent a range of experiences. Australia is an industrialised economy liberalising by 2010, Taiwan is a developing economy liberalising by 2010, China is a developing economy liberalising by 2020 and Indonesia is a developing country but also part of the ASEAN regional bloc.

The first point to note is that GDP rises in each of these countries in the medium term and the more countries participating, the greater the increase. ASEAN liberalisation has a tiny impact on non-ASEAN economies and even for Indonesia, leads to small gains relative to its own liberalisation.

We now focus on the results for Australia in Figure 8.1. In the short run, the credible announcement of future tariff reductions leads to a reduction in GDP as firms begin to restructure in the early period. The gains to tariff reduction only accumulate over time as tariffs are cut, although some of these gains are bought forward through access to forward-looking asset markets. In the short run from 1996 to 1997, GDP grows less quickly than the base but after 1997 it grows more quickly than the baseline. By the year 2000, GDP is equal to the baseline GDP and after 2000, it is permanently above the baseline. For Australia and a range of countries not shown here, own liberalisation is costly in terms of GDP loss in the short term but substantially more beneficial in the medium and long term. Secondly, this figure and other results indicate that the more that other countries liberalise, the smaller the loss in short-run GDP and the larger the gain in long-run GDP. This is true for all countries in the model. Depending on the discount rate of political leaders, this may explain why countries are reluctant to undertake trade without liberalisation taking place in other countries. The problem with this strategy is that although all the short-term costs are the result of own liberalisation, most of the medium- and long-term gains are also due to own liberalisation. Thus free riding on the liberalisation of other countries may be an inferior policy strategy in the medium term. Unfortunately, short-sighted policy makers usually choose not to liberalise because of the short-term costs of own liberalisation.

The results for Australia also apply for each other economy although, in some cases such as Taiwan, China and Indonesia, the short-run losses disappear quickly. In the case of Indonesia, where there is a lot of growth already in the baseline, the absorption of dislocated resources occurs more quickly.

Figure 8.1 *Effects on GDP of trade liberalisation under alternative regional groupings, 1996–2020, per cent deviation from baseline*

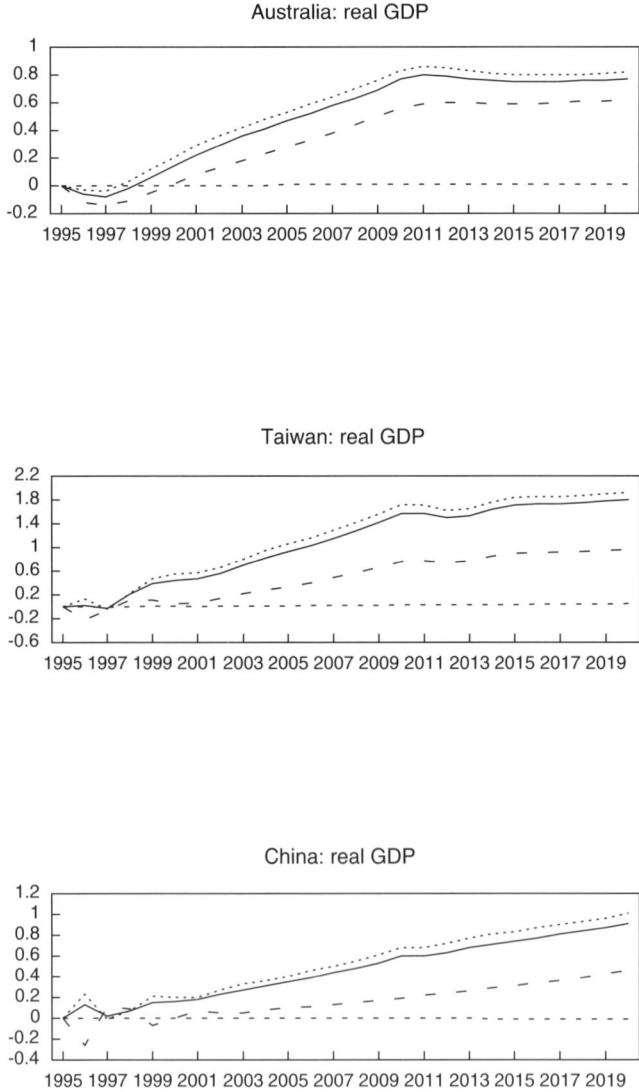

Australia: real GDP

Taiwan: real GDP

China: real GDP

Figure 8.1   *Effects on GDP of trade liberalisation under alternative regional*
groupings, 1996–2020, per cent deviation from baseline (cont.)

Indonesia: real GDP

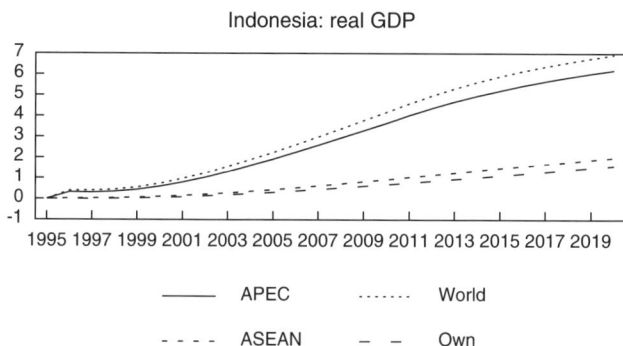

The results for consumption are shown in Figure 8.2 for the same group of countries. This is similar in many ways to the path of GDP (note the different scales) except that for some countries, the large future gains in income cause consumption to rise more quickly than GDP. These are also the countries that experience a trade balance deficit in the early period of liberalisation as consumers borrow from the rest of the world to take advantage of future income gains. In Australia the pick-up in consumption relative to GDP occurs from 2002. Before that year, the Keynesian style business cycle induced by sticky nominal wages leads to a low consumption path for a number of years. Most household consumption is constrained by the short-term slowdown in economic activity and the short-term rise in unemployment caused when prices fall but nominal wages are sticky. This effect is dampened in other economies by more rapid labour market adjustment.

Next, it is interesting to look at what adjustment occurs in the trade accounts of a representative economy under own liberalisation. Results for changes in exports, imports and the trade balance (as a percentage of GDP) for own liberalisation in Taiwan are contained in Figure 8.3. After the announcement of a policy on future tariff reductions in 1996, there is a realisation that in the future, the real exchange rate will depreciate. Financial markets are rational in this model and therefore the current nominal exchange rate depreciates in anticipation. With sticky nominal wages, the real exchange rate also depreciates in 1996. This reduces imports initially and increases exports. The trade balance improves slightly. Over time, as the tariff cuts are implemented, exports continue to rise through reduced input costs and imports also rise due to the fall in home prices for these imports. The trade

Figure 8.2   *Effects on private consumption of trade liberalisation under alternative regional groupings, 1996–2020, per cent deviation from baseline*

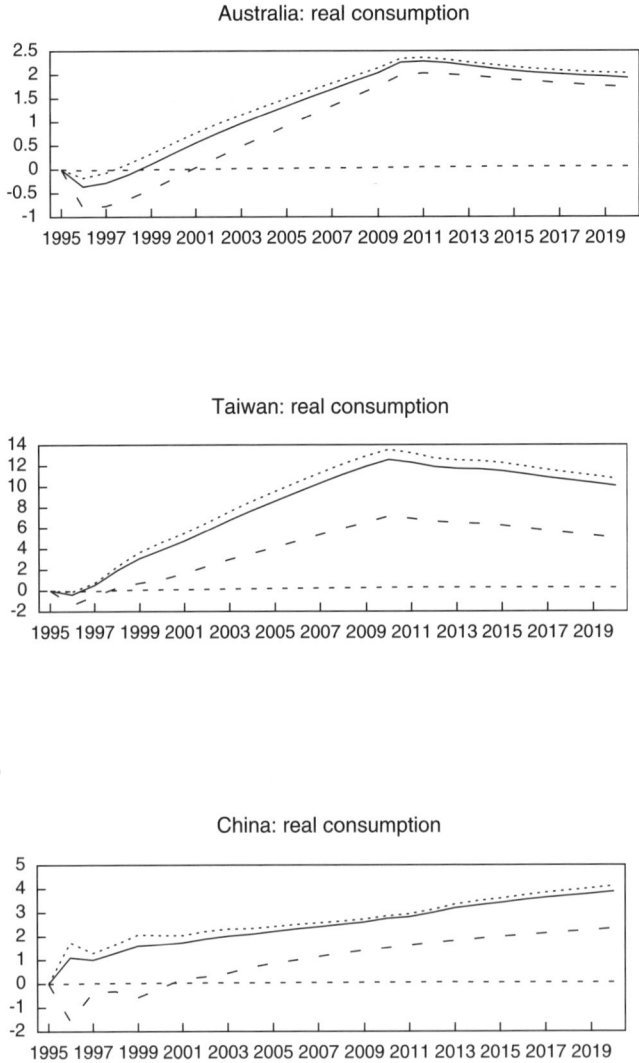

Australia: real consumption

Taiwan: real consumption

China: real consumption

Figure 8.2   *Effects on private consumption of trade liberalisation under alternative regional groupings, 1996–2020 (cont.)*

Indonesia: real consumption

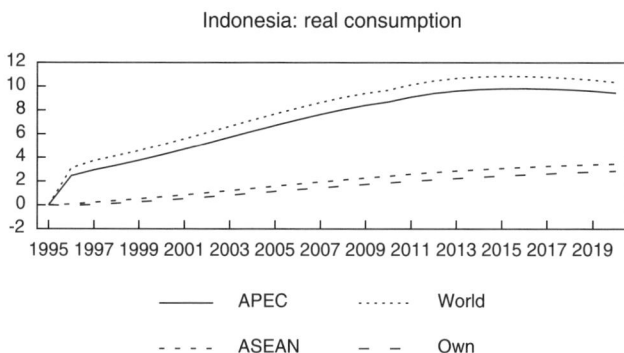

------- APEC   ······· World

- - - - ASEAN   – – Own

balance begins to deteriorate as households raise consumption relative to income in anticipation of future wealth gains and as the fiscal deficit marginally worsens due to the loss in tariff revenue. This borrowing against future income is not concentrated in the first few periods because households in this model are relatively myopic and future income only raises perceived wealth over relatively short time horizons. Once liberalisation is complete in 2010, note that the trade balance begins to improve again, reflecting the fact that debt accumulated before 2010 to raise consumption and investment levels must be serviced over time. The trade balance improvement reflects this repatriation of borrowing as well as repatriation of returns to equities from foreign direct investment in Taiwan. While the trade balance improves, this is reflected in both higher exports and imports.

Similar qualitative results for own liberalisation can be found for the other economies, although there are quantitative differences across economies.

Results for the trade balance adjustment in Taiwan under the alternative regional groupings are shown next in Figure 8.4. The case of own liberalisation is the same as that shown in Figure 8.3. In the case of both APEC and multilateral liberalisation, the deterioration in the trade balance is much greater. In this case the expected gains are also much greater and thus households borrow more to raise consumption and domestic firms borrow more to raise investment. Foreign capital also flows into Taiwan to take advantage of the higher expected returns in Taiwan. The real exchange rate depreciation is smaller in the short run because the inflow of capital tends to bid up the price of the Taiwanese dollar in real effective terms.

Figure 8.3   *Trade adjustment in Taiwan during unilateral liberalisation, 1996–*
            2010

Taiwan: trade flows

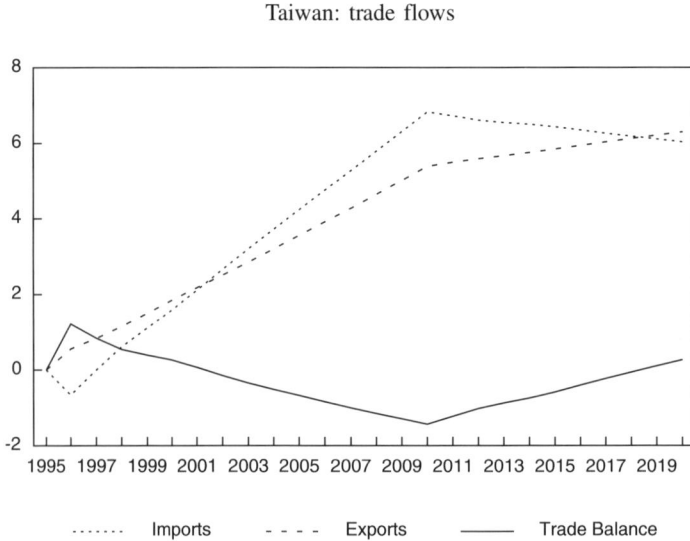

.... Imports   - - - - Exports   ——— Trade Balance

Similar patterns occur for other economies, although those economies undertaking more thoroughgoing liberalisation tend to attract greater capital inflows and countries such as the United States and ROECD regions tend to supply the capital to these liberalising regions.

Conclusion

This paper has offered empirical estimates of the long-run gains to trade liberalisation for a range of countries, primarily in the Asia Pacific region, under alternative assumptions about the grouping of countries. It is found that in the medium to long term, substantial gains are realised from own liberalisation *and* additional gains emerge for all countries from other countries' liberalisation. Multilateral liberalisation leads to larger overall economic gains for each country.

Figure 8.4 *Trade balance adjustment in Taiwan under alternative regional trade liberalisations, 1996–2010*

Taiwan: trade balance

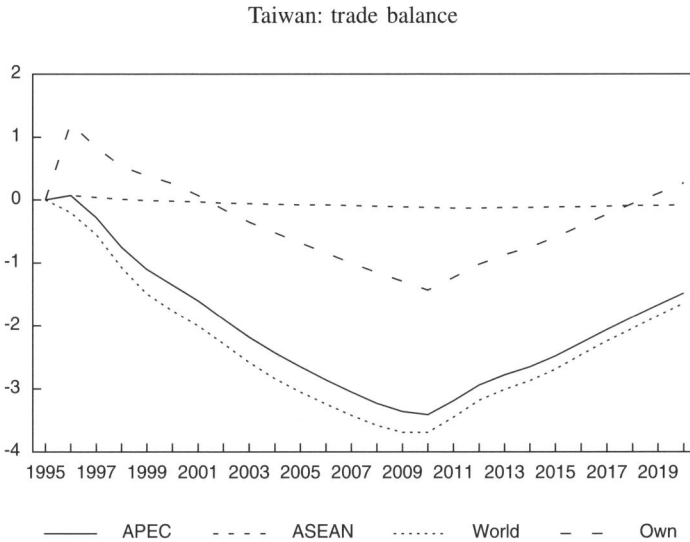

It is also found that the adjustment path to a phased liberalisation can exhibit short-run costs as resources begin to be reallocated before the trade reforms are implemented. To the extent that this is a problem, liberalisation by other countries at the same time as own liberalisation helps to reduce the short-run adjustment costs. There is an irony for some countries, such as Australia, in that a substantial part of the long-run gains are the result of own liberalisation. However, this liberalisation is also the source of short-run costs. These costs are related directly to the extent of labour market rigidities.

A significant amount of further research is required. The nature of the adjustment path is likely to be importantly affected by the timing of tariff cuts. In this chapter a simple linear implementation is assumed but the issue of optimal timing of tariff reductions is not addressed (see Wong 1997). Also, the role of macroeconomic policy adjustment in the short run is suggested by the results for this chapter but not directly evaluated. These issues will be explored in future research.

Notes

* This chapter is a revised version of the paper prepared for the CEPR/ESRC/GEI conference on 'Europe, East Asia, APEC and the Asia–Europe Meeting (ASEM) Process', London, 20–21 May, 1997. This chapter uses the Asia Pacific version of the G-CUBED Multi-country Model and data from the International Economics Databank (IEDB) at the ANU. I thank David Pearce at the Centre for International Economics (Canberra) for helpful discussion and Peter Sinclair and other participants at the conference for helpful comments. The views expressed are those of the authors and do not in any way reflect the views of the above-mentioned individuals or institutions nor the staff or trustees of the Brookings Institution or the Australian National University.

1 Trade in services is assumed not to be liberalised even though we can explore this in the modelling framework. This will be explored in future research.

2 Strictly speaking, public debt must be less than or equal to the present value of future budget surpluses. For tractability, we assume that the government is initially fully leveraged so that this constraint holds with equality.

3 In the model the tax is actually levied on the difference between interest payments on the debt and what interest payments would have been had the debt remained at its base case level. The remainder, interest payments on the base case debt, is financed by ordinary taxes.

References

Anderson, K. and R. Blackhurst eds (1993) *Regional Integration and the Global Trading System*, London: Harvester Wheatsheaf.

Armington, P. (1969) 'A theory of demand for products distinguished by place of production', *IMF Staff Papers*, vol. 16, pp. 159–76.

Bagnoli, P., W. McKibbin and P. Wilcoxen (1996) 'Future projections and structural change', in N. Nakicenovic, W. Nordhaus, R. Richels and F. Toth, eds, *Climate Change: Integrating Economics and Policy*, CP 9 6-1, International Institute for Applied Systems Analysis (Austria), pp. 181–206.

Bergsten, C.F. and M. Noland (1993) *Pacific Dynamism and the International Economic System*, Washington DC: Institute for International Economics.

Brown, D., A. Deardorff, A. Fox and R. Stern (1995) 'Computational analysis of goods and services liberalisation in the Uruguay Round', in Martin and Winters, pp. 365–82.

Campbell, J. and N.G. Mankiw (1987) 'Permanent income, current income and consumption', Working Paper 2436, National Bureau of Economic Research (NBER).

Deardorff, A.V. and R.M. Stern (1986) *The Michigan Model of World Production and Trade*, Cambridge: MIT Press.

Dee, P. and A. Welsh (1994) 'Implications for Australia of regional trading arrangements in Asia', in *Regional Trading Arrangements*, Office of EPAC, Canberra: AGPS, Background Paper No. 40, pp. 35–60.

Dervis, K., J. de Melo and S. Robinson (1982) *General Equilibrium Models for Development Policy*, Cambridge: Cambridge University Press.

Dornbusch, R. (1976) 'Expectations and exchange rate dynamics', *Journal of Political Economy* 84(16), pp. 1161–76.

Drysdale, P. and R. Garnaut (1994) *Asia Pacific Regionalism: Readings in International Economic Relations*, Australia: HarperEducational.

Fane, G. (1995) 'APEC: regionalism, globalism, or obfuscation?', *Agenda* 2(4), pp. 399–409.

François, J., B. McDonald and H. Nordstrom (1995) 'Assessing the Uruguay Round', in Martin and Winters, pp. 117–214.

Garnaut, R. (1996) *Open Regionalism and Trade Liberalisation*, Singapore: Institute of Southeast Asian Studies.

Goldin, I. and D. van der Mensbrugghe (1995) 'The Uruguay Round: an assessment of economywide and agricultural reforms', in Martin and Winters, pp. 25–52.

Harrison, G., T. Rutherford and D. Tarr (1995) 'Quantifying the Uruguay Round', in Martin and Winters, pp. 215–84.

Hayashi, F. (1979) 'Tobin's marginal q and average q: a neoclassical interpretation', *Econometrica* 50, pp. 213–24.

—— (1982) 'The permanent income hypothesis: estimation and testing by instrumental variables', *Journal of Political Economy* 90(4), pp. 895–916.

Hertel, T., W. Martin, K. Yanagishima and B. Dimaranan (1995) 'Liberalising manufactures trade in a changing world economy', in Martin and Winters, pp. 73–96.

Huff, K.M. et al, (1995) 'Medium-run consequences for Australia of an APEC free-trade area: CGE analysis using the GTAP and Monash models', Centre of Policy Studies and the Impact Project Working Paper G-III, April.

Jorgenson, Dale W. and Peter J. Wilcoxen (1990) 'Environmental regulation and US economic growth', *Rand Journal*, 21(2), pp. 314–40.

Lucas, R.E. (1967) 'Adjustment costs and the theory of supply', *Journal of Political Economy* 75(4), pp. 321–34.

—— (1973) 'Econometric policy evaluation: a critique', Carnegie Rochester Series on Public Policy, vol. 1, pp. 19–46.

Manchester, J. and W. McKibbin (1995) 'The global macroeconomics of NAFTA', *Open Economies Review* 6(3) pp. 203–23.

Martin, W. and L.A. Winters (1995) *The Uruguay Round and the Developing Economies*, World Bank Discussion Paper No. 307, Washington DC: World Bank.

McKibbin, W.J. (1994) 'Dynamic adjustment to regional integration: Europe 1992 and NAFTA', *Journal of the Japanese and International Economies* 8(4), pp. 422–53.

—— (1996) 'Quantifying APEC trade liberalisation: a dynamic analysis', *Working Paper in Trade and Development*, No. 1, Economics Department, Research School of Pacific and Asian Studies, ANU. Also *Brookings Discussion Paper in International Economics*, No. 122, Washington DC: The Brookings Institution.

—— and T. Bok (1993) 'The Asia–Pacific region in an integrated world economy', paper for the Economic Modelling Bureau of Australia Conference on the Asia Pacific Economy, Cairns, Australia, 25–28 August.

——, D. Pearce and A. Wong (1995) 'The economics effects of APEC', Canberra: Centre for International Economics.

—— and J. Sachs (1991) *Global Linkages: Macroeconomic Interdependence and Co-operation in the World Economy*, Brookings Institution, June.

—— and D. Salvatore (1995) 'The global economic consequences of the Uruguay Round', *Open Economies Review* 6(2), pp. 111–29.

—— and M. Sundberg (1995) 'Macroeconomic linkages between the OECD and the Asian Pacific region', in D. Currie and D. Vines, eds, *North–South Linkages and International Macroeconomic Policy*, CEPR and Cambridge University Press, pp. 235–72.

—— and P. Wilcoxen (1992) 'GCUBED: a dynamic multi-sector general equilibrium growth model of the global economy', *Brookings Discussion Papers in International Economics*, No. 97.

—— and P. Wilcoxen (1995) 'The theoretical and empirical structure of the GCUBED model', *Brookings Discussion Paper in International Economics,* No. 119, Brookings Institution.

—— and A. Wong (1997) 'Modelling Asia Pacific interdependence: the Asia–Pacific GCUBED model', mimeo, forthcoming, ANU, Canberra.

Murtough, G., Y. Mai, S. Zheng and D. Vanzetti (1994) 'APEC trade liberalisation post Uruguay Round: a general equilibrium analysis', paper presented to the Conference of *The Economist*, September.

Shoven, J. and J. Whalley (1984) 'Applied general equilibrium models of taxation and international trade: an introduction and survey', *Journal of Economic Literature*, vol. 22, pp. 1007–51.

Treadway, A. (1969) 'On rational entrepreneurial behaviour and the demand for investment', *Review of Economic Studies* 36(106), pp. 227–39.

Vines, D. (1994) 'Australian trade liberalisation, APEC and the GATT', Shann Lecture.

Whalley, J. (1985) *Trade Liberalisation among the Major World Trading Areas*, Cambridge: MIT Press.

Wong, A. (1997) 'The dynamics of trade liberalisation: a multi-country dynamic general equilibrium growth model analysis', unpublished seminar paper, Australian National University.

Part IV

Linkages between Europe and East Asia

9 Europe's trade, investment and strategic policy interests in Asia and APEC

ROLF J. LANGHAMMER

Introduction

For many years, Asia in general and East Asia in particular were able to sidestep policy pressures from Europe. Asia was too poor to absorb high fashion European consumer goods and sophisticated European technology. It was too rich in terms of its own resource mobilisation to be a major recipient of concessional European funding. It was too fragmented to negotiate with Europe on equal terms. It was too homogeneous in terms of growth dynamics to be convinced by the European Union (EU) that 'Fortress Europe' was not in decline. It was too passive in Geneva at the GATT (General Agreement on Tariffs and Trade) to be integrated into the EU strategy of *de facto* bilateral (EU–US) trade negotiations ('principal supplier rule') within a *de jure* multilateral framework. Finally, it was too active in penetrating the EU market to be exempted from the EU toolbox of contingent protection in food products, steel, textiles, clothing and footwear.

Profound changes were needed both on the EU and the Asian side to relinquish this stance of 'benign neglect', to re-shape mutual perceptions and interests and to participate in the tango called ASEM (Asia–Europe Meeting). Such changes have taken place under conditions of globalising production and markets, an unprecedented rise in Asian income levels, sustained growth differentials between Asia and Europe, a deepening and widening of the process of EU integration, the transformation of former centrally planned economies in both Europe and Asia into market economies and, finally, some attempts in Asia to coordinate and articulate common interests *vis-à-vis* the European Union at a sub-regional or bilateral level. Since 1996 this has also occurred at a regional level.

This chapter highlights Europe's recent economic performance in Asia and identifies some of the driving forces behind Europe's heightened interest in Asia. Euro–Asian relations have not been analysed to the same extent as Asian interest in EU markets. This chapter examines European interests in

Asia and identifies the main actors. The broad statistical trends in European exports to Asia are then outlined, followed by an analysis of European investment patterns in Asia. The next section points to features of recent policy changes in foreign relations initiated by Brussels and examines their possible underlying motives. Before presenting some conclusions on these findings, some questions are raised about ageing Europe's interests and expectations in regard to financing pensions through investment in high growth and lower income Asia.

Disentangling the actors

The European Union has no telephone number. Henry Kissinger's famous answer to the question of differences between the United States and the European Union comes to mind when analysing Europe's policy stance towards East Asia.[1] A European perspective on Asia is more complex than the view held by a single country. As well as the private household view (often neglected but politically increasingly important), the domestic company view, the traders' view and the national politicians' view, an additional layer is the perspective of official EU institutions (the Commission, the Ministerial Council and the Parliament).

Private households in Europe have ambivalent views about emerging Asia. First, it is seen as a source of rising real consumer income due to the fierce competition between Asian economies on the international goods markets (and including services like tourism and transport). There is a general understanding among European consumers that due to Asia's supply power they have enjoyed gains in terms of trade. Second, and increasingly important in the debate on 'fair' standards, Asia is seen as a threat to European factor income levels. European trade unionists, environmentalists and other lobby groups are alert to two key messages arising from the globalisation of production and markets. The first is that low-skilled European labour in import-competing industries has to cope with an abundant Asian labour supply in the finished goods trade and in the outsourcing of intermediate industries. In future, such competition may be extended to include embodied services if Asian migration is allowed after the liberalisation of trade in services scheduled by the World Trade Organization (WTO). Furthermore, modern telecommunications technology has unleashed the prospect of the production of disembodied services which are tradeable in the European Union regardless of the source of supply. In addition, private households in Europe, primarily the younger ones, are coming to see Asia as an emerging location for investment of pension funds and other instruments of old age insurance.

This perception is not always accompanied by an appreciation of the fact that investment returns will be curtailed if protectionist standards are imposed. These messages have proliferated in the absence of a Europe-wide lobby group. Brussels-based consumer associations and trade unions have not yet established a firm basis in political decision making.

The other group of actors comprises EU-based private companies. They may be either national or global players but they are not 'EU' companies and hence do not usually see the world from Brussels. They compete with each other as they compete with US or Japanese companies. Strategic alliances between EU-based companies do not embrace a specific EU philosophy. This does not preclude the possibility that they might use the EU framework to influence the regulation of market access, for instance in filing anti-dumping complaints, or to benefit from EU subsidies granted under the condition that they do not enter into strategic alliances with non-EU companies operating in the same market (see below). Traditionally, European companies have preferred direct exports over investment in Asia because of their small and medium-sized scale of operations and because of incentives to invest at home. As will be shown below, this preference seems to have been gradually eroded in recent years. In their view Asia is becoming their most buoyant export market, not simply because of strong import demand following high growth, but because of emerging growth bottlenecks in Asian infrastructure and environment — two sectors where European companies offer state-of-the-art technology. To exploit the market potential and to adapt technology to local conditions, production in the host country is indispensable. Unlike the situation a couple of years ago, Asian markets today have reached income levels which are rated sufficient and sustainable to host high technology EU-based companies profitably.

National policy views on Asia usually respond to domestic industry demands for 'gate-opening' support from politicians. Such support ranges from subsidising the establishment of a network of market information building to political lobbying for large-scale national 'champions' such as the French defence industry, the German railway/transrapid industry or the British telecommunications industry. Again, EU companies compete against each other and there is no EU umpire in such competition.

What distinguishes the 'Brussels' view from the EU country view is what I call the Triad perspective. EU institutions almost unanimously take the United States and/or Japan as their yardstick when assessing Europe's performance in third markets. Trade analyses and studies on foreign direct investment (FDI) are structured in this way. In financial markets, the euro is assessed in terms of its capability to match the role of the dollar as an invoice currency as well as a transactions currency in international bond markets. Second, there is a tendency to see bilateral relations in terms of balances or imbalances in trade and investment. This view is not as pronounced as in US trade policies but persistent imbalances are regretted and monitored if they show up in a deficit for the European Union (for instance, *vis-à-vis* Japan [WTO 1995: 12]). Official EU policies tend not to recognise that such a view is economically meaningless and that it reflects mercantilism. Third, elements of a common foreign and security policy enter EU negotiations on external relations with Asian countries — for instance, when a minimum consensus on human rights is adopted by the European Union (or by a blocking minority of EU member states) — as an essential prerequisite for institutionalised economic relations. Such firm positions do not seem to be apparent at the individual EU country level. Overall, at the EU level, 'big' foreign affairs issues are merged with 'down to earth' issues in negotiations on economic cooperation to achieve parity with the two other members of the Triad.

Europe's export performance in Asia

Asian and European export markets

In 1980, Japan and developing Asia as two sub-regions of total Asia were of minor importance as markets for EU exports compared with the importance of the European Union as a market for Asian exports. Given the large differentials in income levels and absorptive capacity, this was not surprising and held for trade between Asia and the United States, too. What has been remarkable in the EU–developing Asia context, is the speed with which developing Asia has emerged as an export market for the European Union.

Table 9.1 tries to capture these shifts by calculating a ratio of 'bilateral export market convergence'.[2] Rising ratios indicate the growing importance of developing Asia and Japan as export markets to the European Union (using the United States as a yardstick) relative to the importance of the European Union (and the United States) as export markets for Asia. This rise was much more pronounced in bilateral trade between the European Union and Asia than in trade over the Pacific with the United States.[3] Hence, while it is correct to say that the importance of each to the other has converged (AJRC 1996: 1), it has to be added that by 1994 the European Union was closer to 'full' convergence (taking a ratio of one as full convergence) than the United States. For EU trade with Japan, the old divergence (the Japanese market being much less important for the European Union than the EU market for Japan) still holds but ratios have tripled from a very low base. This is in contrast to the situation in 1980 when the European Union was nine times as

Table 9.1   *'Bilateral export market convergence'[a] ratios in trade between Asia and the EU, and Asia and the US, 1980–94*

	Total trade				Trade in manufactures (SITC 5+6+7+8-67-68)				Trade in machinery and transport equipment (SITC 7)			
	Dev. Asia/ EU	Japan/ EU	Dev. Asia/ US	Japan/ US	Dev. Asia/ EU	Japan/ EU	Dev. Asia/ US	Japan/ US	Dev. Asia/ EU	Japan/ EU	Dev. Asia/ US	Japan/ US
1980	0.35	0.11	0.40	0.39	0.33	0.17	0.40	0.22	0.44	0.10	0.27	0.15
1990	0.48	0.29	0.47	0.39	0.46	0.29	0.39	0.29	0.49	0.24	0.36	0.23
1991	0.49	0.27	0.51	0.39	0.46	0.27	0.43	0.29	0.51	0.22	0.40	0.23
1992	0.53	0.25	0.50	0.38	0.51	0.25	0.43	0.28	0.57	0.19	0.42	0.23
1993	0.63	0.29	0.52	0.36	0.62	0.29	0.47	0.26	0.68	0.24	0.49	0.20
1994	0.67	0.33	0.53	0.35	0.68	0.33	0.46	0.27	0.76	0.27	0.47	0.23

Note: a   Ratio between the share of developing Asia in extra-EU (or US) exports and the share of the EU (or US) in extra-developing Asia's (or Japanese) exports (columns 1,3,5,7,9,11) and ratio between the share of Japan in extra-EU (or US) exports and the share of the EU (or US) in Japanese exports (columns 2,4,6,8,10,12). Developing Asia excludes Middle East and includes China. As in the EU case, trade within developing Asia (intra-trade) is excluded.

Source: UN, *Monthly Bulletin of Statistics*, various issues. Author's calculations.

important as an export market to Japan than vice versa. The ratio was only three to one fourteen years later. Such swings could not be observed in trade over the Pacific. By 1994, the US market remained significantly more important for developing Asia's exports than the converse. There were ups and downs with no clear trend in trade between the United States and Japan, but recent shifts seem to point to a higher relative importance of the United States in Japanese exports.

A sectoral breakdown supports these observations for trade in manufactures and its most dynamic sub-category, trade in machinery and transport equipment (Standard Industry Trade Classification [SITC] 7). Looking at the latter category, the shift to convergence in trade between the European Union and developing Asia is even more pronounced, showing the extent to which developing Asia has emerged as an export market for European products compared with trade in the other direction. Again, the trend in convergence holds for Asian trade with the United States, but without such a rapid increase. In technical terms, the ratios do not show much dispersion and range below 0.5.

The strong convergence between the European Union and developing Asia is not due to the disproportionate increase in developing Asia's absorption of European products but reflects weak EU import demand relative to the import demand of developing Asia's other trading partners. The EU share in extra-developing Asia's manufactured exports stagnated at the 25 per cent level for the 1980–94 period and the small increase in shares in total exports was entirely due to temporary hikes in commodity prices for oil. Hence, as manufactured products gained a greater share in the export supply of developing Asia, the importance of the European Union as an export market for developing Asia has stagnated. The question as to which factors in above average 'resistances to trade' (Fukasaku and Martineau 1996: 7) are binding, growth induced or policy induced (or exhibit 'objective' versus 'subjective' distance, [Drysdale and Garnaut 1993]), deserves special attention but is not the subject of this chapter. In any case, for this trade, traditional gravity type models which include 'objective' (geographical) distance as a trade resistance factor are likely to raise more questions than offer answers.

Is the European Union really looking east?

Without doubt, Asia has emerged as an increasingly important export market for Europe in recent years. Yet, given that the European Union is behind Japan and the United States in penetrating developing Asian markets, one may ask whether the gap between the other two economies of the Triad has been closed or at least narrowed over the same period. Such catching up could be measured by comparing Asia's shares in the world exports of the Triad. Table 9.2 suggests that, in spite of the increasing importance of developing Asia in EU exports, in 1994 developing Asia in general had not yet attained an importance as an export market comparable with that for the United States and, in particular, for Japan. Changes in Asia's shares in Triad exports between 1991 and 1994, the period for which the EU Commission has published a detailed Triad comparison (EC 1995), have generally been smaller for the European Union than for Japan, and they have been only slightly higher than for the United States. The European Union failed to catch up with the Asian share in Japanese exports and the catch-up in relation to the United States was not sufficient to match the United States' advantage as an earlier starter in developing Asia.

Table 9.2 allows for regional disaggregation among Asian economies. In this respect, it is striking how far ASEAN (Association of Southeast Asian Nations) and especially the original four newly industrialising economies (Hong Kong, Korea, Singapore, Taiwan) or NIE4[4] are ahead as destination

Table 9.2 *Share of Asian sub-regions in Triad world exports, 1994, per cent and percentage point change over 1991*

	EU		US		Japan	
	1994	Change over 1991	1994	Change over 1991	1994	Change over 1991
China	2.3	+1.0	1.8	+0.3	4.7	+2.0
ASEAN	5.2	+1.1	6.2	+1.3	15.3	+3.3
NIE4	7.6	+1.5	11.6	+0.8	23.6	+2.4
South Asia	1.9	+0.1	0.7	-0.1	1.0	-0.2
ANZ	1.9	+0.2	2.2	0.0	2.6	+0.2

Source: EC (1995). Author's calculations.

areas in US and Japanese exports compared with the European Union. Two 'outlier' results deserve attention. First, South Asia has a much higher weight as an export market for the European Union than for the other two members of the Triad, and this gap has even increased because the region has declined in the export baskets of the United States and Japan while it has risen in the EU basket. This discrepancy mirrors a familiar pattern in the regional export structure of the European Union: in the past, the European Union seems to have been strong in weakly growing markets and weak in strongly growing markets. Compared with developing East Asia, South Asia definitely has been a weakly growing market. Second, compared to China's position in US exports, the largest economy in Asia has become more important for EU exports during the early 1990s. But still, China plays a much larger role in Japanese exports than in EU exports.

While the European Union has begun to look east, the other two members of the Triad still seem to look more sharply in this direction, with the exception of South Asia, which has remained a traditional European export stronghold.

Sectoral and sub-regional heterogeneity: a closer look at export structures

Developing Asia is known for its heterogeneity in income levels, market size and openness. Given this heterogeneity, it is of interest whether EU exports position themselves differently in different sub-regions and whether Japanese and US competitors follow similar diversification paths as EU suppliers, or go their own way.

Table 9.3 introduces a ratio between 1991–94 growth rates of aggregate product category exports to Asian sub-regions and the world (as the normaliser) for each of the Triad members. Beyond specific features, a number of common elements in the specialisation profiles of Triad members emerge.

First, among the sub-regions and across almost all product categories, Triad member exports to Japan have grown less than world exports, in contrast to exports to the other sub-regions, which have grown disproportionately. There is the notable exception of the disproportionately high growth in US transport equipment exports to Japan, which may reflect the outcome of the bilateral US–Japan deal in automobiles under the Structural Impediments Initiative (SII) talks. Second, the Chinese market in general and its market for transport equipment in particular has been a principal target of export offensives of all Triad members, with the European Union showing the highest increase in exports relative to its world exports. Third, the chemical industry emerges as the counter pole to transport equipment. It has been a slow mover in exports to Asia and for some sub-regions even shows negative export growth rates. It seems that the chemical industry meets stronger demand in high-income areas such as Japan, Australia and New Zealand than in developing Asia. Fourth, some bilateral supplier–destination country relations are worth mentioning. While the European Union is strongly positioned in South Asia, Japan and the United States seem to by-pass this sub-region (again, except in transport equipment). EU suppliers have made strong efforts to catch up with Japan and the United States in penetrating NIE4 markets in which the two other countries had already marked their claims before the entry of the European Union.

The extent to which shares of the European Union in Triad exports to individual Asian sub-regions differ from each other is demonstrated in Table 9.4. At one extreme, there is the dominant and even strengthened position of the European Union in South Asia, the most weakly growing market among the sub-regions. In 1994, the European Union accounted for about two-thirds of Triad exports. The other extreme is marked by ASEAN and the NIE4. Only about a quarter of Triad exports to these two sub-regions came from the European Union. In ASEAN, the EU export share was even declining while for exports to the NIE4, EU gains in shares were small in spite of the low base. In between these two extremes are EU shares to Japan, China, Australia and New Zealand. Overall, there is no convergence in shares between the sub-regions. Neither is there sectoral homogeneity in the sense that the European Union shares a common specialisation profile with the other Triad members in all sub-regions. The EU chemical industry tops Triad exports in Japan, South Asia, Australia and New Zealand but not in ASEAN,

Table 9.3   *Relative growth^a of EU, US and Japanese exports to Asia and Asian sub-regions, by product categories, 1991–94, per cent*

From	To	Japan	China	ASEAN	NIE4	Sth Asia	ANZ
EU	Total trade	0.74	3.68	2.05	1.98	1.25	1.39
	Manufactures	0.69	3.47	1.79	1.84	1.24	1.37
	Machinery	0.83	3.95	1.63	1.52	1.20	1.68
	Transport equipment	0.46	5.24	2.21	2.16	2.41	1.34
	Chemicals	0.84	-0.36	1.41	1.21	1.09	1.30
US	Total trade	0.63	1.86	2.03	1.32	0.44	0.96
	Manufactures	0.75	1.82	1.84	1.37	0.55	0.89
	Machinery	0.55	2.48	1.84	1.42	1.42	1.07
	Transport equipment	2.31	4.51	1.49	1.64	4.15	0.31
	Chemicals	0.39	-0.30	1.67	0.99	-1.30	0.70
Japan	Total trade	–	3.28	1.95	1.41	0.34	1.30
	Manufactures	–	3.32	1.99	1.40	0.38	1.25
	Machinery	–	3.54	1.95	1.40	0.25	0.84
	Transport equipment	–	5.95	2.24	1.75	0.00	2.07
	Chemicals	–	0.55	1.53	1.03	1.15	0.80

Note: *a* Ratio between average annual growth rates of product category exports to the sub-region and to the world (EU: extra-EU exports).
Source: See Table 2.

China or the NIE4. Similarly, EU machinery exports are leading in China and South Asia while they are far behind the US and Japanese supply in the NIE4. The same weak position applies in exports of transport equipment to Australia and New Zealand. Obviously, Asian sub-markets are still heterogenous in spite of intra-area trade expansion. Barriers to dismantling market segmentation seem to be particularly strong between South Asia and the rest of developing Asia. Anecdotal evidence from technology used in Indian metal manufacturing suggests the existence of some sort of path dependence once a particular technology (in this case a European one) has been established.

Patterns in Triad sectoral export patterns to Asian sub-regions

EU supply in Asia does not only differ regionally from that of the other Triad members. There are also distinct differences in the sectoral pattern of Triad exports. Table 9.5 tries to capture the degree of such differences by measur-

Table 9.4   *EU share in Triad exports to Asian sub-regions, by product categories, 1994, per cent and percentage point change over 1991*

	Japan		China		ASEAN		NIE4		South Asia		ANZ	
	1994	Change over 1991	1994	Change over 1991	1994	Change over 1991	1994	Change over 1991	1994	Change over 1991	1994	Change over 1991
Total Trade	37.0	+0.6	34.5	+2.7	26.3	-0.6	23.9	+1.8	63.3	+4.6	35.3	+0.9
Manufactures	43.5	-0.3	34.9	+3.8	25.5	-0.5	23.8	+2.2	64.6	+5.1	34.8	+2.0
Machinery	28.8	+1.0	40.4	+2.1	20.8	-2.2	17.3	-0.1	59.6	+3.2	35.2	+3.4
Transport equipment	47.7	-6.5	35.9	+7.4	24.7	+3.2	25.1	+4.6	50.0	+11.5	16.7	+0.7
Chemicals	51.6	+4.9	22.6	-3.2	36.4	0	29.7	+2.0	61.9	+11.9	50.0	+6.0

Source: See Table 2.

ing ratios between product category shares of the EU and US (and Japanese) exports to Asian sub-regions. Deviations from unity indicate the degree of difference.

Overall, they are substantial, both for exports to a single sub-region over product categories and for exports in a single product category over sub-regions. To begin with the latter, machinery exports, for instance, have a much higher weight in EU exports to China (relative to the United States or Japan) than in EU exports to ASEAN and the NIE4. In the latter sub-region, however, EU chemical exports play a relatively stronger role than in exports to China. With respect to the former, it seems to make a difference whether US or Japanese export structures are taken as the yardstick. EU exports of transport equipment to China are low if US exports are taken as the yardstick, but high if measured against Japanese exports.

What can we learn from such differences? In part, they seem to reflect the normal diversification strategies of suppliers but, as mentioned above, they may also result from establishing and defending technological leadership in some industries in the Asian sub-regions. It is remarkable that differences seem to be largest in South Asia, which is considered to be the most heavily regulated and the least dynamic of the four sub-regions of developing Asia. This gives rise to the hypothesis that efforts to erode market leadership established by a Triad member may also face policy-induced access barriers which act against leadership erosion even if they are not targeted against individual suppliers. To analyse this hypothesis, however, is outside the scope of this chapter.

Table 9.5   *EU sectoral export profiles in Asia relative to the US and Japan,[a]
1991–94*

		China	ASEAN	Machinery	NIE4	South Asia	ANZ
EU:US	1991	1.90	0.87	0.97	1.47	0.92
	1992	1.88	0.83	0.90	1.34	1.04
	1993	1.58	0.85	0.86	1.02	0.88
	1994	1.66	0.76	0.81	1.07	0.93
EU:Japan	1991	1.09	0.78	0.64	0.68	0.85
	1992	1.02	0.74	0.62	0.68	1.00
	1993	1.22	0.77	0.62	0.78	1.02
	1994	1.15	0.73	0.60	0.73	1.07
		Transport equipment				
EU:US	1991	0.61	0.75	0.69	0.83	0.50
	1992	0.70	0.77	0.71	0.76	0.38
	1993	0.54	0.66	0.63	0.32	0.74
	1994	0.77	1.09	0.83	0.69	0.64
EU:Japan	1991	1.23	0.75	1.17	0.31	0.27
	1992	1.82	0.87	1.09	0.28	0.22
	1993	1.30	0.69	0.99	0.31	0.23
	1994	1.32	0.85	1.31	0.51	0.25
		Chemicals				
EU:US	1991	0.52	1.29	1.23	0.43	1.06
	1992	0.56	1.38	1.25	0.61	1.28
	1993	0.57	1.37	1.24	0.80	1.23
	1994	0.34	1.41	1.26	0.72	1.26
EU:Japan	1991	1.10	1.76	1.45	1.67	3.11
	1992	1.00	1.70	1.41	1.71	3.74
	1993	0.87	1.71	1.43	1.26	4.70
	1994	0.80	1.73	1.40	1.32	3.70
		Other manufactured products				
		(textiles, clothing, iron, steel, paper, non-metallic mineral products)				
EU:US	1991	1.21	1.44	1.79	2.33	1.79
	1992	1.26	1.55	1.89	2.84	1.70
	1993	1.58	1.65	1.91	4.39	1.48
	1994	1.35	1.62	2.02	2.55	1.41
EU:Japan	1991	0.39	1.00	1.06	1.74	1.55
	1992	0.41	1.02	1.14	1.59	1.73
	1993	0.53	1.12	1.24	1.77	1.88
	1994	0.40	1.19	1.32	1.61	1.87

Note: a   Ratio between the shares of the product category in total EU exports and
of US–Japan exports to the Asian sub-region.
Source: See Table 2. Author's calculations.

Have EU exporters chosen the right product mix in developing Asia?

The above analysis has shown that Asian markets are still far from homogeneous for EU exporters. Traditionally, EU exporters have maintained strong positions in South Asia and relatively weak positions in the NIE4, and their supply patterns vary across markets. Yet, one cannot deny that recent developments show that the European Union is slowly catching up with the two other Triad members, in particular with the United States. Relatively neglected markets such as the NIE4 have been given more attention and the European Union's performance in China is among the best in the Triad group.

A synopsis of these developments is presented in Figure 9.1 in which the horizontal axis shows 1991–94 average annual growth of import demand in Asian sub-regions for 12 manufacturing industries approximated by the export growth rates of the Triad countries. This proxy excludes imports within developing Asia and is therefore biased towards capital goods imports from OECD (Organisation for Economic Cooperation and Development) countries only. The vertical axis shows average annual growth rates of EU exports in the same industries and to the same sub-regions. The vertical line indicating average Triad export growth rates to all developing Asian countries for all products (15.8 per cent) and the horizontal line indicating average EU export growth rates (17.5 per cent) divide the graph into four quadrants of either disproportionate or less than proportionate export growth. Export growth on the 45° dotted northeast line comprises all industries in which EU suppliers would have achieved the same growth rate as all Triad suppliers. Deviations from this line indicate differences between EU growth performance and the Asian sub-region's demand for OECD imports. For the sum of 48 observations, the figure shows that, by and large, EU suppliers follow Triad patterns of exports. Given that there are more observations above the 45° line than below, one can even identify a small catching-up process characterised by more than proportionate EU growth of exports particularly to ASEAN and NIE4 countries. Hence, it seems that in recent years EU exporters have chosen the appropriate product mix to challenge US and Japanese shares in Asian export markets.

Trade in services: a promising export field?

Trade in services is part of the most rapidly growing segment in total trade. This is in part due to a new quality in cross-border mobility of persons, goods and physical capital. Human capital has become mobile, too, obviating the

Figure 9.1 *EU and Triad export growth to Asia 1991–94 by manufacturing industries and Asian sub-regions*

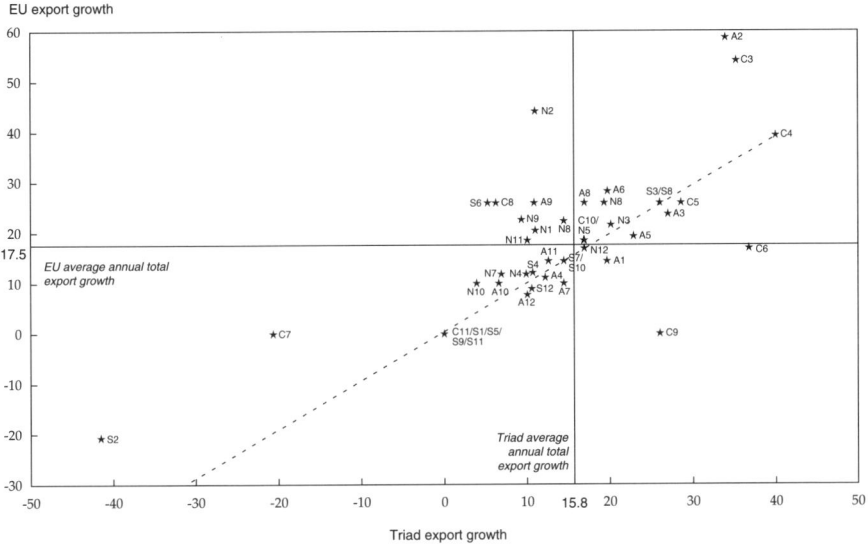

Notes: Exports in the following industries: 1 Non-ferrous metals, 2 Fuels, 3 Office/ telecom. equipment, 4 Power//Non-elect. machinery, 5 Elect. machinery/ apparat., 6 Automotive products, 7 Medical pharm. products, 8 Plastics, 9 Textiles and clothing, 10 Iron and steel, 11 Paper/articles of paper, 12 Non-metal. min. manuf.
Exports to: C = China, A = ASEAN, N = NIEs 4, S = South Asia.

Souce: See Table 9.2.

need for consumers of services to move to producers and vice versa and without requiring the physical movement of goods. Such disembodied services owe their existence to the revolution in information technologies which has made knowledge a tradeable good and shifted production from centralised plants to decentralised 'networks'. To the extent to which trade in these technologies becomes disembodied, trade in services is stimulated. Asia is known for bottlenecks in infrastructure and it was recently identified as such a market when urban life and urban technology were chosen as leading issues in fairs to promote the technological potential of the European Union.

There are significant (but not insurmountable) statistical hurdles to quantifying the amount of knowledge traded cross-border, since many of these 'goods' are intangibles and their movement from residents to non-residents goes unreported. Disaggregated EU data on trade in services in general, and of disembodied services in particular, are flawed, dated and incomplete. Hence, any fresh information on bilateral trade in services has to rely on individual EU country data which may not be representative of the European Union as an entity. Bearing these caveats in mind, one can nevertheless try to estimate the importance of Asia as an export market for European services from the few available national sources. One such source is the German Bundesbank, which offers a relatively detailed statistical breakdown of reported payments related to flows of so-called technological services including payments for patents, licences, engineering services, research and development (R&D) and data processing services (Table 9.6). Between 1992 and 1995, total Asia comprised about one-fifth of German extra-EU 'exports' of technological services (with a slightly rising trend). Roughly the same share is reported for total non-factor service income, which includes tourism, transport, banking and insurance, as well as for German merchandise exports. Interestingly, China and other Asia rather than Japan purchased the lion's share of such services from Germany. Among the NIE4, it is not the main recipient of German FDI, Singapore, which appears as the major customer, but Korea. Again, bearing all qualifications concerning data quality in mind, one can argue that service exports to Asia are growing at least as fast as merchandise exports and that Asia will become an increasingly important market for technological services.

EU foreign direct investment in East Asia: latecoming, but slowly gathering speed

EU company presence in Asia in the past

For many years, observers of EU performance in Asia have monitored low EU foreign direct investment (FDI) in Asia. The controversy over whether this has been due to either demand-side conditions (less favourable treatment of EU potential investors in Asia compared with US or Japanese companies or a general latecomer disadvantage) or whether supply-side conditions (incentives to prefer other hosts) have worked against EU investment has been settled in favour of a majority conclusion: supply-side conditions matter much more. To mention a few of the arguments in support of supply-side effects:[5]

Table 9.6   *Share of Asia in German income from extra-EU countries for patents, licences, engineering services, R&D and data processing services, 1992–95, per cent*

Importing country	1992	1993	1994	1995
Japan	7.0	8.1	7.9	8.3
China	0.9	1.0	1.7	2.5
Other Asia	10.9	12.2	13.3	10.9
of which				
Singapore	0.3	0.5	0.6	0.5
Korea	1.8	2.3	1.8	2.6
Total Asia	18.8	21.3	22.9	21.7
Share of Asia in total German extra-EU non-factor				
service income	19.9	21.4	21.6	22.8

Source: Deutsche Bundesbank (1996).

- EU investors, especially small and medium-sized companies, which are typical of many European countries, generally prefer direct exports over outward investment because of their lack of managerial and financial capacity to run companies abroad. When they do invest outside the European Union, they follow traditional customers (intermediate suppliers in the automobile industry, for instance) after a time lag and opt for hosts with absorptive domestic markets (for instance Brazil).

- Since the mid-1980s, the probability of deepening integration in the form of a single EU market and later integration widening towards Central Europe have offered easy alternatives to go abroad (actually, next door) without much risk.

- The European Union's structural and regional policies have helped to attract FDI to countries on the periphery of the European Union provided that domestic policies of these countries were coherent and predictable. Such conditions were fulfilled in Ireland, and to some extent in Spain and Portugal, but not in Greece.

- EU companies seem to give short-term transaction costs a higher weight in decision making than medium-term market prospects. This leads to preferences for 'safe haven' hosts, even if these hosts show much less dynamism and a more inward orientation. A relatively high dependence on own earnings and less access to parent company loans to finance foreign investment may have triggered such risk-averting behaviour.

• The different perceptions of potential EU investors and their Asian counterparts (both companies and governments) may have deterred EU investors. EU investors seem to prefer equity-type arrangements and majority ownership of companies abroad while their Asian counterparts prefer non-equity arrangements and minority participation in foreign companies in joint ventures. Again, these different perceptions mirror different degrees of risk assessment and differences in time preference rates, with those of European companies probably higher than those of their Asian counterparts.

• EU R&D programs have witnessed 'partial understanding' (as Sigurdson [1996: 3] puts it nicely) of the globalisation of technological and industrial progress linking EU-based and Asian companies in strategic alliances. Under the ESPRIT program (European Strategic Programme for Information Technologies), EU subsidies were subject to conditionality in the sense that alliances between EU recipient companies and non-EU companies which were intended to be 'defeated' by ESPRIT made the European companies ineligible for further membership in ESPRIT. Sigurdson refers to the case of a strategic alliance between two computer companies from the United Kingdom and Japan which induced the EU Commission to exclude the UK company from ESPRIT.

EU FDI in Asia: upward changes since the 1990s

What holds for data on services holds for FDI. Data are often incomprehensive, incompatible, dated and aggregated because of legal barriers to disclosure. But irrespective of the source of FDI (OECD, EU, or UNCTAD, TNCI) and regardless of whether stocks or flows are taken into account, the message is crystal clear: until 1993, the EU was a lagger in investing Asia with only a 3.8 per cent share of developing Asia in EU total outward FDI stock in 1993 (EU UNCTAD TNCI 1996: 23) and even less for EU outward flows (2.2 per cent in 1990–93). US and Japanese shares were very much higher. Viewed from the Asian hosts' inward investment perspective, the European Union did not comprise more than 10.5 per cent of total 1990–93 FDI flows to Asia or more than 12.9 per cent of total FDI stocks held in Asia in 1993 (EU UNCTAD TNCI 1996: 29).

Beyond this general message, all data are sensitive to aggregation at the EU level. To minimise flaws due to aggregation, EU country data are applied in Table 9.7. Extra-EU investment serves as the denominator when calculating shares. Thus, intra-EU investment, defined narrowly as well as broadly to include EU investment in former European Free Trade (EFTA) countries, is excluded. Second, we rely on flow data from the OECD FDI Yearbook as an authoritative source. The latest year available is 1994.

In general, the latecomer position of EU investors appears to be unchallenged if the US shares before 1994 are taken as a yardstick. Yet 1994 marks a clear rise in Asian shares *vis-à-vis* previous years. In this year, German investment flows in Japan amounted to 4.6 per cent of the country's extra-EU investment compared with the 1991–94 average of 3.3 per cent. US investment was at a similar level. EU countries' FDI to the higher-income developing Asian economies reached levels between 7 and 13 per cent (excluding the downward outlier France) compared with 11 per cent in the US case. For lower-income Asian economies, 1994 shares of EU countries were even higher than for the United States. Of course, this result hinges critically upon excluding EU country investment in other EU countries. Such a net figure should be used if the European Union in total is the reporting unit. If, as a back-of-the-envelope calculation, FDI flows from all reporting EU countries were converted into US dollars and then summed up to form an EU figure, and if intra-EU investment flows were then excluded, the above impression of European investors bypassing Asia would have to be corrected for the year 1994. Total Asia (developing Asia plus Japan), for instance, would have then kept a share of about 14 per cent in extra-EU investment, which is not far from the US level. Different concepts of FDI measurement in EU countries make such calculations dubious, however. While any reliable recent figure on extra-EU investment would probably lead to qualifications concerning Asia's under-representation in EU outward investment, it cannot be denied that EU investment dynamics have tended to favour the Central European transition countries.

As an example, by 1994, German FDI stocks in these countries (basically Hungary, Czech Republic, Poland) were already at the same level as stocks in developing Asia (excluding China and Japan) and the latest German flow data (for 1995 and 1996; [Deutsche Bundesbank 1997]) indicate that flows to the three leading transition countries (Czech Republic, Poland, Hungary) were 18 per cent higher than German FDI flows to total developing Asia plus China. Even if one assumes that German investment behaviour is not typical of the rest of the European Union because of close German cross-border relations

Table 9.7   *Share of Japan, developing Asia and Australia in extra-EU12 FDI outflows of major EU countries, 1985–94*

to	from	France	Germany	Italy	Nether-lands	UK	US
Japan	1985–87[c]	0.8	1.5	1.9	1.4	0.4	3.1
		(0.8)	(1.6)	(2.0)	(1.4)	(0.4)	
	1988–90[c]	0.3	3.4	14.8	-0.1	1.6	2.7
		(0.3)	(4.2)	(18.9)	(-0.2)	(1.6)	
	1991–94[c]	1.0	3.3	0.7	-5.1	0.5	2.2
		(1.1)	(4.4)	(0.8)	(-7.2)	(0.6)	
	1994	0.9	4.6	6.1	0.3	2.0	4.8
		(0.9)	(5.9)	(7.1)	(0.6)	(2.2)	
Advanced Asian developing economies[a]	1985–87[c]	5.5	1.6	–	–	3.3	3.2
		(6.1)	(1.7)	–	–	(3.4)	
	1988–90[c]	2.3	2.1	–	–	3.6	5.4
		(2.7)	(2.7)	–	–	(3.6)	
	1991–94[c]	3.4	5.0	3.5	5.9	10.9	8.0
		(3.9)	(6.6)	(3.9)	(8.3)	(11.5)	
	1994	3.3	7.2	13.5	8.0	9.8	11.2
		(3.2)	(9.2)	(15.9)	(14.9)	(10.9)	
Other Asian economies[b]	1985–87[c]	0.8	0.5	–	5.5	0.1	0.4
		(0.8)	(0.5)	–	(5.7)	(0.1)	
	1988–90[c]	0.1	1.2	–	7.6	0.6	1.0
		(0.1)	(1.5)	–	(8.7)	(0.6)	
	1991–94[c]	1.6	4.4	1.9	8.0	2.9	2.3
		(1.8)	(5.9)	(2.1)	(11.3)	(3.0)	
	1994	2.4	9.5	8.6	11.7	3.3	2.6
		(2.3)	(12.1)	(10.2)	(21.8)	(3.7)	
Australia	1985–87[c]	1.0	1.9	0.1	–	6.1	2.1
		(1.1)	(2.1)	(0.2)	–	(6.2)	
	1988–90[c]	2.0	1.6	2.2	–	10.7	4.0
		(2.3)	(2.0)	(2.8)	–	(10.9)	
	1991–94[c]	0.3	0.9	-0.5	2.4	14.3	2.5
		(0.3)	(1.2)	(-0.5)	(3.5)	(15.1)	
	1994	0.0	0.4	-3.0	2.8	15.6	1.4
		(0.0)	(0.5)	(-3.6)	(5.3)	(17.2)	

Notes: Shares with EU country FDI in EFTA countries are counted as intra-EU investment and are in parenthesis.

    a NIE4, Malaysia, Taiwan, Thailand.

    b China, India, Indonesia, Philippines.

    c Annual average.

Source: OECD 1996. Author's calculations.

with neighbouring Central Europe, OECD investment statistics for the sum of all EU members suggest that over the 1991–94 period, the transition countries were roughly on a par with the advanced developing Asian countries in attracting FDI from the European Union.

From Brussels to Asia: how far is it today?

For many years, 'Brussels' approximated to Asian perceptions of 'Fortress Europe'. Such perceptions were fuelled by the MFA (Multi-fibre Arrangement), the CAP (Common Agricultural Policy) and anti-dumping policies.[6] In addition to such 'grandfather' problems, statements like that attributed to former EC (European Community) Commissioner for Foreign Relations Willy de Clerq relating to the Single Market were not helpful in dissipating fears of aggressive bilateralism.[7] They coincided with estimates based on the static trade effects of completing the Single Market that Asia would suffer from trade diversion (Kreinin and Plummer 1992). After 1992, the eastern enlargement issue has fuelled further concerns in Asia that any sort of discriminatory trading arrangements with lower-income countries would end in welfare losses for Asia due to trade and investment diversion. Partial equilibrium models and Computable General Equilibrium (CGE) models focusing on static effects support this view (Horne and Huang 1996), though their explanatory power is necessarily limited. In addition, in many Asian circles, Europe is still perceived as a group of countries in decline facing an uphill task in coping with a massive task of adjustment. There are still fears that the Union is liable to shift some of the burden of adjustment to non-members. EU technical jargon like 'trade defence legislation' can easily be interpreted as an element of such endeavours. On the other hand, while not denying progress made in recent years, the European Union has closed ranks with the United States in protesting the difficulties of penetrating Asian countries' markets.[8]

For quite some time, academics have sought a balance between well-founded criticism of EU contingent protection on the one hand and unfounded 'Fortress Europe' perceptions on the other. But it was not until July 1994 that such endeavours, supported by the conclusion of the Uruguay Round (UR), began to show the first signs of success in terms of transmitting this view to Asia. The 'New Asia Strategy' (NAS) proposed by the Commission at that time (Kommission 1994) and endorsed at the Essen Summit in December 1994, together with the March 1996 First ASEM Meeting in Bangkok, have contributed to opening new channels for dialogue, stabilising expectations on both sides and to ruling out the imposition of unilateral measures.

For a number of reasons on the Asian side, the European Union began a fundamental reshaping of its policy towards Asia after 1992, a policy which began two decades earlier with the decision to exclude the seven Asian Commonwealth members from preferential European Economic Community (EEC) treatment in the context of UK accession in 1973 and the 1975 ACP Agreement (Tulloch 1973; 1975).

Sustained economic dynamism

Economic size, potential and sustainability of growth are the three key characteristics which underlie the EU position in its NAS document. Of the three, sustainability stands out. Many countries have recorded growth for a few years. Yet, when faced with setbacks, growth has often proved unsustainable, as was the case in Latin America. The degree of sustainability in Asia has been unrivalled and is seen as durable by the European Union. This assessment is based on the European Union's profound understanding of the depth of institutional integration. If integration is economically understood as the trend towards the Law-of-One-Price, then the European Union implicitly recognises that deep and wide integration are under way not only in Europe but also in Asia. The degree of economic interaction in goods and factor markets within Asia has risen markedly and has been accompanied by a network of cooperative efforts ranging from almost region-wide consultations to binding sub-regional commitments (such as in ASEAN). Such institutional steps have been accompanied by market-driven integration deepening which can be measured, for instance, by the growing convergence in exchange rate movements within Asian sub-regions (Green 1994; Langhammer 1997). The NAS also recognises that integration is widening with the integration of Indochinese countries and China into the Asian business network. A multiple strategy of bilateral, sub-regional and multilateral cooperation (the latter represented by ASEM) is seen as necessary to take care of European interests in penetrating the integrating and enlarging markets of Asia. It is a level playing field argument: the more Asian countries engage in raising issues collectively, the more Brussels feels compelled to reciprocate on behalf of its members. This should not be confused with trade policy negotiations (Pelkmans and Fukasaku 1995: 157) but should be understood as a general support of micro-level relations between EU and Asian companies.

Asia in the Uruguay Round

The UR was the first multilateral trade negotiations (MTN) round in which Asian countries took common positions and were actively involved in reciprocally negotiating tariff cuts and dismantling non-tariff barriers (NTBs). Common ASEAN positions presented in the UR, the leading role of Asian countries in the Cairns Group and the Asia Pacific Economic Cooperation (APEC) commitment to 'open regionalism' consistent with the Geneva consensus of multilateralism are three examples of a supra-national stance which have gained credibility in Brussels.

Japan and the United States in Asia

The European Union has closely observed Japan's strong role as a capital provider and the strong role of the United States as an absorptive export market for Asia. In addition, trade links between the United States, a WTO member, and China, which has yet to be admitted, have been vigorously employed by the United States in recent years to open Asian markets to US technology. Such roles have not been matched by the European Union so far. As neither a strong capital and technology exporter nor a dynamic export market for Asia, it is not clear how the European Union should define its role within the Triad. Obviously, the European Union considers that it can offer its vast experience in supra-national institution building,[9] including dispute settlement and hopes for an improved standing of its single currency in Asian financial markets.[10] Yet, the euro's performance in a beauty contest against the dollar will be greatly affected by the success in overcoming the European Monetary Union (EMU) 'trilemma': starting EMU on schedule, having more first round members than the *de facto* core group of European Monetary System (EMS) countries and, finally, convincing financial markets that the euro will remain as stable as the most stable national currency.

Effectiveness of EU development aid

The European Union stresses its role as the second largest donor next to Japan but far ahead of the United States. Aid has mainly gone to South Asia, with mixed results, as the NAS paper admits. Tighter EU and EU member states' budget constraints in addition to increasing demand for aid from former socialist economies have raised the necessity to submit aid to Asia to more stringent efficiency criteria than in the past.

Negative cross-border externalities from Asia

Some of the negative cross-border externalities which are mentioned as reasons for concern to Europe include drug trafficking, proliferation of banned weapons and weapon technology, non-compliance with economic sanctions raised by the international community against third parties, organised crime, prohibited trade in endangered species, rising pollution intensities and illegal migration. In negotiating these issues with sovereign Asian governments, the European Union faces the 'victims pay principle' as it cannot charge the country of origin according to the 'polluter pays principle'. Hence, by investing in resource-saving technology in Asia (stimulated, for instance, by the instrument of 'joint implementation' of the Rio environmental targets), by compensating Asian losers for adhering to multilateral rules and by trying to gain influence – jointly with Asian governments – in supra-national rule making and enforcement, the European Union tries to contain the supply-side momentum of such externalities.

Smoothing the impact of locational competition

The domestic price of immobile factors is a decisive element in international competitiveness. Immobile factors comprise the entire regulatory system for trade and investment, including standards for immobile labour and the environment. In raising these issues in Asia–Europe fora, the European Union has responded to frequently articulated complaints within Europe about 'ecological and social dumping' and exchange rate protectionism in Asian economies. Allegations of Asian countries' deliberately adopting 'beggar-thy-neighbour' policies have been raised by some French economists (Lassudrie-Duchêne and Lafay 1995: 12–13). The basis of these complaints has been the assumed negative impact of merchandise imports and capital outflows on European labour markets. Tabling such complaints has never been very successful, as the long history of misperceptions between ASEAN and the European Union on human rights has demonstrated. Furthermore, the fear of creating a new opening for ethical or environmental protectionism has induced Asian economies to unite in utmost scepticism against the 'fair standards' debate. Within the WTO framework, the European Union can count on

US support on these matters. Consequently, Asian countries may prefer to discuss them bilaterally rather than run the risk of tacit alliances between the United States and the European Union against Asia.

Stabilising transition in the former Soviet Union

Europe has a genuine interest in stabilising and stimulating the transition process in the successor states of the former Soviet Union. This is demonstrated by its role as the largest donor in this region. At the same time, geography, culture and history provide justification for labelling parts of the former Soviet Union as truly Asian territory. This is the case in the Asian part of the Russian Federation and in particular in Central Asia, where overlapping membership in European and Asian-based institutions is common. Since 1992, two Central Asian economies (Kazakhstan and Kyrgyz Republic) have been members and aid recipients of the European Bank for Reconstruction and Development which is basically funded from European sources, while they have also been regional members and aid recipients of the Asian Development Bank since 1994. Politically, influence in Central Asia is a matter of contest between Iran on the Asian side and Turkey, which strongly identifies itself as a prospective EU member. Finally, on Russian territory, European and Asian interests in exploiting the natural resource base in the Asian part of the country are sometimes said to be governed by different time preference rates, with those of Asian investors in the resource sector of the Russian Far East being higher than those of European investors. This could lead the European Union to try to influence Asian countries to accept common minimum standards for sustainable resource management in the Asian part of the former Soviet Union.

Europe and APEC: the tyranny of geography

The NAS document mentions APEC only once, in the context of the role of the United States in Asia. The remark is brief and cautious, as by 1994, the direction of APEC policies was not yet clear except for the (correct) assumption that APEC would not pave the way to a treaty-based free trade area like EFTA. Meanwhile, the target of non-discriminatory trade liberalisation under the 'open regionalism' principle within APEC has become clearer than the instruments to achieve it. The latter is essential for the European Union as in the European tradition of institutionalised regionalism, trade policy instruments are legally binding and subject to a fixed timetable. This approach is not necessary in APEC, which is a voluntary and evolutionary means of unilateral decision making supported by monitoring and peer pressure and aimed at deepening, broadening and widening economic cooperation (Elek 1996). For the European Union, however, this definition does not answer the question of whether it is an invisible or visible hand which conducts the APEC orchestra, and if it is a visible hand, whose hand it is. Given APEC's soft profile, the European Union seems to want to be as close as possible to the decision-making process within APEC. But apart from the tyranny of geography which excludes the European Union from the Pacific Rim, it is precisely this softness which prevents a removed observer from gaining much more insight into the process than can be afforded by being informed *ex post* by the players in various systems for EU–Asian dialogue. What APEC (or more exactly, the Asian group within APEC) intends to achieve is essentially a 'shallow' process of GATT/WTO Pacific Plus, that is a transpacific liberalisation initiative following the UR commitments with the intention of trying to accelerate and enforce them. As long as APEC maintains its soft institutional underpinnings, sub-regional fora offer more substance in trade and investment dialogues between Europe and Asia.

Ageing Europe's interests in Asia beyond 2000

Demographic changes documented, for instance, by rising age dependency ratios in Europe, and the critical state of Continental European PAYE (pay as you earn) social security systems challenged by mass unemployment make fiscal adjustment in Europe during the next decade imperative.

To meet the future commitments of large accumulated unfunded public pension liabilities inherited from PAYE systems, fiscal deficits in Europe must be redressed, private savings must be raised, and the profitability of present savings must be increased. An essential element of fiscal adjustment is the gradual replacement of increasingly unprofitable forced savings in PAYE systems with voluntary private savings profitably invested outside the home country. This requires substantial liberalisation of investment opportunities on the part of European institutional investors like insurance companies and pension funds. Such liberalisation would not only raise incentives to mobilise more private savings but would also induce more capital to flow into emerging markets, including Asia, where returns could be expected to be higher and relatively uncorrelated with EU home investment returns. Yet, for a long time, liberalisation of portfolio investment has been anathema in many

European countries with the exception of the United Kingdom, which has been a forerunner in funded social security systems and portfolio liberalisation. As a study by Davanzo and Kautz (1992: 83) states: 'Outside the UK, the European pension fund sector is generally underdeveloped relative to the size of local economies, as well as [being] under-diversified, highly regulated, and subject to wide divergence in national practices and policies'. High mandatory percentages of corporate plan assets to be held in own government bonds or restrictive caps on assets held in international papers are common in all Continental Europe countries. Chuhan (1994: 25) and Reisen (1994: 95) list tight regulatory constraints on foreign investment by private pension funds in Denmark, Finland, Germany and Sweden, with high matching requirements (adjustment of the currency mix of assets with the currency mix of pension commitments) and restrictive caps on assets held internationally. By 1994, even countries like France and Italy had negligible privately funded pension schemes. It is also true that even in the absence of governmental restrictions, a rapid rise in investment in emerging markets is impeded by self-imposed prudential restrictions. This would explain why even under relatively liberalised conditions such as in the United States, institutional investors still invest probably less than 1 or 2 per cent of their portfolio in emerging markets (Khan 1995: 49). A specific European reluctance to invest abroad is said to be due to high risk aversion, which is only slowly being eroded in countries like the Netherlands and France but is still dominant in other Continental European countries like Germany (Eurobonanza 1992).

The high degree of policy inertia in Continental Europe also explains why, in spite of increasingly manageable risks due to reliable investment grade ratings, Continental Europe is not expected to match US or UK levels of outward portfolio investment in the years ahead. Davanzo and Kautz (1992) estimate that the share of Continental Europe in total pension assets held in major markets by the year 2000 will not exceed 13 per cent: a modest increase over its 10 per cent share in 1990. This compares with 28 per cent for Japan, 44 per cent for the United States and 11 per cent for the United Kingdom by the year 2000.

A push factor to liberalise the portfolio investment of institutional investors in Europe seems to be a necessary but insufficient condition for an increase in EU assets held in Asia. Complementing a multi-country growth model by demographic assumptions, Börsch-Supan (1996: 133) concludes that his scenario of ageing-related capital flows would primarily favour flows between OECD countries. However, this could change dramatically if large Asian countries such as India or China started to offer productive investments which would absorb large amounts of capital from the OECD area. Such a pull factor is not an implausible scenario if estimates of domestic savings–

investment gaps in East Asia beyond the year 2000 are taken into account (Lam and Teh 1996). Lam and Teh take as their starting point assumptions on slower future income growth, demographic changes towards ageing, increasing labour force participation and rises in incremental capital–output ratios due to more capital-intensive industrial production and infrastructure investment. These assumptions impact upon the investment–savings gap and lead the authors to conclude that East Asia excluding Japan will be a net borrower in the 1994–2010 period. Developments in the three sub-regions (NIEs, ASEAN, China) are likely to differ. NIE current account surpluses are expected to dwindle and even disappear by the year 2010 while ASEAN countries including Vietnam will continue to be net borrowers, although to a lesser extent at the end of the period (2 per cent of GDP [gross domestic product]) than the beginning (3 per cent). Demand for external savings will be driven by China, whose current account deficit by the year 2010 is estimated to be twice as large as the sum of deficits of all ASEAN countries, though in relative terms it is expected to decline and not to exceed 2 per cent. Deficits of such magnitude could be sustainable provided that domestic macroeconomic policies remain coherent. This includes sustained efforts to mobilise domestic savings in order to counter the effects of a non-saving ageing population (particularly in the NIE4), to raise factor productivity and to continue to liberalise domestic capital markets.

With respect to South Asia, Qureshi (1996) estimates the amount of annual investment in 1996–2005 at about one-quarter of investment in East Asia. If domestic savings ratios in South Asia countries remain significantly lower than in East Asian countries (a difference of ten percentage points in 1986–95), South Asia's contribution to rising demand for external savings in Asia will be significant.

Both push and pull factors suggest that future European retirees will ultimately accept Asia as an important source of pension income and that this will be a win–win strategy. Changing perceptions in Europe in favour of Asia as a host for private European household savings will accelerate slowly, starting with reforms to Continental European PAYE systems giving greater weight to individual precautionary savings than to forced savings in public schemes. Savings diversification on a large scale, however, is not possible without the removal of policy-induced barriers to portfolio diversification by institutional investors. Some movement towards reform has been facilitated by competition between different national regulatory systems in life insurance contracts under the Single Market Program. This has allowed UK companies to offer innovative insurance contracts in other EU member states under the home country rule with different regional asset spreads and different risk grades. But more reforms are necessary to prove that risk aversion is not a specific characteristic of European savers but the outcome of both delayed financial and social reforms and the lack of incentives for individual precaution.

Conclusions

The European Union still has no telephone number in terms of a common foreign and security policy which encompasses commercial policies. Nor has East Asia. Economic relations between the two regions will therefore continue to remain strongly decentralised and multi-faceted, whether Asia is defined as East Asia or total Asia as in the NAS document. Hence, there will be many commercial and political avenues linking Asia and Europe. The Brussels avenue will be but one of them. Increasingly, institutionalised relations are deepened at sub-national levels, for instance, between European and Asian municipalities or between provinces and states in European countries such as those between Chinese provinces and German *Länder*.

Europe's commercial interests focus on sustaining the momentum of buoyant import demand in open markets and obtaining competitive returns from FDI and portfolio investment in Asia. Political interests basically comprise the minimisation of negative cross-border externalities and the conveyance of the message that Europe is neither a victim of economic decline nor of cultural decay. 'Eurosclerosis' is not a term the European Union would like to be associated with in Asia. Nor is the catchword 'clash of civilisations' a promising point of departure. The prospects for achievement are not bad. EU-based companies including banks and insurance firms operate globally and are now less hesitant to adopt an Asian style of company management and motivation in their affiliates than they were some years ago. In spite of the eastern enlargement of the European Union, Asia stands to gain in their investment portfolios. Private European households are beginning to think more seriously about their future as retirees and will slowly begin to accept offers from financial markets to position part of their savings directly in Asia via equity funds or bonds. National governments, especially those representing Continental European countries, will start to liberalise the asset allocation of national pension funds and finally, the European Union will offer its experience in supra-national institution building.

The failure to 'sell' Europe in Asia is basically a product of the success of domestic adjustment in Europe and further progress in integration deepening based on subsidiarity. To begin with the latter, the direct impact of the introduction of EMU upon business with Asia may be smaller than its psychological effect. If the European Union can cope with the EMU 'trilemma' and introduce a stable common currency, this will anchor Europe as an entity in Asia far more than the rather intangible 1992 completion of the Single Market. This also means that deeper EU integration would probably lead to a loss of credibility in Asia in the event of EMU failure. The former is definitely more important. Europe's most important adjustment issue is the problem of mass unemployment. It stigmatises Europe as anti market-oriented in Asia, where high employment and flexible labour markets have contributed significantly to skill formation and income gains. There is no better way to be discredited in Asia as a region depreciating its skill stock than to leave domestic labour markets inflexible and let unemployment rates rise. Under such conditions, can Europe regain its past (not to say historical) attractiveness as a place of learning for Asian students who are tomorrow's commercial and decision makers? The answer goes without saying.

Notes

* The author acknowledges helpful comments from both discussants and participants at the London and Brussels conferences and the Paris seminar.
1 Viewed from Europe, East Asia is not clearly defined as a region. EU policies relate either to Asia in total, as in the 1994 New Asia Strategy (NAS) including South Asia, or to institutionalised schemes like ASEAN and APEC. Hence, for analytical purposes and for easier data handling, 'developing Asia' is used as the regional aggregate which includes China but excludes Japan, Australia and New Zealand.
2 This Table and Tables 9.3 and 9.5 construct ratios between different regionally and structurally disaggregated trade flows. Their purpose is to capture developments in trade performance with a few statistical indicators instead of displaying them in absolute terms. Such ratios by no means signal a normative purpose, that is to suggest that approaching specific numerical values of ratios would be desirable.
3 Note that developing Asia is taken as a single unit so that trade among developing Asian countries is excluded. World trade of developing Asia equals extra-developing Asia's trade.
4 Both sub-regions include Singapore. Hence, it is not possible to add the sub-regions to total developing Asia because of double counting.
5 A detailed discussion of this controversy based on company questionnaires and other micro-level data can be found in EU UNCTAD TNCI (1996: 47–62). This enquiry supports the main thrust of two earlier Kiel Institute studies by Hiemenz and Langhammer et al. (1987) and Nunnenkamp, Gundlach and Agarwal (1994).
6 For a discussion of the prominent role of Asia as a target of EU anti-dumping policies, see Pelkmans and Fukasaku (1995: 155–57).
7 'We are not building a Single Market in order to turn it over to hungry foreigners', quoted in Hamilton (1991).

8 Conditions of market access are closely monitored by the European Union. For example, an EU GD I report of December 1996 lists both improvements and continuing barriers to entry for European suppliers in Japan. It differs from the annual US Trade Representative Report by giving due attention to improvements and opportunities (EC 1996).

9 This experience seems to have met relatively strong demand in ASEAN, especially after the decision to implement AFTA. See Langhammer (1996) and Pelkmans (1996).

10 There is no systematic empirical evidence on the extent to which EU currencies have been used by Asian actors as invoice currencies in goods markets and transaction currencies in financial markets. Anecdotal evidence summarised by Black (1991) for the 1980s suggests that the use of EU currencies as invoice currencies for Japanese exports and imports was smaller than the share of the European Union in Japanese trade. In internationally syndicated loan markets, the US dollar (with about 75 per cent) remained the most important currency of denomination (OECD 1997: 74), albeit along a slightly declining trend. The use of ECU (European currency unit) shrank from 15 per cent in 1992 to 0.2 per cent in 1996. Finally, in Asian Development Bank borrowings, EU currencies lag far behind the yen, dollar and Swiss franc. By the end of 1994, less than 10 per cent of Asian Development Bank borrowing principal outstanding was denominated in deutschmark, guilder and pounds sterling (ADB 1995).

References

Asian Development Bank (ADB) (1995) *Annual Report*, 1994, Manila.

Australia–Japan Research Centre (AJRC) (1996) 'Europe, East Asia and APEC: initial report', prepared by Andrew Elek, Canberra: AJRC.

Black, Stanley (1991) 'Transaction costs and vehicle currencies', *Journal of International Money and Finance* 10, pp. 512–26.

Börsch-Supan, Axel (1996) 'The impact of population ageing on savings, investment and growth', in *Future Global Capital Shortages: Real Threat or Pure Fiction?*, Paris: OECD, pp. 103–42.

Chuhan, Punam (1994) 'Are institutional investors an important source of portfolio investment in emerging markets?', Policy Research Paper No. 1243, Washington DC: World Bank.

Davanzo, Lawrence E. and Leslie D. Kautz (1992) 'Toward a global pension market: stirrings of transformation in North American, Japanese, and European markets', *Journal of Portfolio Management* 18(4), pp. 77–85.

Deutsche Bundesbank (1996) 'Technologische dienstleistungen in der zahlungsbilanz', *Statistische Sonderveröffentlichungen* 12, May.

—— (1997) *Zahlungsbilanzstatistik*, March.

Drysdale, Peter and Ross Garnaut (1993) 'The Pacific: an application of a general theory of economic integration', in C. Fred Bergsten and Marcus J. Noland, eds, *Pacific Dynamism and the International Economic System*, Washington DC: Institute for International Economics, pp. 183–223.

EC (1995) 'The European Union and world trade: European Union trade developments for the year 1994, comparison with the United States in Japan', Luxembourg: EC Directorate General for External Economic Relations, Unit for Analysis and Policy Planning.

—— (1996) 'Market opportunities in Japan: improvements in access to the Japanese market and opportunities for European companies', mimeo, GD I External Relations, Unit for Relations with Japan, 17 December.

Elek, Andrew (1996) 'APEC and the European Union: shared objectives within the international economic system', paper presented at the conference on Europe, East Asia and APEC organised by the Australia–Japan Research Centre, ANU, 28–29 August.

EU, UNCTAD TNCI (1996) 'Investing in Asia's dynamism', Luxembourg: European Union Direct Investment in Asia.

'Eurobonanza? What Eurobonanza?' (1992) *Institutional Investor*, April, pp. 50–56.

Fukasaku, Kiichiro and David Martineau (1996) 'Forging trade links between Europe and Asia', paper presented at the conference on Europe, East Asia and APEC organised by the Australia–Japan Research Centre, ANU, 28–29 August, mimeo.

Green, David Jay (1994) 'Convergence and cohesion with the ASEAN-4', *Journal of Asian Economics* 5, pp. 119–45.

Hamilton, Carl B. (1991) 'European Community external protection and 1992: voluntary export restraints applied to East Asia', *European Economic Review* 35, pp. 378–87.

Hiemenz, Ulrich, Rolf J. Langhammer, Jamuna P. Agarwal, Martin Groß and Friedrich von Kirchbach (1987) *The Competitive Strength of European, Japanese and US Suppliers in ASEAN Markets*, Tübingen: J.C.B. Mohr.

Horne, Jocelyn and Yiping Huang (1996) 'East Asia and Eastern Europe: a global trade analysis', paper presented at the conference on Europe, East Asia and APEC organised by the Australia–Japan Research Centre, ANU, 28–29 August.

Khan, Mohsin S. (1995) 'Recent developments in international financial markets', *Asian Development Review* 13(1), pp. 36–53.

Kommission der Europäischen Gemeinschaften, Mitteilung der Kommission an den Rat (1994) Auf dem Weg zu einer Neuen Asien-Strategie, EC Document, Kom(94) 314 endg. Brüssel, 13 July.

Kreinin, Mordechai E. and Michael G. Plummer (1992) 'Effects of economic integration in industrial countries on ASEAN and the Asian NIEs', *World Development* 20, pp. 1345–66.

Lam San Ling and Teh Kok Peng (1996) 'The savings and investment outlook in developing East Asia', in *Future Global Capital Shortages: Real Threat or Pure Fiction?* Paris: OECD, pp. 103–42.

Langhammer, Rolf J. (1996) 'What can ASEAN learn from the experience of European integration?', paper presented at the 1996 ASEAN Roundtable 'ASEAN & EU: Forging New Linkages and Strategic Alliances', jointly organised by the Institute of Southeast Asian Studies, Singapore, and the OECD

Development Centre, Singapore, 16–17 September, forthcoming in ISEAS Conference Proceedings.

—— (1997) 'The expansion of intra-Asian trade: An analysis of structural patterns and determinants', *Kiel Working Papers* 792, Kiel: Institute of World Economics.

Lassudrie-Duchêne, Bernhard and Gérard Lafay (1995) 'Les limites du libre echange', in *La Négociation Commerciale et Financière Internationale*, Publié à l'initiative de Michael Rainelli, Paris: Economia, pp. 3–26.

Nunnenkamp, Peter, Erich Gundlach and Jamuna P. Agarwal (1994) *Globalization of Production and Markets*, Tübingen: J.C.B. Mohr.

OECD (1996) *Foreign Direct Investment Yearbook*, Paris.

—— (1997) *Financial Market Trends* 66, March.

Pelkmans, Jacques (1996) 'A bond in search of substance: reflections on EU's ASEAN Policy', paper presented at the 1996 ASEAN Roundtable on 'ASEAN & EU: Forging New Linkages and Strategic Alliances', jointly organised by ISEAS Singapore, and the OECD Development Centre, Singapore, 16–17 September, forthcoming in ISEAS Conference Proceedings.

—— and Kiichiro Fukasaku (1995) 'Evolving trade links between Europe and Asia: towards "Open Continentalism"', in Kiichiro Fukasaku, ed., *Regional Cooperation and Integration in Asia*, Paris: OECD, pp. 137–74.

Qureshi Zia (1996) 'Global capital supply and demand: directions in development', Washington DC: World Bank.

Reisen, Helmut (1994) 'On the wealth of nations and retirees: finance and the international economy', *The AMEX Bank Review Prize Essays*, Oxford, pp. 86–107.

Sigurdson, Jon (1996) 'Scope and relevance of strategic alliances: European viewpoint', paper presented at the 1996 ASEAN Roundtable 'ASEAN & EU: Forging New Linkages and Strategic Alliances' jointly organised by ISEAS, Singapore, and the OECD Development Centre, Singapore, 16–17 September, forthcoming in ISEAS Conference Proceedings.

Tulloch, Peter (1973) *The Seven Outside: Commonwealth's Asia Trade with the Enlarged EEC*, London: ODI.

—— (1975) *The Politics of Preferences*, London: ODI.

WTO (1995) 'Trade policy review: European Union', report by the European Communities, WT/TPR/G/3, 30 June, mimeo.

Part V

Global issues

10 China and the global system

JUSTIN YIFU LIN

China's integration with the global economy has become a hot topic both because of the success of China's recent reform in stimulating economic growth and the failure of China's reform to address some major economic issues.

China's transition from a planned economy to a market economy started in 1979. This transition has transformed China from a poor, agrarian, inward-looking economy to one of the most dynamic economies and one of the largest trading powers in the world. It is recognised that the World Trade Organization will not be a truly global trade organisation if China is not a part of the system.

Chinese negotiation for accession to the General Agreement on Tariffs and Trade (GATT), and later the World Trade Organization (WTO), started in 1986. Despite its commitment to the basic principles of free trade, the Chinese government has demanded that China be treated as a developing country so that it can enjoy the same period of grace for the removal of domestic protection as that allowed for other developing countries. The Chinese government insists that such a period of grace is necessary because, in spite of the dynamic growth which reform has brought about, the transition to a market economy is not complete and the economy has inherited many problems from the planned system. However, some advanced countries insist that China should follow the rules for developed countries as a precondition for her accession to the WTO, citing as reasons China's strong domestic growth and trade expansion in the past one and a half decades. These countries argue that if allowed to free ride the 'loopholes' in the WTO's regulations, China will expand her trade rapidly at the expense of other countries.

This chapter analyses China's rapid growth in the past decades, why the Chinese government insists on being treated as a developing country in her accession to the WTO, and the gains for China and other countries of China's integration with the global system.

To understand why China has achieved such dynamic growth in the reform era and what the remaining problems in the economy are, it is necessary to have an understanding of the economic system before reform. Like other socialist countries, China followed the Stalinist model of economic development in the early 1950s during the period of postwar recovery and reconstruction. The main goal of Stalin's model was to accelerate the growth of capital-intensive industries. However, the Chinese economy was a capital-scarce economy. To make possible the priority growth of capital-intensive industries, the government instituted a distorted macroeconomic policy environment, including an artificially suppressed interest rate and an overvalued exchange rate. It also set artificially low prices for raw materials, wages and basic necessities. Given this distorted macroeconomic policy environment, demand for credit, foreign exchange, raw materials and living necessities far exceeded supply. The Chinese economy became what the Hungarian economist, Kornai, describes as a shortage economy.

To guarantee a limited supply of credit, foreign exchange, and other resources to the targeted industries, the government first needed to have a plan that ranked projects according to the government's priorities, and second needed to use administrative controls to replace the market for the allocation of resources according to the plan. Because prices were distorted, an enterprise's profit or loss was largely determined by the policy-determined prices of the enterprise's outputs and inputs. Therefore, profits ceased to be the indicator of an enterprise's managerial efficiency. This lack of an objective indicator of enterprises' efficiency was one reason the government deprived state-owned enterprises of their autonomy and managerial discretion. In rural areas, the government instituted the collective farming system to facilitate the implementation of low-price procurement of grain, cotton and other agricultural products.

The above-mentioned trinity of the macroeconomic-policy environment, the resource allocation system, and micro-management institutions were induced institutional arrangements. They were designed to facilitate the pursuit of a capital-intensive, heavy-industry-oriented development strategy in a capital-scarce economy. Under the institutional arrangements outlined above, China was able to establish a complete set of heavy industries despite her low income. However, this came at a high price. The major problems were low efficiency due to distortions in the industrial structure and the suppression of incentives (see Lin, Cai and Li 1996). Moreover, the Chinese economy was basically an inwardly-oriented, closed economy.

China started the transition from a traditional planned economy to a market economy in 1979. Instead of adopting a big-bang approach, which characterised the transition in the Eastern European countries and the former Soviet Union, China adopted an incremental approach. The government first increased the autonomy of the state-owned enterprises and replaced the collective farming system with a household-based farming system as a means of providing incentives. This improvement in the incentive structure was found to be very effective in stimulating output growth. Initially, part of the new income stream was controlled and invested by the micro-management unit. Reform was then gradually extended to the resource allocation system and the macro-policy environment, but in a piecemeal manner. The relaxation of the administrative controls on resource allocation stimulated the development of township-and-village enterprises, joint ventures and private enterprises. Driven by the profit motive, investments made by the enterprises and farmers were largely in the labour-intensive service and light manufacturing sectors, which were more consistent with the comparative advantage of the Chinese economy but which had been suppressed under the previous system. The subsequent improvement in the resource allocation system further stimulated economic growth.

At the beginning of the reform period, the government adopted a policy of opening up to foreign investment. This policy was also implemented in a gradual manner. The government first set up four special economic zones to attract foreign investment and to facilitate technology transfer. After gaining some experience and success, the policy was then extended to other cities in the coastal provinces and along the major rivers.

This gradual approach to transition created a dynamic, outward-looking non-state sector alongside an inefficient state sector. This prevented the collapse of the Chinese economy, as occurred during the transition of Eastern European countries and the former Soviet Union, and also ushered in dynamic growth in the transitional period. The average annual growth rate of GDP (gross domestic product) reached 9.7 per cent in 1979–96, equalling growth in Japan and the four East Asian Tigers at the height of their performance. National income quadrupled and the Chinese economy became the second or third largest in the world, depending on whether the calculation is based on purchasing power parity or the official exchange rate. With the current momentum, the Chinese economy is likely to become the largest in the world early next century. The growth of trade has been even more remarkable. The average growth rate in the same period was 15 per cent per year. Trade volume increased tenfold in the 17 years between 1979 and 1996. In terms of trade volume, China now ranks eleventh in the world. It is projected that China's economy will become the world's largest around 2020.

Chinese reform and open-door policies have also contributed to overall Asian dynamism in recent years. The possibility of relocating labour-intensive manufacturing industries to China made the upgrading of industries in Hong Kong, Taiwan and other Asian newly industrialised economies easier. In addition, China also became their major export market.

The Chinese approach to transition has not been without drawbacks. Reform started in the micro-management institutions and then gradually extended to the resource allocation system and the macro-policy environment. Because of the lag in the reform of the macro-policy environment and resource allocation system, institutional disparities emerged. Moreover, reform of micro-management institutions is incomplete. The ownership structure of the state-owned enterprise has not changed. State-owned enterprises still have to carry many policy-determined burdens. As a result, the Chinese economy faces several serious problems. The major ones are as follows:

• The economic performance of the state-owned sector is extremely poor. More than one-third of the state-owned enterprises registered explicit losses. Another third of enterprises are implicitly loss-making. Only a small proportion of the state-owned enterprises is profitable. Without the state's subsidies and protection, the majority of the state-owned enterprises would collapse. State-owned enterprises currently employ 100 million workers in urban areas. Despite September 1997 decisions on the reform of the state-owned sector, the collapse of the majority of state-owned enterprises would be socially and politically unacceptable.

• The government understands that the liberalisation of interest rates and the commercialisation of banking are necessary for the stability of the Chinese economy. For this reason it attempted financial sector reform in 1994. However, low interest rate soft bank loans are the major source of subsidies. To ensure the survival of state-owned enterprises, financial sector reform has been postponed.

• Regional disparities have widened. Gradualist reform and the open-door policy have unevenly favoured the coastal provinces, causing a widening income gap between the coastal provinces and the hinterland. This regional disparity may become a serious social and political problem.

Looking to the future, if China can maintain political and social stability and adopt measures to solve these problems gradually, the economy is likely to maintain its dynamic growth. The main reasons for this optimism are the advantages of backwardness. To benefit from the existing technological gap, the Chinese economy needs to have access to foreign markets and capital so that China can acquire enough foreign exchange to import technology and equipment. Membership of the formal world trade organisations would greatly facilitate China's export of goods and import of technology and capital. To meet GATT/WTO membership requirements, China moved from a dual-track system to a unified foreign exchange rate system, made the current account convertible, cut unilaterally the average tariff rate from 45 per cent to 23 per cent, and committed to full convertibility of Chinese currency by 2000. China is also actively involved in APEC (Asia Pacific Economic Cooperation) and other regional and international economic forums.

In spite of the Chinese government's efforts, China has yet to conclude the negotiation successfully. The main issues raised in the negotiation process have been intellectual property rights, market access and developed or developing country status. However, the fundamental problem is whether or not China's dynamic growth and integration with the global economy is beneficial to other economies. It is inevitable that the dynamic growth of the Chinese economy will reduce the gap between China and advanced countries. However, even if China becomes the largest economy in the world, its productivity and per capita income will only be about one-fifth that of advanced countries. China still has a very long way to travel from being a large economy to being a strong economy. Therefore, looking at its endowment structure, the Chinese economy will largely be complementary to other economies. In particular, to sustain growth, China needs to import US$100 billion or more of equipment and technology each year in the near future. China also needs to make a major investment in infrastructure, estimated at US$250 billion in the coming five years alone. Most of the equipment imports and a substantial amount of the capital for infrastructural investment will come from advanced countries. As income levels rise and the comparative advantage of the Chinese economy changes, China will also increase its imports of grain, and other land-intensive agricultural and mineral products. China will become the largest market for the exports of capital-abundant and land-abundant countries.

To conclude, the gradualist approach to reform and the open-door policy have contributed to the dynamic growth of the Chinese economy in the past 17 years. The continuing dynamic growth of the Chinese economy in the future depends on the government's ability to maintain economic stability on the one hand and to resolve the remaining problems inherited from the planned system on the other hand. The removal of protection to the state-owned sector, the liberalisation of the financial sector, and the narrowing of regional income gaps can only be achieved gradually. The Chinese government's demand for a period of grace, which is granted to other developing countries in the negotiation for accession to the WTO, is therefore justifiable. The dynamic growth of the Chinese economy will contribute to the dynamic growth of the world economy. The integration of the Chinese economy with the world economy will benefit not only China but other economies in the world. It is to be hoped that economic wisdom will prevail and the deadlock on China's accession to the WTO can soon be successfully resolved.

Note

* A version of this chapter was presented at the panel on 'Europe, East Asia and APEC: A Shared Global Agenda' at the conference on 'Europe, East Asia, APEC and the Asia–Europe Meeting Process', London, 20–21 May 1997.

Reference

Lin, J. Yifu, Fang Cai and Zhou Li (1996) *The China Miracle: Development Strategy and Economic Reform*, Hong Kong: Chinese University Press.

11   Regionalism and the world trading system: reflections on trends in EU, US and APEC policy

JIM ROLLO

Regionalism is all around us: the European Union (EU), APEC (Asia Pacific Economic Cooperation), Free Trade Area of the Americas (FTAA) and Mercosur. It remains a potent subject in the political economy of trade. Exchanges between Bergsten and Bhagwati published in the *Economist* in late 1997 show that the subject still has the capability to raise controversy. The on/off pursuit of fast-track liberalisation by the US administration, and the tying of the timetable to the potential for progress on free trade in the Americas, equally point to the importance of regionalism in trade policy choices. In this chapter I attempt an overview of some of the underlying trends in the main centres of regionalism and ask what this might mean for the future of the world trade system and the work of the WTO (World Trade Organization). Without being at all analytical, the underlying presumption in the chapter is that multi-lateral trade liberalisation is the goal which all groupings eventually share but that regionalism presents either short-term political and economic gains and/or a strengthening of bargaining power in the multilateral system, which makes it desirable in itself. This applies as much to APEC, despite its open regionalism rhetoric, as it does to the European Union or any putative Western Hemisphere preferential trading arrangement.

There are three broad sections. The first is a survey of the pressures for widening and deepening in the European Union and what that might mean for attitudes to the world trading system. Second, there is a discussion of the US concentration on reciprocity and its implications for regionalism in the Western Hemisphere and hence the world trade system. The third section discusses APEC and, in particular, how the American fear of free riders may affect the longer-term approach of APEC, despite the current rhetoric of concerted unilateralism and/or open regionalism. Finally, I ask if there is some way in which we can close the circle on regional groups and end up in a multilateral nirvana.

The European Union: widening and deepening

Let me begin with the widening agenda, since that is directly relevant to the trade system. The European Union is about to enter into enlargement negotiations with five countries in Central and Eastern Europe (Czech Republic, Estonia, Hungary, Poland and Slovenia) plus Cyprus. In the wings are five further Central European countries (Bulgaria, Latvia, Lithuania, Romania and Slovakia) plus Malta, should it wish to apply. Other countries with potential claims on EU membership are Turkey, Switzerland, Norway, Iceland and Liechtenstein. The immediate focus is on the first wave of enlargement to the east. Those negotiations will not open until the spring of 1998 and, for the moment, there can be no certainty about when they might end. The political problems surrounding Cyprus may slow the whole process. Difficulties, particularly over the application of the Single Market among the Central Europeans as well as free movement of labour among current members, may also have an impact on the timetable.

EU enlargement: good or bad for the world trade system?

This is a difficult balance to draw at this point. There will be good aspects to bringing the Central and East Europeans into the European Union from a trade policy perspective. First and foremost, it is likely that average tariffs in Central Europe, as well as tariff peaks, will fall. The assessment of the impact of EU enlargement carried out using a GTAP (Global Trade Analysis Project) model by Baldwin et al. (1997) makes this point strongly. Further, moving from a system of hub-and-spoke free trade areas to a single customs union will also bring advantages. Most notably, the disappearance of rules of origin along with the implementation of the Single Market will end recourse to contingent protection. So, overall, average protection should fall and administrative protection be reduced. The main impact of the latter will be to make inward investment a more attractive option for third countries because of the disappearance of local content rules and contingent protection by the EU15.

More speculatively, there is the potential impact of enlargement on the political economy of the Common Agricultural Policy (CAP). This partly derives from the budgetary pressures that would be imposed, in the current CAP, upon Eastern Europe. These could be significant. Median estimates (see Baldwin et al. 1997 and Rollo 1997) put the likely cost of the first wave of the order of 15 billion ECUs (European currency units). Perhaps more importantly, it seems likely that application of the current CAP to Central Europe, alongside the negotiated disciplines under the Blair House Agreement in the Uruguay Round, would make it impossible for an enlarged European Union to meet its combined commitments under export subsidies and perhaps even the total volume of support. It is these arguments, as well as both the probability of emerging suppliers in the EU15 and the opening of the next round of global agricultural negotiations in 2000, which have pushed the EU Commission to propose further reforms to the CAP. These are contained in the Agenda 2000 document released at the end of the summer. The proposals are an extension of the MacSharry reforms of 1992. Price cuts of around 20 per cent are proposed for cereals and beef, with smaller price cuts for dairy products and a reduction in recourse to supply controls. This may not amount to free trade in agricultural products but it is a further, and significant, step in the direction of reducing the trade distortive effects of the CAP. And if it is not driven by enlargement alone, that is an important element in the equation.

If there are positive elements to enlargement, what are the negatives? These are more difficult to be precise about but reference to past enlargements gives at least some indication of the issues that may need to be watched. Opportunities for trade diversion are obviously the most important. In general terms one would not expect these to be large (outside the CAP) since most of the economies joining are small. (Even Poland is not large, in economic terms, at market exchange rates.) But it is worth reflecting on the example of Portugal which, before membership, was an ardent proponent of liberalisation of the Multi-fibre Arrangement and, after membership, was an equally ardent opponent of such liberalisation. It is entirely possible that for some relatively sensitive products, EU membership will bring low-cost producers in from Central Europe and increase pressure for sectoral protection.

It is even more difficult to be specific about the other potential downside. It relates to the question of decision making within the European Union. The agricultural negotiations in the Uruguay Round demonstrated some of the difficulties that the European Union faces in internal decision making and then in negotiations with the rest of the world. A European Union that expands from 15 to 20 seems likely to increase those problems, if only because of the increased number of interest groups that enlargement will involve. These groups' interests would have been represented in a WTO negotiation by their national governments in any case but it is arguable that EU decision-making methods, even with qualified majority voting on trade policy issues, will increase their leverage rather than reduce it. In any case, sheer numbers might make internal decision making more difficult.

At a more general level, a larger membership with more dispersed interests might have wider effects. The difficulty of pursuing the domestic integration of the European Union, both economically and politically, might act as a distraction from global policy issues. That is, the sheer complexity of managing a larger union will by itself reduce the importance of external policy in EU counsels.

EU deepening

To complicate matters even further, the European monetary union (EMU) project will add to the complexity of the European policy context and hence to the insularity of the European Union. The early years of the monetary union will be taken up with the inevitable learning-by-doing process of making it work. This will take much time and effort, not just at the technical level but also at the highest levels of government. I expect this to be true even if things go well. Should things go badly, particularly with inconsistencies between monetary and fiscal policy, the problems faced by policy makers could be significant indeed. As far as the rest of the world is concerned, the outcome most to be feared would be a mix of tight monetary policy and loose fiscal policy. That contains within it the seeds of a strong euro with all that this might imply for the competitiveness of euro-area traders on world markets. In turn, this might have implications both for attitudes to trade policy and potentially also for tensions between EU members who are in the euro-area and those outside it. It is easy to make flesh creep in this context but it is sufficient to say that managing EMU, particularly with the potential for a stream of new members throughout the first decade of the next century, will be a significant drain on EU decision-making resources. If it also results in a drive for deepening of the political institutions, then that would be a double hit.

Reasons for optimism

It is too easy to be pessimistic about the role of the European Union in the world trade system. The Commission above all is well seized of the importance of a well-functioning trade system for the European Union. The Commission's record in the post-Uruguay Round period has been good. Most importantly, it has been pro-active on behalf of the WTO, which is a significant change from the historically defensive role the European Union played in the GATT (General Agreement on Tariffs and Trade) in the years since the Kennedy Round. Starting from the beginning with unfinished business from the Uruguay Round, the European Union kept the WTO show on the road, pushing forward with a plurilateral agreement on financial services when the United States stood aside from that negotiation in 1995. That has made it easier to reopen the negotiation now, and it is arguable that we will get a better deal in 1997 or early 1998 than would otherwise have been possible.

Equally, at the Singapore Ministerial the European Union played an important role in pushing the built-in agenda. It was a leading player in two areas in particular. The Telecoms Agreement would not have been possible without a good offer from the European Union, and that was forthcoming. More innovatively, the European Union and the United States collaborated on an Information Technology Agreement which, in conjunction with the APEC countries, was driven to a conclusion in the immediate aftermath of Singapore. These two sectoral agreements depended crucially on pro-active EU engagement.

Inside the European Union, the Commission has been active in promoting WTO rules-based solutions. This is expressed in two types of issue. The first is the question of free trade areas between the European Union and other countries. In this, Directorate General I and the Article 113 Committee of the member states which deals with trade policy have both been insistent that any free trade areas negotiated by the Union should be consistent with WTO rules. In particular, the 'substantially all trade' rule, in essence requires that agriculture be part of any free trade area. This is close to a veto since pressures on the CAP from such preferential liberalisations could damage it fatally.

The other area where the Commission has been insistent that WTO rules are paramount is dispute settlement. The most significant test of this so far has been the ruling on the EU bananas regime. This provides particularly acute problems for internal EU policy consensus. Nonetheless, the Commission has made it clear in its statements to the Dispute Settlement Committee that the EU regime will be brought into compliance with WTO rules.

Finally, the EU Commission is among the foremost proponents of a new round of global trade negotiations beginning with the new century. There are practical reasons for this. Nonetheless, it expresses a commitment to pursuing a long-term goal of global trade liberalisation and signals that the European Union will not easily stand aside from the multilateral process.

The US and reciprocity

The American focus on reciprocity shows itself both in issues of market access and in issues of regulatory harmonisation. Of course, it is not a new subject. To restate the obvious, the GATT and now the WTO is in essence a reciprocity game. The difference is that, in the early days of the GATT, this was based on principal supplier negotiations with most favoured nation (MFN) application and laterally it has taken the form of tariff formula cuts and similar approaches, which leave individual members of the GATT or the WTO to make such offers as they feel they are able. As globalisation has advanced and more and more countries play a fuller part in the world trade system as their trade volumes increase, the importance to the United States of the free riders created by the MFN principle has become increasingly significant.

This has led, over the years, to a multi-faceted approach to trade policy. The key issue has become market access for US exporters and the main performance measure is the bilateral trade balance (despite everything that economists can do to destroy the concept that such bilateral balances have any relevance at all). This policy was pursued most consistently in relation to Japan and, with the current weakness of the yen, may re-emerge in that context. More recently, China has been the focus of attention. The response to these pressures by successive US administrations has been to pursue unilateral, bilateral and multilateral policies simultaneously. The notorious Article 301 which gave the administration the ability to employ unilateral trade measures against countries that did not allow equivalent access to US exporters is the most obvious example. That has recently been made subservient to the WTO dispute settlement mechanism, but nonetheless, it remains relevant for commerce not covered by WTO rules. It is still there in the background if the dispute settlement mechanism does not result in a satisfactory outcome.

In the multilateral sphere, the issue of reciprocity has shown itself in two ways. The first is that, in the context of the Uruguay Round, the United States has shown itself to be unwilling to enter into multilateral negotiations unless they included sectors or areas which were either outside WTO rules or which had not shown sufficient liberalisation and where the United States was a competitive exporter. Hence, there has been strong pressure for agriculture, intellectual property, financial services and overseas investment to be included in the Uruguay Round. The second element in US reciprocity in the WTO reveals itself in unwillingness to sign up to agreements unless there is a sufficient liberalisation effort on the part of others, for example in financial services; or not to allow agreements to come into effect unless there is a critical mass (usually 90 per cent of the relevant trade) covered by the agreement, for example the Telecoms and the Information Technology Agreements.

Somewhat separately, because it represents a new agenda for the multilateral organisations, the other element of reciprocity which the United States has been pursuing is that of regulatory harmonisation. The most troublesome areas here are trade and environment and, more particularly, trade and labour standards. Trade and competition policy is also part of this agenda, and this is of some relevance given the competition policy elements in US policy towards Japan and Korea.

The final area in which reciprocity shows strongly in US policy is bilateral agreements. Here the benefits of open trade with the United States can only be garnered if that open trade is completely reciprocated. Free trade between Canada and the United States, NAFTA (North American Free Trade Area), free trade areas with Chile, and now the pressure for a free trade area of the Americas, perhaps as part of a US economic engagement with Africa, all point in this direction. All of this has come into being despite the well-known economists' objections to free trade areas, most notably trade diversion and rules of origin.

It is clear that there is immense suspicion in the American body politic of the potential for free riding created by the MFN principle in the multilateral system and in APEC. This perhaps is reinforced by the fact that tariffs are still, on average, high in emerging markets while they are low in OECD (Organisation for Economic Cooperation and Development) members' more generally and hence the bargaining power of the OECD is reduced in a multilateral negotiation. APEC attempts to deal with that by a program of concerted unilateralism or open regionalism. While this policy would benefit the United States, there are clearly those who would prefer that it were preferential. Fred Bergsten is the main proponent of this view (World Economy 1997, as well as the *Economist* article referred to above). It is clear that at the Manila Summit of APEC in 1997, the United States was not willing to go beyond existing Uruguay Round commitments. Up to a point that is understandable, since it was already the most liberal of the large countries in APEC and it could reasonably expect to see some progress from others towards the APEC objectives of free trade by 2010 and 2020 before moving itself. It is clear, however, that there is an unwillingness in the United States to see the benefits of that liberalisation achieved through APEC negotiating processes — if they can be so described — being handed on a plate to others and, above all, to the European Union. It is this risk which has led Bergsten, among others, to suggest that APEC liberalisation should only be made available to those non-APEC members who offer equivalent liberalisation in return.

None of this is to say that the United States has stood out from the multilateral system. It is still the most important player. It does seem, however, that the US agenda in the WTO is increasingly oriented towards results. The focus is on sectoral agreements and on critical mass as well as the degree of liberalisation. Similarly, the suspicion of a new round, since that might prevent the early harvest of sectors which are ready for further liberalisation, is yet another indicator of this focus. The question, however, is whether these are circumstances in which, in an inversion of the cliché, the good is the enemy of the best. A focus on sectors where liberalisation can go ahead quickly may mean that difficult sectors are left unresolved because there are no exporting pressure groups in the protectionist countries to argue for a liberalisation package. The danger with the US approach must be that it stymies this problem and we are left then with only regional groupings with protectionist policies covering different sectors.

Whither APEC?

It is not surprising that the outsider finds APEC hard to understand. Geographically it covers a huge region. The distances are immense; San Francisco is closer to Europe than it is to Singapore or Beijing. More importantly, there does seem to be a number of distinct economic regions as measured by trade intensities: ASEAN, greater China, NAFTA/FTAA. Furthermore, there are large differences in average levels of protection. Hong Kong and Singapore are at one end with China perhaps at the other, and sectoral peaks are extreme. Korea and Japan take agricultural protectionism to degrees that only the Swiss in Europe think normal, let alone reasonable.

All of that said, the APEC vision of MFN liberalisation by 2020 is one which the rest of the world can only applaud. Of course there is scepticism outside APEC, but then that has been true at every point since APEC was formed and progress to date has been significant. The Manila action plans contain real progress. At a more general level, the engagement of China in APEC has very strong externalities for the rest of the world. Similarly, and this was apparent in the run-up to the Singapore Ministerial, APEC has put global liberalisation on the agenda and this can only be a good thing in terms of long-term strategy for the WTO. Finally, you don't have to be Fred Bergsten to believe that the existence of APEC, which contains many of the important players in the WTO outside the European Union, puts pressures on the European Union to come to the negotiating table. The Seattle Summit in 1993 may have helped to close the Uruguay Round. APEC has certainly raised the profile of Asia in Europe and may be an important element in the politics behind the Asia–Europe meetings (ASEM).

There are serpents in this paradise, however. I have already noted that agricultural protectionism in northeast Asia is very high and while no-one talks of excluding agriculture from the liberalisation process, there is no doubt that the presence of important agricultural exporters in APEC who are unlikely to let agricultural liberalisation go slow could be a cause for dispute. And there are sectoral pressures in other parts of the APEC area. Even Australia, a major proponent of the APEC process, has found it difficult to liberalise as fast as it had originally intended in sensitive sectors. Perhaps as important, though as yet undeveloped, is the question of preferential trading areas within APEC. NAFTA already exists. Chile is trying to join and has a free trade area arrangement with Mercosur. The ASEAN Free Trade Area (AFTA) is in existence and liberalising at increasing speed, while New Zealand is certainly open to the idea of free trade areas with countries ready to negotiate. One of the benefits of free trade areas, of course, is that either party can go to zero protection at any point it wants. So these preferential agreements do not of themselves necessarily prejudice the long-term objectives of APEC. They do, however, have something of the air of an insurance policy against a possible breakdown in the overall APEC project. The last issue in this category is that of free riders referred to above. The open question for the future is whether US dislike of free riding as against the fear, particularly in the Western Pacific, of being sucked into a free trade area with the United States contains within it the seeds of a breakdown of APEC.

The question that emerges from the discussion above is whether the Western Pacific would go it alone if the United States decided that the costs of free riding were too high and decided to focus its liberalisation agenda on the Western Hemisphere. The question would then be whether open regionalism would remain the driving force of trade policy in the region. There is a case, and it is made perhaps most forcefully by Drysdale and Garnaut (1993), that open regionalism is the right answer for the emerging economies of the Western Pacific. It offers a way of liberalising at a rate and with a sectoral balance that suits the economies in the region without tying them up in legal commitments.

That may be convincing at an economic level, but it leaves open the question of politics. If the United States lost interest, how would Japan or China react? Similarly, would ASEAN give up AFTA in such circumstances? It would presumably be brave for one member of AFTA to liberalise unilaterally with the effect of destroying the preferences to other members of ASEAN. Finally, would there be enough balance in the relationships within the Western Pacific to allow agriculture to be dealt with without the presence of the United States to keep up the pressure? It is arguable that all of these points would equally weigh in US counsels in deciding whether to stick with an open regionalism APEC or focus on a preferential FTAA. Nonetheless, there must be a suspicion in the rest of the world that if the United States were to stick with APEC, it will have to become at least an open club if not a preferential trading area *per se*.

Regionalism and the world system

The possible trends in trade policy within the regional groupings outlined above could point to the emergence of two possible groupings of trade blocs. The first is that US fear of free riding, combined with political pressures within APEC to keep the United States on board, pushes APEC in a preferential direction. Whether this would be APEC as a full-blown free trade area or APEC as some form of open club which non-members could join by making equivalent liberalisations might not make much difference to the potential outcomes. The circumstances would effectively mean there were two blocs in the world: the European Union and APEC, with some potential non-members in South Asia and Africa, the Middle East, Latin America and the former Soviet Union (FSU), which might be connected perhaps through their own free trade areas with either of the larger blocs. The dangers of this are clear. The WTO would become moribund since APEC and the European Union would between them internalise more than three-quarters of world trade. The internal politics of both regions would leave little time or capacity for multilateral trade politics. More important, it is likely that trade politics would become unstable. Work by Krugman (1993) suggests that a two-bloc world in which the blocs play non-cooperative games is likely to lead to trade diversion dominating trade creation. So, as well as being bad politics, a two-bloc world is bad economics.

The second alternative is in essence a three-bloc world. Here the European Union and FTAA would form preferential regions while the Western Pacific would pursue the current APEC agenda, but potentially with preferential elements, particularly in AFTA, and possibly also greater China. Here, an inward-looking European Union accompanied by an inward-looking Western Hemisphere would be the real driving forces. There might be more potential for cooperation in the WTO if the Western Pacific remained with relatively high tariffs. The pressures, however, for the Western Pacific to hang together rather than hang separately when confronted with the European Union and the Western Hemisphere blocs would be pretty strong, so there would be a tendency, if nothing more, towards a three-bloc world. Krugman (1993) suggests that, if anything, a three-bloc world is more unstable than a two-bloc world in political terms and of course the economic disbenefits remain.

Approaching nirvana

As Hugh Patrick pointed out at the conference which gave rise to this volume, each of these three routes to regionalisation is a dead end. If this is so, the question is how to build on the trends outlined above towards a multilateral system which encompasses free trade and global regulatory rules that allow commerce to take place freely. The key issue is the US attachment to reciprocity. The Western Pacific shows engagement with the MFN principle while the European Union shows increasing appreciation of the importance of the MFN principle in its longer-term trade policy. The United States, however, appears unconvinced. There are no doubt many ways in which these problems could be tackled, but I will focus on two main strategies. The first is to deal directly with the American fear of EU free riding on APEC and the second is a more traditional route of strengthening the WTO by making it at least as liberalising as regional agreements.

Transatlantic liberalisation and global free trade

As noted above, the United States seems particularly concerned that, in the process of APEC liberalisation, the European Union will gain advantages from MFN liberalisation which it will not reciprocate. One way of dealing with that fear is to liberalise across the Atlantic so that, for the United States at least, the reciprocity question is dealt with directly. Of course there are considerable problems with this. Reinforced disciplines under Article XXIV of the GATT would require that agriculture be part of such an agreement and that would cause very significant difficulties within the European Union, so much so that one has to suppose that a transatlantic free trade area is unlikely to make an early appearance on the agenda. This point is reinforced by the fact that, a few tariff peaks aside, trade barriers across the Atlantic are not high (Baldwin and François 1996). If that is so, from where exactly would the liberalisation benefits come? Here, perhaps, we must look for intensification of the transatlantic market place agenda. The focus here is on sectors where liberalisation is possible and, more importantly, can be extended to the rest of the world, most notably information technology. The second area where the transatlantic market place has demonstrated progress has been mutual recognition agreements. These of course are not MFN. Nonetheless, they develop an approach to regulatory integration that avoids the almost insuperable problems of complete harmonisation, while reducing significant barriers to trade. It might also be possible to further intensify cooperation on competition policy issues. With these sorts of advances, it might then be possible to consider setting up a transatlantic single market after the style of the EU single market. This would eventually have to include trade in goods and, above all, agriculture, but only after a significant period of confidence building (and agricultural reform in Europe).

Such a transatlantic agreement, however, would have strong demonstration effects for the rest of the world. It could also cause problems for the WTO since the two largest trading entities in the world, the United States and the European Union, would have something close to common interests and concerns in the WTO. The threat of their hegemony could leave others unwilling to engage in multilateral negotiations with them. For that reason, if for no other, such a transatlantic agreement would at a minimum have to have the characteristics of an open club; that is to say, anyone who was willing to abide by the rules could be a member. If the rules proved attractive to others, then in time, and perhaps even quite rapidly, it could all be folded into a WTO negotiation that made those rules world-wide. In all of this I assume the United States would be unwilling to make transatlantic liberalisation MFN.

Written out boldly, such a progression does not by itself look very likely, but it is worth bearing two points in mind. Looked at in the same light in 1989, APEC did not seem to have much of a future and the open regionalism concept looked as if it had no legs at all. More speculatively, policy is often defined by the constraints imposed on policy makers. The policy which often emerges is often neither the best nor even the most popular, but rather the policy which most effectively deals with the political constraints facing policy makers at the time. Hence, if reciprocity does bind the Americans firmly, then a transatlantic agreement is one way of slashing those cords.

Strengthening the WTO

A more traditional and perhaps more likely route would be a further bolstering of the WTO to accelerate the multilateral liberalisation agenda and hence persuade the Americans that their reciprocity concerns can be met in the multilateral arena. The first point in such a strategy would be to convince the political classes in the United States that the recent successes of the WTO (the Information Technology Agreement; the Telecoms Agreement; a possible Financial Services Agreement; but above all perhaps the dispute settlement mechanism) all indicate the relevance of the organisation to US concerns. The second approach would be to demonstrate that the WTO takes the new subjects and, above all, the question of regulatory integration seriously. This would mean engaging all members of the organisation in a process of rule making for issues such as investment and competition policy, as well as more work on standards, perhaps including rules for mutual recognition agreements. It might also mean dealing with even more controversial issues such as rules governing trade and labour standards, and trade and the environment. There would also have to be convincing progress on traditional issues, notably agriculture in relation to Europe and North Asia, and tariffs, particularly in the context of Asia and Latin America where reducing bound tariffs would be a priority.

The complexity of that agenda suggests that the current American approach of taking early harvests where they can and leaving the difficult areas for later may not be entirely convincing. Equally, however, the complexity of the agenda raises fear among American negotiators that any global round would be a recipe for infinite delay. This suggests that if the WTO is to make progress, it needs to put some timetables and some specific targets in place. One obvious approach might be to adopt the APEC target of MFN free trade by 2020. Such a goal was certainly discussed in the run-up to the Singapore Ministerial. Even that, however, worries American negotiators since it might imply that little, if anything, would be done until the run-up to the final date. That should not be an insuperable problem if something like the Manila action plans approach of APEC were adopted. Thus there would be some forward commitment and a requirement to meet intermediate targets on the way.

Thus, as with a transatlantic approach to global free trade, the traditional WTO approach contains its own difficulties. Writing down the sort of process that might be required to make policy credible in the United States underlines the difficulty of getting there with the traditional WTO approach and given the conflicting interest of developing countries in Asia and Latin America and those of OECD members (let alone conflicts within the OECD).

Conclusion

The purpose of this chapter has been to sketch some of the underlying tendencies in trade policy in Europe, the Americas and the Western Pacific and to ask what this might mean for the future shape of the world trade system. It has deliberately taken a rather pessimistic view of those trends, adopting the traditional economist's approach of looking at worst cases (the dismal science), but with the intention of asking what policies might be used to avoid such outcomes. This is not done with the intention of sketching out wholly formed policies but rather exploring approaches that might deal with the dangers identified. The two suggested solutions, one via transatlantic liberalisation and the other via an intensified global liberalisation, both demonstrate difficulties. In any case, neither is likely to be adopted on an exclusive basis: that is seldom the way of trade policy. The question remains whether there are ways of short-circuiting the global liberalisation process so as to bring free trade and consistent and liberal rules for commerce into being at the global level and in a realistic time frame. Nothing in the discussion above suggests that reaching such an objective will be easy.

Note
* This paper represents the personal view of the author. It is not an expression of official British Government policy.

References

Baldwin, Richard and Joseph François (1996) *Transatlantic Free Trade: A Quantitative Assessment*, London: CEPR.
—— Joseph François and Richard Portes (1997) 'The costs and benefits of EU enlargement to the east', *Economic Policy*, April.
Bergsten, Fred (1997) *Economist*, 27 September.
—— (1997) 'Open Regionalism' *World Economy* 20(5), August.
Bhagwati, Jagdish (1997) *Economist*, 21 October.
Drysdale, Peter and Ross Garnaut (1993) 'The Pacific: the application of a general theory of economic integration', in F. Bergsten and M. Noland, eds, *Pacific Dynamism and the International Economic System*, Washington: IIE.
Krugman, Paul (1993) 'Regionalism versus multilateralism: analytical notes', in J. de Melo and A. Panagariya, eds, *New Dimensions in Regional Integration*, Cambridge University Press for Centre for Economic Policy Research.
Rollo, Jim (1997) 'Economic aspects of EU enlargement to the east', in Marescau, ed., *Enlarging the European Union*, London: Longman.

12   Europe and Asia Pacific economic cooperation

ROSS GARNAUT

Europe in mid-1997 is pre-occupied with the European project and, in particular, the challenge of monetary union. This is understandable, as there is much at stake.

There are powerful reasons why, as Europe grapples with the challenges of continental integration, its vision should lift beyond Europe. This is a time of unprecedented expansion of production and trade beyond Europe. There is a large agenda of trade policy issues affecting Europe's relations with the rest of the world. This is a pivotal time in the evolution of the international trading rules and institutions, in the formative years of the WTO (World Trade Organization), when the basis of Chinese and Russian membership of the WTO is being settled. And it is a time when the future of economic and political stability in Russia is in the balance — surely still the biggest open issue in European as it is in East Asian security, and one that will be influenced profoundly by European and global trade policy. It is also a time of proliferation and high legitimacy of regional trading arrangements that have the potential to negate the global trading rules.

The British economy's greater structural flexibility and improved economic performance, and the enhanced self confidence in the international economy that has accompanied these developments, have made Britain a more forceful and influential participant in the shaping of global trade policy and institutions. The United Kingdom in 1996 became the first state to commit itself explicitly to the vision of global free trade — in this case by 2020. This commitment, neatly complementary to Asia Pacific Economic Cooperation's (APEC) goal of free and open trade by 2020 in the Asia Pacific region, could, if it were confirmed by the Labour government, play a significant role in shaping the international institutions and rules that are necessary in the era of the global economy.

The second section of this chapter examines the achievement of the European partners, notably Britain, in expanding intra-regional trade over the past several decades. It raises some questions about the extent to which this has been achieved at the expense of trade beyond Europe.

Section 3 looks to the future development of the European Union, including geographic broadening, monetary union, and the momentum for greater coordination of economic rules and standards.

Section 4 introduces some major contemporary developments beyond Europe which, if managed well by Britain and her European partners, can complement European integration — containing its costs and adding new gains.

Finally, section 5 points to a destination of global free trade, which will arise naturally through the interaction of an outward-looking Europe with contemporary developments beyond Europe.

The (qualified) European achievement

The value of trade in amongst EC12 members has expanded on average since the mid-1960s at a touch below 5 per cent per annum, substantially faster than Europe's total output or its intercontinental trade. Intra-EC12 trade represented a shade below half of the region's total trade in 1965, and had lifted to 57 per cent in 1995. The rate of increase in intra-European trade slowed with each passing decade — less than Europe's intercontinental trade, but a bit more than economic output. Imports from outside the EC12 as a proportion of regional GDP (gross domestic product) rose from 7.3 per cent in 1965 to 13.8 per cent in 1985, before easing back to 12.5 per cent in 1995 (Table 12.1).

The United Kingdom, outside the original six, was at first a laggard in intra-European trade expansion. In 1965, UK exports to countries that later were part of the EC12 represented 4.1 per cent of GDP, only half the ratio for others of the 12. As intra-European trade expanded rapidly for Britain and for the other 11, the gap in European orientation narrowed: 10.8 per cent and 13.8 per cent of GDP respectively in 1995, by which time the British proportion was similar to the average of the other large Europeans, Germany, Italy and France (Table 12.2).

The rapid expansion of intra-European trade, and Britain's 'catching-up' with the three large continental Europeans, are qualified achievements, because they were accompanied by sluggish growth in intercontinental trade.

For the purposes of this story, I have divided the world into four large 'regions': The EC12; North America; East Asia; and the Rest of the World. The fourth is not a region, but a diverse grouping of the Former Soviet Union

Table 12.1 *Exports: GDP ratio for selected economies by export destination, 1965–95, per cent*

Importer	EC12				East Asia				North America				E. Europe & FSU				Rest of the World				World			
Exporter	1965	1975	1985	1995	1965	1975	1985	1995	1965	1975	1985	1995	1965	1975	1985	1995	1965	1975	1985	1995	1965	1975	1985	1995
EC12	7.2	10.5	13.9	13.4	0.4	0.6	1.1	1.9	1.5	1.4	3.0	1.9	0.4	1.0	0.7	0.8	5.0	6.7	7.0	5.6	14.5	20.2	25.7	23.5
East Asia	0.7	1.6	2.0	2.3	1.3	4.1	6.2	8.0	1.4	2.7	6.2	4.0	0.1	0.3	0.3	0.2	1.3	3.5	3.4	2.1	4.7	12.2	18.1	16.6
North America	1.3	1.6	1.3	1.6	0.5	1.1	1.2	2.4	1.6	2.7	3.1	4.9	0.1	0.2	0.1	0.1	1.4	2.2	1.4	1.6	4.8	7.9	7.1	10.6
E. Europe & FSU	0.5	1.3	2.4	6.7	0.1	0.2	0.4	1.5	0.0	0.1	0.2	0.9	0.1	2.3	4.5	5.9	0.6	1.7	3.1	4.2	1.3	5.7	10.6	19.2
Rest of World	0.7	2.8	4.6	6.5	0.1	1.1	1.9	3.5	0.2	1.1	1.9	2.3	0.1	0.4	1.0	0.6	0.4	2.1	3.6	4.8	1.5	7.5	13.0	17.7
World	1.4	3.7	4.6	5.9	0.3	1.2	2.1	3.9	0.6	1.6	3.0	3.3	0.1	0.6	0.8	0.5	1.0	3.0	3.4	3.4	3.3	10.2	14.0	17.0

Notes: East Asia includes Japan, Korea, China, Taiwan, Hong Kong, Thailand, Malaysia, Philippines, Indonesia, Singapore and Vietnam.

North America includes the United States, Canada and Mexico.

Data for Germany after 1991 refer to Unified Germany.

Eastern Europe includes Albania, Bulgaria, German Democratic Republic, Hungary, Poland, Romania, Czech and Slovakia. FSU represents the Former Soviet Union.

Data for Taiwan are not available in the IMF database and are estimates based on *Taiwan Statistical Databook*, 1996.

World GDP data are from World Development Report 1996 (World Bank) where only two data points, 1980 and 1994, are available. World GDP in 1980 is US$10,759,322 million and US$25,223,462 million in 1994. The estimates for other years are based on this benchmark figure, taking into account growth rate and inflation rate provided by IMF, *World Economic Outlook* (October 1996).

GDP data for Eastern Europe and Former Soviet Union are based on World Bank's estimate of GNP per capita population in 1990 for these countries and take into account the growth rate provided by *World Development Report* 1996.

Source: IMF, Direction of Trade and International Financial Statistics, International Economic Data Bank, Australian National University, Canberra.

Table 12.2 *Exports: GDP ratio for selected regions by export destination, 1965–95, per cent*

Partner	EC12				East Asia				North America				Rest of the World				World			
Reporter	1965	1975	1985	1995	1965	1975	1985	1995	1965	1975	1985	1995	1965	1975	1985	1995	1965	1975	1985	1995
France	5.3	8.1	10.0	11.2	0.2	0.4	0.9	1.4	0.8	0.8	1.9	1.3	4.1	6.2	6.7	4.8	10.3	15.6	19.5	18.7
Germany	7.3	10.2	14.7	10.2	0.5	0.8	1.5	1.8	1.5	1.6	3.5	1.8	6.3	9.2	9.9	7.0	15.6	21.6	29.7	20.9
Italy	5.9	8.1	9.0	11.6	0.3	0.4	0.8	1.8	1.2	1.3	2.6	1.9	4.2	6.7	6.3	6.5	11.5	16.5	18.7	21.8
Japan	0.9	1.3	1.6	1.3	1.8	2.7	3.2	3.1	3.0	2.6	5.4	2.6	3.1	4.7	3.1	1.1	8.9	11.3	13.2	8.1
Taiwan & Korea	1.1	4.2	3.8	3.9	5.9	9.3	10.2	15.4	3.0	10.3	17.8	7.6	1.0	5.5	7.3	5.9	10.9	29.2	39.1	32.9
United Kingdom	4.1	6.6	10.8	10.8	0.5	1.0	1.2	2.0	2.1	2.3	3.8	2.9	6.8	9.1	6.3	5.8	13.4	19.1	22.1	21.5
EEC excl UK	8.1	11.2	14.6	13.8	0.3	0.6	1.1	1.7	1.3	1.3	2.8	1.7	5.1	7.4	8.0	6.4	14.8	20.4	26.5	23.7

Notes: East Asia includes Japan, Korea, China, Taiwan, Hong Kong, Thailand, Malaysia, Philippines, Indonesia, Singapore and
Vietnam.
North America includes the United States, Canada and Mexico.
Data for Germany after 1991 refer to Unified Germany.
Data for Taiwan are not available in the IMF database and are estimated using data from *Taiwan Statistical Databook 1996*.

Source: IMF, Direction of Trade and International Financial Statistics, International Economic Data Bank, Australian National
University, Canberra.

and Eastern Europe, South Asia, the Middle East, Africa, Latin America and the Caribbean, and Oceania. In subsequent tables, some further detail is provided by separating out 'Eastern Europe and Former Soviet Union' from the 'Rest of the World Economy' (ROW).

I call trade within each of these 'blocs' intra-regional, and trade between them intercontinental.

The European 12 represented 41.9 per cent of global intercontinental imports in 1965. This was more than twice the North American share, and more than five times that of East Asia (Table 12.3). Europe's share of the increment in intercontinental trade fell in each successive decade: 29.9 per cent in 1965–75; 24.3 per cent in 1975–85; and 19.4 per cent in 1985–95.

As a result, Europe's share of global intercontinental trade was down to 27.9 per cent in 1995. By the mid-1990s, North America and East Asia were each almost as large as Europe in intercontinental trade. The ROW was larger than Europe and growing much more rapidly.

The share of intercontinental imports in GDP was initially far higher for Europe (8.9 per cent) than for any other region (East Asia 3.9 per cent, North America 2.5 per cent, ROW 1.2 per cent).

By the mid-1990s, the other regions had mostly (North America, East Asia) or more than (ROW) made up the gap.

In the mid-1960s, prior to entering the European Community (EC), the proportion of the United Kingdom's GDP imported intercontinentally (11.9 per cent) was almost one and a half times as high as the total of others of the EC12 (8.1 per cent). Other Europe's intercontinental trade grew more rapidly than the United Kingdom's, and by the mid-1990s the margin of difference had shrunk to less than one-third. The United Kingdom's intercontinental trade as a share of GDP fell considerably after 1975, while that of its European partners fell slightly.

It is evident from Table 12.3 that over recent decades the expansion of intercontinental trade has centred on East Asia. East Asia has moved from being a relatively minor player to become the major intercontinental trade partner of both Western Europe and North America. It is a much larger partner for North America than for the European Union. There has also been a substantial lift in the Rest of the World's role in intercontinental trade, with economic reform and trade liberalisation in Latin America, South Asia, Oceania and parts of Africa and Eastern Europe.

So the first broad reality is of fairly rapid growth in intra-European trade, faster for the United Kingdom as it catches up than for other EC members, and for all of Europe slowing over time.

The second broad reality is of rapid expansion of intercontinental trade, if anything accelerating over time. East Asia is the source of much of the

Table 12.3 *Exports of the five trade blocs, 1965–96, US$billion, constant price 1995*

Importer Exporter	EC12					East Asia					North America				
	1965	1975	1985	1995	1996	1965	1975	1985	1995	1996	1965	1975	1985	1995	1996
EC12	196	437	692	1,023	951	10	26	56	148	147	39	60	147	143	143
East Asia	9	27	54	169	166	16	69	166	584	591	17	47	167	289	281
N. America	41	62	72	131	125	17	43	70	196	189	51	103	177	394	407
E. Europe & FSU	17	28	41	56	59	2	5	7	13	13	1	2	3	8	9
Rest of World	191	221	198	330	336	31	85	84	178	198	62	83	83	118	135
World	400	749	1,024	1,708	1,646	76	247	455	1,118	1,131	173	316	665	951	982

Importer Exporter	Eastern Europe & FSU					Rest of the World					World				
	1965	1975	1985	1995	1996	1965	1975	1985	1995	1996	1965	1975	1985	1995	1996
EC12	1	11	41	35	59	133	278	346	425	431	384	843	1,276	1,797	1,739
East Asia	16	60	91	157	162	59	209	486	1,209	1,213	1	5	9	11	14
N. America	45	84	79	129	133	156	298	404	855	862	2	7	6	6	7
E. Europe & FSU	17	35	53	35	44	41	118	180	160	183	5	48	77	49	58
Rest of World	109	162	156	246	287	415	583	563	902	994	23	32	41	30	36
World	303	616	753	991	1,060	988	2,058	3,075	4,923	5,003	35	131	179	155	184

Notes: East Asia includes Japan, Korea, China, Taiwan, Hong Kong, Thailand, Malaysia, Philippines, Indonesia, Singapore and Vietnam. North America includes United States, Canada and Mexico. Eastern Europe includes Albania, Bulgaria, German Democratic Republic, Hungary, Poland, Romania, Czech and Slovakian Republic. FSU represents the Former Soviet Union. Data for Taiwan are not available in the IMF database and the estimate is based on *Taiwan Statistical Databook*, 1996. Data have been deflated using Export Unit Value Index (IFS, IMF, Base year 1995).

Sources: IMF, *Direction of Trade and International Financial Statistics*, International Economic Data Bank, Australian National University, Canberra.

dynamism. Intercontinental trade has been much more sluggish for Europe than for other regions; and has been even slower for Britain as other Europeans catch up.

A European destiny?

There is a strong hint in these data that, especially for Britain, the fairly strong although decelerating growth in intra-European trade was at the expense of relatively weak and decelerating growth in intercontinental trade. The hint is underlined by evidence from econometric tests of the gravity model that *trade diversion* has been important in intra-European trade expansion (Bayoumi and Eichengreen 1995).

There are some costs associated with discriminatory expansion of intra-regional trade that bear closer analysis within Europe. The classical theory of customs unions drew attention to the benefits from trade creation and the benefits as well as costs from trade diversion for members, while pointing unambiguously to disadvantages from trade diversion for outsiders. Later discussion of the economic effects of customs unions and free trade areas pointed to the possibility of another kind of 'trade creation', involving outsiders, as economic growth within the Union expanded opportunities for trade. But the latter was always problematic since it depended on the formation of the regional area raising the incomes of members in the first instance.

The classical theory was a bit too favourable to the effects of customs unions on members' welfare, and perhaps too unfavourable to the effects on outsiders. It did not recognise some important secondary or general equilibrium consequences of formation of a customs union.

Trade diversion within a customs union raises domestic costs, and therefore generates secondary trade diversion within the rest of the world. Trade diversion within the union also reduces the supply prices of some products from the rest of the world, which itself generates both trade diversion and trade creation within the rest of the world. Taking these general equilibrium effects into account, the chances of net loss within the customs union become greater, and net loss in the rest of the world smaller. There is little that can be said in general about whether the total including secondary costs of trade diversion will be greater for the members or the outsiders, except that the costs to members will be greater relative to outsiders the smaller the union relative to the rest of the world.

That development along these lines may have been set in train by regional trade liberalisation developments within the European Community (and later the North American Free Trade Area) is suggested by the intensification of and increase in country bias in the Rest of the World's 'internal' trade over recent decades — overall, as substantial as the intensification of trade within Europe itself (Table 12.4).

Exclusion by secondary trade division from opportunities for efficient trade and specialisation beyond Europe has obvious direct costs. Perhaps less obvious, and undoubtedly large, are the indirect costs of weakening Europe's links to the most dynamic region of the world economy, in East Asia. The attenuation of Europe's links with East Asia lowers Europe's sights in many areas of its own economic performance.

But the costs of the customs union do not loom large on the current policy agenda. The discussion of policy on the customs union is now focused on enlargement, and on engagement in discussions beyond Europe on the height of the common external tariff.

Simple admission of the many European candidates into the established customs union would substantially increase the costs of classical and secondary trade diversion, and further discourage ties to the most economically dynamic of the world's regions. It would concentrate intercontinental adjustment to the former communist economies' emerging powerful comparative advantage in agriculture, and absorption of the inevitable fluctuations and dislocations in reforming Eastern Europe, disproportionately in Western Europe.

These costs of enlargement would be diminished and, at the limit in a free trading Europe, eliminated through reduction in the common external tariff of the European Union. Open external borders would also reverse one other danger of enlargement of the Union: that it would increase still further the difficulties and reduce the incentives of internationally-oriented economic reform in excluded states on the edges of the European Union, most importantly Russia.

Beyond enlargement, other major issues in contemporary discussion of change in the character of the European Union have potentially significant indirect effects on relations with East Asia.

The effect of monetary union on European relations with East Asia will derive mainly from the effects on European economic performance. The danger is that the removal of the capacity for international relative cost adjustment within Europe through national exchange rate changes, together with application of the contractionary demand policies that are necessary to establish the fiscal and monetary base for successful union, will lead to higher average levels of unemployment than otherwise would have prevailed.

If this were an unhappy consequence of monetary union, one could expect a less congenial environment for liberalisation of external barriers to trade It is a common response to economic underperformance in a country or

Table 12.4 *Complementarity, intensity and country bias indices*

Partner		EC12					East Asia					North America					Rest of the World				
Reporter		1965	1975	1985	1994	1995	1965	1975	1985	1994	1995	1965	1975	1985	1994	1995	1965	1975	1985	1994	1995
EC12	B	68	77	95	97	103	26	21	21	23	23	36	28	32	27	27	63	63	70	78	78
	C	105	112	109	112	116	77	75	85	92	91	97	97	100	99	100	107	110	107	110	112
	I	71	86	103	109	119	20	15	18	21	21	35	28	32	26	27	67	69	75	86	87
East Asia	B	35	36	31	33	30	238	223	164	125	116	134	125	112	88	80	72	76	63	49	48
	C	90	85	91	94	95	127	102	105	118	119	101	100	114	110	110	112	107	100	97	96
	I	31	31	28	31	28	303	227	172	147	138	136	125	127	97	88	81	81	63	47	47
North America	B	53	48	38	33	35	90	103	85	71	69	157	171	114	157	149	78	71	62	61	65
	C	97	97	102	102	102	101	93	95	97	97	101	107	126	112	111	103	104	101	99	100
	I	51	47	39	34	36	91	96	81	69	67	159	183	144	175	166	80	73	63	61	66
Rest of World	B	72	60	76	89	88	54	51	37	54	59	58	53	49	56	62	75	95	117	115	117
	C	100	96	103	101	100	111	115	116	106	107	94	95	83	90	92	94	92	104	106	107
	I	72	58	78	91	87	60	59	42	57	63	54	51	41	51	57	71	87	121	121	126

Notes: East Asia includes Japan, Korea, China, Taiwan, Hong Kong, Thailand, Malaysia, Philippines, Indonesia, Singapore and Vietnam.

North America includes the United States, Canada and Mexico.

Self trade is excluded.

B Country bias index

C Complementarity index

I Trade intensity index

Sources: UN trade data, International Economic Data Bank, Australian National University, Canberra.

region to identify 'unfair' advantages in those that are performing better, and to insist on amelioration of those advantages as a condition for the maintenance of open external trade arrangements.

In this way, monetary union could interact with another area of contemporary change in the European Union: the movement towards greater consistency in standards across Europe. Some European standards, for example in labour relations and environmental management, would be highly contentious if efforts were made to extend them as conditions for the maintenance of open trade beyond Europe. Higher unemployment on average within Europe would generate pressures for removing the 'unfair' advantages outsiders were perceived to receive from their different standards.

This would be disastrous for Europe and its relations with East Asia. Harmonisation of standards within Europe may contribute to European political objectives, and to improved economic performance through reduction of transaction costs in intra-European trade. But the reaping of the advantages of economic integration over wider areas, for example encompassing Europe and East Asia, and beyond to the global economy, requires acceptance of diversity in many internal arrangements.

The global complement

Recent developments in the global economy make this a time for productive expansion of Europe's global economic relations. It is a time of economic growth and trade liberalisation beyond the great discriminatory trading blocs of Europe and North America.

Intercontinental imports, as defined in Table 12.3, roughly doubled in real terms in the decade after 1985. The expansion was concentrated in East Asia (31.3 per cent) and the Rest of the World (27.8 per cent), with roughly one-fifth each in the EC12 (19.4 per cent) and North America (21.5 per cent). Total East Asian imports (in very little of which are European suppliers affected by discriminatory regional arrangements in Southeast Asia) increased from US$0.28 trillion in 1985 to US$1.16 trillion in 1996. Rest of World imports (in very little of which are European suppliers affected significantly by the discriminatory arrangements within Latin America, Oceania, South Asia, Africa and Eastern Europe) rose from US$0.47 trillion to US$1.09 trillion over the same period.

The import expansion of the world beyond the great two North Atlantic blocs has been underwritten by mutually reinforcing economic growth and economic reform that has embodied major trade liberalisation.

This is the story of the recent past, but is the foundation of growth being undermined by the financial instability in Southeast Asia in 1997? Analysts have learned to be cautious as major changes in currency and asset markets continue to unfold. Developments in these markets can have large consequences for real economic activity that are not readily foreseeable in the current state of economic science.

From what we have seen so far, however, there is no inevitable and large unfavourable consequence for medium- and long-term East Asian economic growth, trade liberalisation and import expansion. First of all, the Southeast Asian economies, in which the financial market instability has been concentrated, are relatively small players in East Asia's participation in the global economy. The largest of the Southeast Asian economies in international trade, Singapore, imports less than any one of the five Northeast Asian economies that are current members (Japan, Republic of Korea, Hong Kong) or applicants for membership (People's Republic of China, Taiwan) of the WTO. Second, in two of the five largest Southeast Asian trading economies, Singapore and the Philippines, the currency adjustments so far have been little more than is necessary to maintain macroeconomic competitiveness following depreciations elsewhere in Southeast Asia. Third, while there have been pressures for atavistic responses to the new economic circumstances, the effect of the crisis has been, on balance, to underline the importance of continued trade and payments liberalisation. In the largest country, Indonesia, the agreement with the International Monetary Fund announced on 31 October 1997 represents a substantial step forward in trade and investment liberalisation.

The longer-established tendencies are more reliable guides to future developments. These are unambiguously favourable in East Asia. None of the essential conditions for sustained economic growth has been seriously weakened by recent developments: the high savings rates facilitating high investment when other conditions are right; openness to foreign trade, investment and ideas; structural flexibility supported by primary reliance on markets for resource allocation; and strong societal commitment to the national goal of economic growth.

Within this context, trade and investment liberalisation have been primarily unilateral in origin, driven by recognition in each country that liberalisation was necessary for stronger economic performance in the national interest.

Here and there, and in some particular goods and services, the unilateral motives have been reinforced by bilateral pressures, particularly from the United States, or through participation in the Uruguay Round of trade negotiations. The bilateral and Uruguay Round pressures helped to secure some agricultural liberalisation in Japan, Korea and Taiwan, and some additional movement on some items of manufactures and services trade. But even in those cases, the external pressures were on doors the locks of which had already been weakened by recognition within some influential parts of the domestic polities that liberalisation was in the national economic interest. In Southeast Asia, the bindings offered in the Uruguay Round were generally a long way behind the progress in unilateral liberalisation.

In recent years, APEC has reinforced tendencies to unilateral liberalisation in East Asia in ways that invite interest and constructive response from Europe. From the founding ministerial meeting of APEC, in Canberra in November 1989, the strengthening of the multilateral trading system as an instrument of liberal and liberalising trade has been the central theme of trade liberalisation within APEC. At first, the emphasis was on successful completion of the Uruguay Round, with its inclusion of previously excepted or neglected sectors of importance to Western Pacific members (notably agriculture and textiles). More recently, the focus has shifted to WTO initiatives in sectoral free trade, and to extending WTO membership to include China and Taiwan. The understanding on free trade in information technology and the discussion of telecommunications at and around the 1996 APEC Summit in Manila were important foundations for the WTO sectoral agreements that were completed in 1997. More generally, APEC provided important background to Singapore's successful hosting of the inaugural ministerial meeting of the WTO in December 1996.

To recognise the importance of the APEC Summit to the WTO Information Technology Agreement is not to deny the relevance to this important development in the multilateral system of other fora, and in particular of the transatlantic dialogue. Both the Asia Pacific and the transatlantic discussions were necessary to a successful outcome, bringing the three large regional concentrations of trade and economic power into the discussion. The Information Technology Agreement will prove to be a model for future agreements within the WTO, preceded by a clearing of understanding among North America, East Asia and Europe. The current unbalanced trilateral communications, with the transpacific and transatlantic legs each much better developed than the third, could usefully be strengthened by development of the Europe–East Asia dialogue that has taken new forms since 1995.

Importantly for Europe, East Asia's interest in APEC is built around the concept of 'open regionalism', or economic cooperation to promote regional integration without discrimination against outsiders. This conception of regional cooperation is yet neither accepted nor thoroughly understood in the North American members of APEC. APEC's role in global trade liberalisation must be uncertain in some degree until this transpacific conceptual gap has been closed.

In the meantime, APEC has played a substantial role in recent major steps in liberalisation in East Asia's most populous economies, China, Indonesia (with a population as large as Germany, Britain and France together) and the Philippines (with a population soon to be larger than any European country). President Soeharto's leadership of the 1994 APEC Summit in Bogor, Indonesia, that agreed on the goal of 'free and open' trade and investment in the Asia Pacific region by 2010 (for developed countries and 2020 for developing countries) was important to the political economy of trade policy in his own country. The commitments associated with the 1994 meeting were important causal elements in the major Indonesian trade liberalisation packages announced in May 1995 and May 1996. In the Philippines, President Ramos secured congressional support for a radical liberalisation package in the lead-up to the Manila Summit in November 1996. The package committed the Philippines to multilateralise its commitments to free trade within the ASEAN Free Trade Area by 2004 — that is, to reduce manufacturing tariffs to or below 5 per cent. The APEC context helped Ramos to achieve decisively a policy change that had been politically out of reach of his predecessors for over a quarter of a century. The APEC context, too, was helpful for the maintenance of momentum in trade liberalisation in China through years punctuated by tense exchanges with major Western states on trade and other issues. Successive APEC Leaders' Meetings (and the ministerial meetings that preceded them) were used by China to announce new steps in trade liberalisation, most impressively in Osaka in 1995.

Europe has shared in the opportunities for increased trade and specialisation that have opened with trade liberalisation and economic growth in East Asia. This has been a matter of contention in some APEC members, notably the United States, where gains to 'free riders' outside APEC have been seen as a negative consequence of non-discriminatory trade liberalisation. Whether or not APEC continues as an effective instrument of non-discriminatory liberalisation will depend importantly on the European response to its expanding Asia Pacific opportunity.

The opportunities beyond Europe are not solely in the Asia Pacific. Economic reform and trade liberalisation have been associated with stronger growth performance and import expansion to various degrees in Oceania, Latin America, South Asia, the Middle East, and in parts of Eastern Europe, the former Soviet Union and Africa. As in East Asia, the origins of trade liberalisation in these regions have been overwhelmingly unilateral. In most cases, liberalisation was influenced to some extent by the East Asian experience, often transmitted through advice and conditional lending from the international agencies. The fact of expanding global markets, open to international competition, first of all in East Asia, has been important in the dissipation of the 'export pessimism' that had once discouraged outward-looking strategies. Continued commitment to 'open regionalism' in the Asia Pacific and to external liberalisation in the European Union are important to the success of current reforms in South Asia, Russia and other economies without an obvious home in the major regional economic groupings.

A global destination

Europe played a central role in the emergence of the modern world economy. This role left a legacy of close economic ties to all parts of the global economy. These were most general and productive from the United Kingdom, notably from London.

These global links weakened as the European project took shape. This has had some short-term costs. Without special efforts, the costs will rise, as the centre of world economic and trade dynamism disperses through East Asia and what this paper has described as the 'Rest of the World'.

The maintenance of trade liberalisation in East Asia is now critical to the health of the multilateral trading system, most importantly in China and Southeast Asia, which remain highly protectionist despite significant reform. Amongst much else, the prospects for reform, trade liberalisation and economic growth in the 'Rest of the World' depend on an effective multilateral trading system.

Commitments that have already been announced unilaterally or in an APEC or WTO context will maintain momentum in Asia Pacific trade liberalisation into the early years of the next century. In the important case of the North American APEC members, these announcements have been made in the context of global negotiations, with APEC so far playing a relatively unimportant role in the political economy of policy making.

It is important to the continued success of APEC that, by early next century, the United States polity has noticed and been impressed by the reality of Western Pacific liberalisation. This is the necessary condition for the United States to judge whether playing a leading role in movement towards a goal of global free trade is worth the domestic political cost. The well-established American political preference for 'reciprocity' in trade negotiations will require that the final realisation of non-discriminatory Asia Pacific free trade be achieved through multilateral negotiations. At this point, not many years away, the future of the multilateral trading system will depend on the European Union's readiness to join APEC in achieving global free trade alongside Asia Pacific free trade by 2020.

Global free trade is a natural consequence of recent developments in regional and global trade relations. It would be a destination of great value for Europe. Amongst much else, it would allow full utilisation of Europe's historical legacy of close global economic ties, and ease the immediate dilemmas associated with the widening and deepening of European integration.

Reference

Bayoumi, T. and B. Eichengreen (1995) 'Is regionalism simply a diversion? Evidence from the evolution of the EEC and from NAFTA', Discussion Paper No. 1294, CEPR, London.

Index